D0590718

OUR

A Year in the Life of a Smallholding

ROSIE BOYCOTT

Cork City Libraries
WITHDRAWN
FROM STOCK

BLOOMSBURY

First published in Great Britain 2007

Copyright © 2007 by Rosie Boycott

Illustrations and endpapers by Kate Miller

The moral right of the author has been asserted

No part of this book may be used or reproduced in any manner
whatsoever without written permission from the Publisher except in
the case of brief quotations embodied in critical articles or reviews

Extract on p. 153 from *Charlotte's Web* by E. B. White (Hamish Hamilton, 1952)
Copyright E. B. White. Reproduced by permission of Penguin Books Ltd.

Extract on p. 195 from *Winnie the Pooh* by A. A. Milne
© The Trustees of the Pooh Properties. Published by
Egmont UK Ltd London and used with permission

Extract on p. 205 from 'St Katy the Virgin' from *The Long Valley* by John
Steinbeck (Penguin Books, 2000). Copyright John Steinbeck, 1938. Copyright
renewed John Steinbeck, 1966. Reproduced by permission of Penguin Books Ltd.

Extract on p. 266 from *Black Lamb, Grey Falcon* by Rebecca West, first
published in Great Britain by Canongate Books Ltd, 14 High Street,
Edinburgh EH1 1TE

Bloomsbury Publishing Plc
36 Soho Square
London W1D 3QY

www.bloomsbury.com

Bloomsbury Publishing, London, New York and Berlin

A CIP catalogue record for this book is available from the British Library

ISBN 9780747588979

10 9 8 7 6 5 4 3 2 1

Typeset by Hewer Text UK Ltd, Edinburgh
Printed in Great Britain by Clays Ltd, St Ives plc

The paper this book is printed on is certified by the © 1996 Forest Stewardship
Council A.C. (FSC). It is ancient-forest friendly. The printer holds
FSC chain of custody SGS-COC-2061

FSC

Mixed Sources
Product group from well-managed
forests and other controlled sources

Cert no. SGS-COC-2061
www.fsc.org
© 1996 Forest Stewardship Council

To Charlie Howard, with love

CONTENTS

Acknowledgements   *ix*

1.   Green Shoots in November   *1*

2.   The Cleverest of Animals   *21*

3.   The Luck of the Tailor of Gloucester   *32*

4.   Trees Are Excellent Listeners   *49*

5.   A Christmas Market   *66*

6.   The Nature of Soil   *93*

7.   The First Slaughter   *117*

8.   The Swallows Return   *148*

9.   Bluebell Gives Birth   *173*

10. A Market Stall at Langport   *202*

11. The Midsummer Pig Roast   *238*

12. The Return of the Large Blue   *268*

Further Reading   *295*

Index   *297*

ACKNOWLEDGEMENTS

The Wheel is come full circle, I am here.
Edmond in *King Lear*

The wheel has turned full circle for me. It is a January afternoon; it has been raining and the light has faded early from the
winter skies. I've just come in from our Somerset garden, where
a man called Charlie has been telling me where to plant bulbs
(we are late getting the last lot in the ground). He is, at times, a
bit critical of my technique. Forty years ago, I was also often in
a garden; this one was in Shropshire and I was regularly
instructed in the arts of gardening by another man called
Charlie. He was a bit of an autocrat, too, when it came to
the finer points of rearing and tending plants. The two Charlies
are, respectively, my husband and my late father. In many
ways, therefore, I have not moved forwards, although there has
been a lot of living in between my two gardening phases.
Without the inspiration of my father, I would not have discovered my love of the countryside, which became so vital and
important to me in the early years of the twenty-first century. I
owe him a big debt and I like to think that, were he still alive, he
would have been pleased to see how his youngest daughter's life
turned out. He would certainly have been surprised.

I owe thanks to many people. Our farm would not have
been possible without Ewen and Caroline Cameron, David
Bellew and his mother and father, Dennis and Anne, and
Wayne Bennett, the manager of Dillington Park, as well as
Bob, Adrian, Mark and Julian.

To the many people in Ilminster and around us in Somerset

who have made us welcome, and shared their stories, I owe my thanks: Henry and Elizabeth Best, Clinton Bonner, Joe Burlington, Chris Chapman, Kit Chapman, Ellen Doble, Bryan and Elizabeth Ferris, Mike and Patricia Fry-Foley, Richard Guest, Mark and Yseult Hughes, Nick Lawrence, Liz Leddra, Gillie Minnett, John and Mary Rendell, and Colin and Zoe Rolfe.

I would also like to thank the following for giving me their time and sharing their knowledge: David Attenborough, Chris Blackhurst, Jules Cashford, Monty Don, Andy Gossler, Trevor Grove, Revel Guest, Graham Harvey, Vicki Hird, Patrick Holden, Felicity Lawrence, James Lovelock, Mike McCarthy, John Mitchinson, George Monbiot, Andrew Parker, Rose Prince, Joyce de Silva, Andrew Sims, Thom Steinbeck, Jeremy Thomas, Martin Warren and Francis Wheen.

My thanks are also eternally owing to Bob Simonis, a doctor in an hour of need, without whom I would, literally, not have a leg to stand on in the garden or elsewhere. And to Rowley Leigh, our good friend and great chef, who bought our eggs and vegetables for Kensington Place restaurant.

Many members of my family helped with the writing of this book, in particular Ander and Richard Parker, who spent many hours recalling tales of farming past, and my sister Collette.

Thanks are also owning to Tobyn Andreae, who first encouraged me to write about our farm; Carole Bamford, for her generosity; my friends Hannah Rothschild, Cindy Blake and Jennifer Nadel, who read the manuscript at various stages and were constantly supportive; my cousin Charlie Viney for being both my friend and my agent; my editor at Bloomsbury, Michael Fishwick, for being both patient and wise; my stepson-in-law, Charlie Glover, for taking the pictures for the cover; my stepdaughter, Miranda Glover, for reading the proofs and being such a special friend; Nicola Easton, for all her help with the research; Sue Ayton, for never giving up; and Katie Bond, Minna Fry, Trâm-Anh Doan and

Emily Sweet of Bloomsbury, who made the process so enjoyable.

By the start of 2007, we had ninety-three pigs running around on the farm, so, even though they'll never get to read this, thanks are due to Bramble, Bluebell, Guiness, Babe, the Empress, Hyacinth, Robinson, Boris and Earl for being both excellent pigs and excellent breeders.

I'd like to thank Francesca, Alex and Luke for being wonderful stepchildren, and my daughter Daisy for contributing so much to the sum of my life's happiness. Finally, our farm belongs every bit as much to my husband, Charlie, as it does to me; for that, and for so much more, thank you.

Green Shoots in November

Inside the red van the five pink piglets are asleep, sandwiched together between two bales of straw. It smells bitter, of sour milk. They must have been fed on gruel; normally pigs don't smell at all. On their straw bed they are warm and they don't want to come out. I hold the door open and make encouraging noises. One piglet opens an eye, looks at me and goes back to sleep. I scramble into the van and grab the nearest pig round its fat little stomach. Immediately it starts shrieking and squealing, waking up the others who look around in alarm, staggering to their feet and moving to the back of the van, as far away from the door as they can. I carry the frantically wriggling pig a hundred yards to his new home and push him through the gate into the run where five other Gloucester Old Spot males are watching his arrival with great curiosity.

Two years ago I would never have imagined that I would become the owner of a small group of pigs. In my life I've been many things – mother, wife, journalist, writer, magazine editor, newspaper editor, radio and TV presenter, feminist, hippy, divorcee, junkie, drunk and traveller – but pig-owner was never on the cards. It makes me wonder what really determines the course of our lives – is it chance or the result of careful planning? If I think about my own life I come to the conclusion that it has mostly been determined by chance, more akin to a game of roulette than a game which requires some skill, such as bridge. Things happen for so many seemingly random reasons; choosing to answer the phone at the right moment, casual meetings at parties and on aeroplanes, even having a good night's sleep which means you're more likely to say yes to an offer than no. There's rarely been any strategy involved. The only element that links it all has been my willingness to say yes more often than no.

Due to chance, my husband Charlie and I have a house in Somerset and if I peel back the layers a little more, chance has followed me down the long corridors of years. Charlie is my second husband. We knew each other when we were teenagers, lost touch for twenty-seven years .and met again in 1997. That was chance. I was editing the *Independent on Sunday* and he was sharing his legal chambers with the libel lawyer George Carman. George and I were friends and one day over lunch he suddenly mentioned Charlie Howard. 'He sends you his love . . . you ought to ring him up.' Editing a newspaper doesn't leave you much time for anything else, but I did pick up the phone and we did meet for lunch. Two years later we were married.

By the time of our wedding, in a church in the New Forest with all our respective children playing parts in the ceremony, my father was sliding into the fog of Alzheimer's, moving into a twilight world from which he would never return. While he was able to live on his own, our country weekends were spent with him, at his family house outside Ludlow in Shropshire, but in the spring of 2002, he suffered a series of small accidents. He fell down stairs, bruising his coccyx, then he fell into a ditch in the field where he was walking his dog, and lay there for hours before he was rescued. The ever-present bad chest which he had lived with for years turned into a bronchial infection. He went into hospital in the first week of May 2002 for a course of heavy-duty antibiotics. Charlie and I brought him home on a Friday in mid-May, but as the evening wore on his breathing grew increasingly laboured; he was disorientated and confused and, for the first time, he was having trouble walking. We made a bed for him downstairs and his doctor intimated to Charlie that he might not last the night. He did, but only just. The following day, Dad was back in an ambulance, heading once again for hospital. It was two days before my birthday and I perched beside him in the back of the van, surrounded by tanks of oxygen, stethoscopes and defibrillator machines, certain that this would be the last time he would ever see the home he had loved for the last forty years.

Three months before that May morning, Charlie and I had gone to Somerset to stay with Ewen and Caroline Cameron. I had met them in the 1970s when I'd been going out with one of Ewen's old college friends. Like Charlie and me, we had lost touch, meeting again in the late 1990s in a more official capacity when Ewen was in charge of the Countryside Agency and I was editing the *Daily Express*. The *Express* had just run a hugely successful campaign to keep GM food out of Britain and Ewen, in his capacity as head of the Countryside Agency, had been giving intelligent newspaper interviews as to how New Labour could help revitalise rural Britain. I remembered how much I'd liked him and his wife Caroline and so renewed the acquaintance. They came to dinner with Charlie and me, and a year or so later they invited us down to Ilminster for the weekend.

Charlie was full of enthusiasm for the trip; he had grown up in the village of Charlton Mackrell, just ten miles northwest of Ilminster. It was a cold, grey weekend but the rain held off and we walked extensively round Ewen's family estate which he had been managing since his twenties. The old family home,

Dillington Park, is now leased to the County Council and it operates successfully as an adult education college. We approached the imposing house via the park, where oaks and field maples, walnuts and chestnut trees stood leafless in the winter chill. Off to one side of the park, black-and-white Friesians were grazing outside the gate to a square stone house, appropriately called the Dairy House, set in its own overgrown garden. It was built of the honey-coloured local Ham stone, and in the pale winter light it looked cosy and inviting. Charlie asked who lived there. Ewen said the current tenants were going to leave shortly.

Later that night, when we were getting ready to go to bed, Charlie voiced my own thoughts. Perhaps, even though Dad was still battling on alone in his house, we should think about it. So the following day, before we left, we asked if the Camerons would consider us as possible future tenants of the Dairy House. Two days after my gloomy ride in the ambulance with my father, the phone rang in our London home. It was Ewen. Were we still interested? I knew that Dad would never again be going home and that we would soon be selling his house. What on earth was I going to do with all that furniture? Our London house was already overflowing with books, pictures, furniture and cooking equipment, the contents of both our lives. I said yes: it would be a solution and a way to keep my feet in the country, at least some of the time. You see, chance comes in many forms, and sometimes one gets one's chances from another's misfortunes.

Over the next two months, my elder sister Collette and I packed up our father's house, and at the beginning of August 2002 the removal van moved my half of my parents' home to the Dairy House. But that only explains a part of the story, the how we got to Dillington part. It does not explain the pigs.

The garden we inherited at the Dairy House had been created in the 1980s. Carved out of parkland, the incredibly rich soil, fertilised by livestock for hundreds of years, soon produced a wonder of shapely trees, shrubs and herbaceous flowers. The garden surrounds the house: in the front, to the south, there's a flagstoned terrace which soaks up the sun all year round. Pink roses and mauve wisteria cover the south-facing wall, growing so fast that in summer the long wisteria tendrils sneak in through the open windows and creep along the tops of the bookshelves. The main garden lies to the east, full of curving beds and a circular yew hedge which surrounds the small pond and cuts the garden off from the wood, which you can reach either via a small wooden bridge or through a beech archway that hangs over a wrought iron gate, with upturned horse-shoes soldered on the top. From almost every point in the garden you can look out across the park, at the stately oak trees, which shelter the cattle from rain and sun, and the hill away to the south which rises up steeply towards the tangled hedge marking the end of the open land. It had been a little neglected in the immediate years before our arrival, which, for any aspirant gardener, is a pretty ideal situation. Charlie especially was entranced. He had grown up in the country and had always regarded the city as a diversion in a life that would, eventually, find him back in the countryside. He had long been a frustrated city gardener, growing peppers and tomatoes in pots on his sun-drenched terrace in Shepherd's Bush.

But here work was needed; in particular, several trees needed cutting down or cutting back to open up the views to the parkland. We consulted Chris Wilson, the estate manager, who lives with his wife Rosie in a stone farmhouse on the other side of the park. He dispatched Mark Bellew and Phil Wright, who worked on the estate, to help out. They arrived early one morning, armed with a chainsaw and a fund of knowledge. The chainsaw hummed as the branches fell, our

first steps to putting the garden back to rights. But as each
branch bit the dust, the scale of the work needed became more
apparent. Charlie had been resistant to having any help with
the garden. In a fit of false heroics, he reckoned that, with my
help, he could look after it all on weekend afternoons. Sure, we
needed some help with the trees, but that was only because we
did not own a chainsaw. I wasn't so sure: the garden was
complex and richly planted and clearly high-maintenance.
Over mugs of coffee, Mark told us that his brother was a
gardener and might be interested in helping us. Two days later,
after walking the garden and discussing the possibilities,
David started work.

Two years later, we had restored the main flower garden,
planted an orchard, created a vegetable garden, and embarked
on an ambitious scheme to transform a wildly overgrown
wood into a woodland garden, complete with a large pond,
paths, a living willow house, willow arches and huge sofas
carved out of fallen oak trunks which had been positioned to
look out over the park. Then in the autumn of 2004, just as the
main work was completed, David asked us if we would be
interested in investing in a plant nursery, which he would run
as the full-time manager.

We didn't think about it for long. Both Charlie and I were
already spending some of our happiest weekends digging,
pruning, sowing seeds and transplanting seedlings. Charlie
loves growing plants and vegetables and he seems to have a
knack of making them flourish. Green fingers, my father used
to say, as he'd watch Charlie tidy up his much loved and once
immaculate garden on the weekends we used to spend with
him.

We were too old to have children together and, even
though we had the dogs – my daughter Daisy's old Battersea

rescue dog Bingo, and Dylan, the Labrador that Charlie had bought as a puppy for his daughter Francesca – there was something hugely appealing about the prospect of a project which we could build together. We had first met in 1965, in Ludlow, where I spent most of my childhood. Charlie was an old school friend of the vicar's son, Robin, and when his own parents divorced he became a regular visitor to the tall Georgian vicarage which stood beside the River Teme in the village of Ashford Bowdler. My own father, frustrated that he had never had a son, liked organising cricket matches on the village green and one summer Charlie pitched up for a game. He turned up every summer after that and when Charlie and Robin decided to travel round America in the summer of 1969, I asked to go too. I was only eighteen but, after a great deal of persuasion, my protective and cautious father decided to embrace the proposed adventure with surprising gusto and helped us plan our trans-continental journey with military precision.

Before I left, he handed me a Greyhound bus ticket, valid for three months, for use in any state of the union. In the event, I was the only one with such a ticket and, after travelling over the New Jersey Turnpike to Indiana late one night, bundled together on the back seat of an overcrowded bus, I was easily persuaded to ditch all ideas of the Greyhound bus network in favour of sticking out my thumb. A mutual friend flew out to join us and Charlie and I found ourselves hitchhiking together, crossing the vast plains of the Midwest in an old green Chevrolet with a group of dope dealers, being marooned on a rattlesnake-infested mountain outside Salt Lake City by a gun-toting cowboy, and meeting up with a Harvard student who, weeks later, would be joining Charlie at Cambridge.

My late teenage years were promiscuous in the extreme, but those weeks with Charlie were special because they were wholly platonic: ours was a deep friendship which had been well tested by frustrating hours on lonely roadsides and moments of real danger. We developed the easy-going camaraderie that results from days spent in someone's company: neither of us can recall having a single argument in all those weeks. But when we came home, Charlie returned to Cambridge and I went off to Kent University, to begin a course in pure mathematics. In my second term I dropped out, fled to London, found a job on an underground newspaper and, a little over a year later, founded *Spare Rib* magazine. Our lives diverged: he married, had Franky and Alex, and divorced. I married, gave birth to Daisy and divorced. Twenty-seven years later, chance – this time in the form of a nudge from George Carman – brought us together again.

My father was delighted. He didn't like growing old and seeing his youngest daughter as a single mum, and, though by the time of our wedding Alzheimer's was steadily claiming his sanity, he made it through the day, cheering hugely as George stood up to make a speech. Charlie's son Alex was our best man, his daughter Francesca and my daughter Daisy were bridesmaids. Luke, my stepson from my first marriage, was an usher, as was Charlie, the husband of my stepdaughter Miranda. Robin, who had introduced us all those years ago, was also an usher. Bingo followed us up the aisle with a huge yellow bow pinned to her collar.

Now, almost five years later, those two teenagers who had once thumbed lifts on interstate slipways were setting out on another adventure. Charlie had discovered both his love of plants and his skill in nurturing them; my own interest in the politics of the countryside was growing. The more I discovered about the stranglehold of the supermarkets, the insanity of 'food miles' (the distance that food travels from where it is grown to where it is bought), the lazy greed of our consumer society which demands strawberries and green beans in January without thinking of the environmental consequences, let alone the taste, the more I felt a sense of anger and sadness. It seems to me that we live in increasingly schizophrenic times: wanting our countryside to remain for ever like the pictures Constable lovingly painted so long ago, yet standing by while agri-business, responding to our demands for ever cheaper and more available food, rips up hedges and chemically destroys our wildlife. Every year, twenty-one square miles of country-side, an area the size of Southampton, is lost to developers. Investing in a nursery seemed a good way to start to redress the balance.

David is a proud and conscientious single parent, and lives with his nine-year-old son, Josh, for whom he is the primary carer. They live in a sprawling village called South Petherton, which is about four miles from Dillington and boasts a fish shop and a deli. He did have his eyes on a floundering nursery there, but it quickly became apparent that buying an already existing nursery made little economic sense. Over 50 per cent of the £90,000 asking price was for the plant stock, which would have been hard to turn a profit on. The idea lapsed, but not for long. At the end of November 2004, David arrived one Saturday morning with a new idea. Across the park, to the north of Dillington House, was a Victorian walled garden almost two acres in size and unused since the early 1960s.

In the pale, late autumn sunshine we walked over to inspect the site. The walls were made of mellow old red brick, marks still visible where once ornate glasshouses had stood. It was built on a slight slope, angling downwards to the north, which allowed the heat of the day to pool into its corners. Even in the thin November sun, the bricks on the north wall were warm to the touch and as we leant back we could feel the heat stored within. To the west the wall had collapsed – a previous estate manager in a hurry had driven straight through it to provide easy access to the lower pastures – but apart from that they stood solid and intact.

Inside the old tumbledown potting shed, a wooden door

was covered with spidery inscriptions, records of the weather and the movements of migrating birds, dating back to the 1850s: 'April 12, 1851, first swallows arrive.' They had been written by James Kelway, then the eighteen-year-old head gardener at Dillington House, later to become one of the great Victorian gardeners and founder of Kelway's Nurseries at Langport, breeder of peonies and irises and inventor of the cineraria plant. When Kelway came to Dillington the house was owned by an ancestor of Ewen's, Vaughan Hanning Vaughan Lee, a keen gardener who built two grape houses and grew peaches, melons and even bananas in the walled garden. He was particularly partial to his grapes, and one day while shopping in Jackson's of Piccadilly his eye was drawn to a display of large, especially succulent ones. Recently, he had been annoyed that his own grapes weren't as perfect, so he decided to buy them to show Kelway just what really good English-grown grapes could look like. On enquiring where they came from, he learned that these were the 'famous Dillington grapes', possibly the best in the whole of England. Later that night, Kelway was unceremoniously sacked for stealing.

Ewen was happy to extend a long lease on the walled garden and the surrounding five acres, which comprised a very old orchard, and two wooded areas to the north and south. Our rent was set at a nominal £1 for year one, to compensate for the amount of work needed, rising to £3,000 by the third year. Old fridges, dead sheep, countless plastic sacks, bits of metal and other assorted rubbish had been dumped in the area immediately outside the garden over the last few decades. Occasionally local people, like David's brother Mark and his girlfriend Louise, had arranged to keep their sheep in the garden, but apart from that the whole area had remained untouched and derelict since the early 1960s.

The clearing began in earnest in January 2005: Mark and David borrowed a digger from the estate, and the rubbish was soon safely sunk twelve feet down. We rotavated the rest of the ground. Inside the nursery, years of couch grass broke up under the blades into tiny little white roots, each one a new weed. There was no option but to delay planting while we zapped the weed with Round-up, the most powerful weed-killer on the market. What to do with the woods? We all wanted to keep pigs, so the wood to the north was fenced off, a timbered house erected and muddy wallows dug out along the path of the underground spring. The first three Gloucester Old Spots, Bluebell, Bramble and Guinness, arrived in early April. Chickens were the next, seemingly logical, step, so a half-acre site outside the walls, once an old orchard but now just an unused area with a walnut and chestnut tree, was fenced off and secured from foxes by an electric wire circling the enclosure a foot above the ground. More huts and coops needed building. We didn't stop at chickens: twenty noisy geese, seven ducks and an assortment of 'rare breeds' arrived at regular intervals over the next three months. Josh Bellew's grumpy angora rabbit, Gus, moved in as well, as David couldn't cope with having yet another animal needing feeding and cleaning at home. Most days Gus sits with his back to the assembled throng, occasionally joining in round the feeder when he's hungry.

Inside the walled garden, the old shed was stripped down, re-roofed and re-pointed. We divided it into a tiny office, storage and potting shed. We bought and erected three poly-tunnels inside the garden, where tomatoes, cucumbers, courgettes, melons, peppers, chillies and three types of lettuce were soon sprouting in the almost tropical heat contained in the plastic frames. Seed planting began in earnest in the spring and by June there were rows of carrots, beans and onions outside the garden walls, sandwiched into the space between the chickens and the pigs.

And, of course, with more animals and more vegetables, we needed more help. By midsummer, David's mother Anne had quit her job as a cleaner and was working in the nursery twenty hours a week. His father Dennis looks after the small blue tractor and the electrics, feeds the animals when his son is not there and helps out with the planting. Since Dennis was waiting for his hip replacement, what he could do was initially circumscribed. Ian, a fireman from Taunton, helped out periodically and Stuart, a friend of David's, did shifts. Charlie and I made some fifteen hundred cuttings over the summer, starting the long, slow but ultimately rewarding process of building our own plant stock. Hydrangeas, boxes, bays, different herbs and herbaceous plants were snipped off at the growing point, the leaves trimmed back, the stems doused in rooting powder and planted in potting soil in seed trays.

There was a moment in July when it looked like our little farm was growing out of control, too many small feet moving in too many directions and all too fast. Certainly that was the view of many of our friends, who saw our hobby, as they called it, turning into a hugely expensive exercise that would ultimately go nowhere. But it wasn't as haphazard as it sounds. It seemed to Charlie and me, as it seemed to David, that to make a smallholding work in the twenty-first century you have to try everything and be prepared for some things to fail. We weren't just looking at intensive farming of a small five-acre plot, we were looking to make every square inch become as productive as possible and we were looking to find as many ways as possible to generate an income.

On a monthly basis the costs in early July 2005 worked out like this:

David is paid £1,000 (but this obviously needs to increase as soon as possible).
Anne is paid £384, as is Dennis.
Animal feed: £80
Electricity: £25
Insurance: £62
Water: £25
Phone: £50
Fertilisers: £100
Vet: £30
Car: £134
Tractor: £5
Jam jars, egg boxes and extras: £50
Total: £2,329

The set-up costs, to date nudging £60,000, have included:

Clearing: £2,018 (although this work went on till autumn)
Rental of digger: £550
Timber for fencing: £815
Sand, cement, props, fixings: £1,140
Rebuilding wall: £641.75
Timber for office: £802
Purchase of small cement mixer: £236
Roofing sheets for shed: £275
Polycarbonate sheets: £457
Tractor and rotavator: £2,100
Tractor shed: £500
Trailer: £50
Polytunnels (3): £2,900
Tractor delivery: £40
Day-old chicks from Piggots: £290

Grass seed: £38.98
Putty and glass for windows: £48
Seeds from Thompson and Morgan: £258
Pigs: £225
Greenhouse: £1,789
Digger rental: £669.75
Heated benches and watering system for potting shed:
    £1,693
Water pipe: £106
Tozer seeds: £777.69
Timber for fencing: £2,019
Compost and wheelbarrows: £443
Box plants: £800
Vets' bills: £42
Office furniture: £140
Chickens: £267
Rare-breed chickens: £235
Lavender bantams and Apricot ducks: £50
Electric fencing and installation: £900
Seven Gloucester Old Spots: £450
Fencing for pigs/chickens: £1,509
Timber: £950
Chickens: 200
Rare-breed chickens: £86
Two Berkshire pigs: £140
Timber: £907
NFU insurance: £741
NFU membership: £188.49
Egg boxes: £73.70
Fruit trees: £493
Fruit trees (soft): £195
Roof for new shed: £327
Straw: £35
Egg stamp: £47

When we first embarked on the venture in the early months of the year we approached Wayne Bennett, the manager of Dillington House adult education centre, and secured his agreement that we could supply his chef with vegetables and, in due course, with 750 eggs a week. Dillington House runs courses in everything from local history to tracing your ancestry, from art classes to three-day sessions on looking good. They serve roughly two thousand meals a month. Until we started selling carrots to them in July, all their carrots had been imported from Spain. Now their food miles are a short walk up the garden path.

The income from Dillington House underpinned all our calculations about how we were going to break even. The initial financial forecast looked like this:

Dillington House: £1,500 worth of vegetables every month

Eggs: 750 eggs a week will yield £320 a month

Pigs: Selling one pig a week from May 2006 makes £150 a week, £600 a month

Vegetable boxes: 20 a week at £7.50 a box makes £600 a month

Rare breeds: should start breeding in spring 2006. Each pair can produce 20 pairs a year, selling at (average) £50 a pair

Plants: plant stock to build up over the next two years, earning £5,000 a year

This makes it sound very easy; it wasn't. To start to pay back the capital and to increase David's salary to a reasonable level we had to be making almost an extra £1,000 every month. By July 2005 we had earned virtually nothing and by the end of October, nine months after the project began, we had earned the following:

June:
Sale of plants at a Garden Open Day at the Dairy House:
　£120
July:
Sale of vegetables to Dillington House: £70

August:
Sale of vegetables to Dillington House: £202
Sale of vegetables to Mr Rendell (the local greengrocer):
　£120.00
Sale of vegetables to individual buyers who visit the
　nursery: £18

September:
Dillington: £202.90
Dillington Open Day: £126
Individual veg sales: £26

October:
Dillington: £252.55
The Popp Inn: £229 (a local pub with which David had
　done a deal)
25 dozen eggs to local households: £37.50
Other vegetables: £28.35
Chickens: £30
Vegetables to Kensington Place restaurant in London:
　£82.50

Total: £1,544.80

I am continually taken aback by how much hard work goes
into making just small amounts of money. Eggs are a good
case in point. We bought our first day-old chicks in May.
They cost us £1 a piece and began their lives balanced on
their spiky little legs, huddled together on sawdust under the

warmth of a heating lamp. Six weeks later they were ready to go outside into their pen. Another two months elapsed before they were ready to lay. Even then, and very endearingly, they had to take a few practice runs, producing eggs that were small, sometimes minus the yolks, sometimes containing two. Every day they need feeding in both the morning and the evening. The electric fence means they don't need locking up at night to protect them from foxes; they just go inside of their own accord into a warm huddle. Twice a day, someone has to collect the eggs. They need washing if they are dirty, they need checking under a sharp light for cracks and they need to be stored in a specially reserved place. Every chicken needs an inoculation and inspection before we are allowed to sell our eggs commercially. Now we have a certified number and this must appear, by law, on the side of every box of eggs we sell and on the egg itself, to certify that we have been inspected for cleanliness and hygiene. Seven hundred and fifty eggs earn us £80.

I am, of course, approaching this with the sensibilities of a Londoner who works in the media and who can earn considerably more than that just for showing up at a radio station and talking about what I happen to think of something in the arts or in politics. If I contribute to a lunchtime radio show, talking about an issue of the day, I can earn fifty quid in a few minutes; a similar item on TV nets much more. So I reckon I'm probably very blasé when it comes to evaluating financial worth, but, whichever way I look at it, it still seems incredibly tough that going through that exhaustive process still nets you only eighty quid.

Now, as the autumn days turn to winter, we are facing the possibility of bird flu and probably having, at best, to move our chickens indoors or, at worst, to have them all killed. We don't have a hut that is big enough to contain them and there isn't land enough to build one. If the order comes to keep all birds indoors, we will have to rent a barn somewhere in the vicinity for the duration of the outbreak. It is hard to imagine them all being slaughtered: far from being headless, chickens have personalities and looks. At any one time of day ours will be busy having dust baths, pecking for grubs in the ground, feeding from the trough, teetering on the ramp which leads into the duck pond for a drink, sitting in twos by the fence, walking gingerly between the legs of the geese, or just jumping up into the air for no good reason at all. We've got one black Maran who hops everywhere, bouncing along on her two feet like a feathery pogo stick. On the odd occasion when I've had to pick them up (usually because their wing feathers need a clip) their hearts beat very fast under their feathers, as though all they are is heart, but this calms down in seconds and they are quite content to lie there, firmly held between my two palms, their intense eyes darting in every direction.

We finish carrying the pigs out of the red van. They are so reluctant to leave their snug temporary home where they've been sleeping in their bed of straw. Pigs are prone to melodrama and, like an opera singer into whose behind someone has stuck a pin, they squeal madly when we pick them up to carry them to their gate. Once on the ground, though, the three boys trot happily into the run. The five resident males, all roughly the same size, come nosing up, sniffing and curious. Within seconds, they are playing tag, pushing each other, chasing this way and that, their tails alternating between curly and straight out, ears forward. Pigs don't exactly grin, but they have an expression which seems to say, 'I'm happy.'

'So that's Boris,' I say to David as we lean on the gate

watching them. Boris was the name we had already given to the boar who would become our breeding male. We had been referring to this mythical male pig as Boris for months, long before we met him, long before this actual Boris had even been born. But there is no doubt now about which pig is going to step into the role. He's small and pink, with a big bunched mass of very black spots on his rump. David is chuffed because one of Boris's ancestors had been bred by Princess Anne, who has a reputation in the pig world as an excellent breeder.

'He'll get to be this big' – David holds his hand out, above the level of the fence. That means Boris is going to be almost three feet six inches tall, and probably very fat with it.

Now it is the turn of the girls, two equally fine little Gloucesters, one with an endearing black splodge over her left ear. We call her Blossom. Like the boys, they squeal as we carry them through a gate and across the vegetable patch to their run. But there the similarities end. The older lady pigs – Guinness, Bluebell, Bramble and Babe – immediately freeze them out. Babe, an Oxford Black and Sandy and my favourite pig, who is now emerging as the unelected queen of the tribe, pushes them to one side, then bites Blossom on the ear. The two little pigs stand there, legs rigid, ears forward, surprised, distressed looks on their faces. They turn to try and join the group who are gathered near the gate, hoping that David or I will feed them the hard little inedible pears that have fallen from the tree growing beside the wall. Babe immediately shoulders them aside and gives Blossom another nip on the back. The two other most recent arrivals – the Empress of Dillington and her sister, Hyacinth, two small Berkshires – stand to one side, and I swear a look of relief can be seen in their eyes. They are no longer the newcomers, the butt of the jokes. Berkshires are black with fabulous white noses, and have an inexhaustible capacity for stuffing themselves. Both she and Hyacinth have literally made themselves sick by eating too many pears. Their hearty appetites make me confident that P. G. Wodehouse's great creation, the Empress of Blandings, best beloved pig of the Earl of Emsworth and three times winner of the Fat Pigs Competition at the South Shropshire Agricultural Show, has a thoroughly worthy namesake.

Charlie has collected a big bunch of the bacon weed which grows so freely all over the nursery and he throws it into the run as a welcome gift for the newcomers. The pigs fall on it with enthusiasm, chomping up the leaves and stalks, emitting grunts of pure happiness. 'Think of it this way,' he says, 'we could have bought a Mercedes instead.'

The Merc might be more appropriate for a QC and a journalist, but, as they say, stuff happens, chances come and go, and here we are with the pigs, the chickens, the newly planted vegetables and a plan but, in truth, very little idea of what we are doing and what is going to happen next.

2

The Cleverest of Animals

The pigs make their first escape on a Sunday morning in October. The week before, the boys' run had been extended back into the wood, in the direction of the main house. It's a thickly wooded area, made up mostly of pines and laurels. A heavy-duty electric fence delineates their area, but not well enough, it turns out. At eight in the morning, before we have even gone downstairs to let the dogs out and collect the Sunday papers, the phone rings; it's one of the staff at Dillington House, calling to tell us that there are seven little pigs out on the main lawn having a field day. And they are. Pigs love worms and grubs, so using their muscular noses they have pushed up the top layer of turf, exposing the new soil underneath for grubbing and rootling. Seven little tails are curled in pleasure as they zip around the lawn, churning up the soil like a fleet of small rotavators. By the time we arrive, they have attracted a small crowd of Dillington House course members. Cameras are out and everyone is laughing, enjoying this laddish bid for freedom.

There's something fascinating about pigs. Churchill memorably remarked that 'cats look down on you, dogs look up to

CORK COUNTY
1165 9361
LIBRARY

you, but pigs treat you as an equal'. They do. Perhaps it's because they're smart – smarter than dogs, as tests have shown – perhaps it's because their faces are so full of expression. Haughty, curious, engaging, surprised, busy: they seem to run the gamut of emotions. All animals are not equal, whether we like it or not. Some are more equal, more interesting, more able to grab the imagination. We all know that dogs have that magic ingredient. Sheep don't. Pigs do. It was no accident that George Orwell cast a pig as the ruler of his farmyard. The task of organising the others 'fell naturally upon the pigs, who were generally recognised as being the cleverest of animals', while the sheep were content to lie around in the field bleating 'Four legs good, two legs bad! Four legs good, two legs bad' for hours on end.

Babe and the other six breeding females, or gilts, have organised their pen with military thoroughness. Not for them any confusion about where they sleep, eat or go to the lavatory. Each area is clearly defined. They have a mud wallow which allows them to cool off in the summer heat and keep their coats clean through regular mud dips, which, once dry, can be scratched off, leaving behind clean, hairy skin. They help each other out with the process, reaching a fellow pig's awkward body parts, like the inside of a back leg, with their snouts. Pigs maintain a definite pecking order: Babe is top pig and capable of horrendous bullying of the smaller pigs and cavalier behaviour when it comes to scrabbling for food. But I imagine that if the herd was threatened it would be Babe who'd be out front leading the defence. And they're social too, keeping in touch with each other through a medley of small, agreeable sounds which rise to squeals if one of the pack feels threatened or if there is the possibility of an unexpected snack.

On the lawn that Sunday morning, the pigs are making small delighted squeals, their snouts working overtime, churning through the turf. The strong, flattened tip of a pig's nose is supported by a tough pad of cartilage which lets them shovel through hard ground. I read a story recently about two wild boar in the Bronx Zoo who took out their boredom on their outdoor concrete run. Beginning with one tiny crack and using only their snouts, they reduced concrete paving four inches deep to rubble in just three weeks. Apart from its strength, the snout is also the pig's main organ of external information. Their sense of smell is acute and the two small nostrils in the middle of the snout close up quickly to prevent dirt getting in. In the same way as a dog can learn from a lamppost just who was there before, how long before, their sex and, amazingly, their class, so a pig's snout can sort out details of his environment. That day their snouts are telling them that the best food is to be found a few inches below the lush green grass of the lawn.

A couple of minutes after Charlie and I arrive, David appears, carrying a bucket of pig nuts. 'Pigs!' he shouts, rattling the bucket, so that the nuts make a satisfactory clanking noise against the sides. Seven heads look up in curiosity. Stuff the worms, they seem to say, as each one falls into line behind the bucket to trot off in the direction of their run.

The fuss over, we walk back across the park to brew coffee and read the newspapers. They're full of stories about a parrot that has died in quarantine in Britain from avian flu. The bird had the lethal form of the virus and the prospect of having to lock up our chickens moves a little closer to reality. At least we have found a suitable place: David's father, Dennis, has a mechanical repair shed in a run-down set of farm buildings in the neighbouring hamlet of Atherston, and there will be room in his shed for the birds if the worst comes to the worst. But what will they then be? We can't describe them as free-range any more, so will we have to take a cut in the price of our eggs? And if that happens will DEFRA, as the old ministry of agriculture is now known, pick up the difference?

What will happen to very small producers who can't afford to build a shed big enough to house their chickens or who can't find one? Since the debacle of the foot and mouth crisis, which so affected farmers, no one has any faith in the government to do the right thing at the right time. Looking back on foot and mouth, it is so clear that the simple act of curtailing all movement of animals around the country from the moment of the first diagnosed outbreak could well have stopped the disease in its tracks. Instead, countless animals were slaughtered, ruining farmers both financially and emotionally. Of course for the beef-buying public, ignorant of the human toll the crisis was creating, life went on as normal. The huge supermarket chains ensured that we never ran out of a single hamburger, steak, or packet of mince. They simply looked abroad for supplies.

'Did you know that the imports of beef from South America have risen by 70 per cent in the last year alone?' I'm in Bonner's, Ilminster's champion butcher's shop, on a Saturday morning in October and the shop, as ever, is heaving with life. The queue for the meat counter stretches out into the street, and inside the store people are jostling between the deli area and the meat counter, picking up food for the weekend. As always, it feels good to be in this shop. The Bonner family is headed by Clinton Bonner, known to me as Mr B. Thirty years ago, when the elder Bonners arrived from Kingston-on-Thames, there were five butchers in the town. Now we just have Bonners. The noticeboard to the right of the cash registers lists the provenance of the meat, game and poultry on sale that morning. Everything is local, everything is sourced. The pork has come from a farm that Mr B has known all his life, the chickens come from Mr Cracknell's and the lamb from Ashill Farms. I am looking forward to the day when Mr B chalks up that the Gloucester Old Spot was reared at Dillington Nurseries, as we've decided to call our smallholding.

As ever, Mr B is in fine form. If you had to paint a picture in your mind of what a classic butcher would look like, an image of someone looking uncannily like Mr B would float into your mind. He's red-faced, with a smile that stretches ear to ear. On his head he wears a white cap, to go with his white butcher's coat, which is usually speckled with red splodges of blood. He doesn't so much talk as boom, with laughter, advice and general bonhomie. Mr B makes entering his shop an experience, something much more than just buying a piece of meat and handing over the money. For a brief moment you sense that you've entered an essential and wholesome part of the old-fashioned ways of commerce where you, the buyer, are part of a chain that supports the local farmer, the local feed-producer, the local abattoir, the man who drives the van and the butcher. With the meat in your basket, that chain extends its way to your family and friends, who feast on the sum total of all those transactions.

Importing beef from South America distorts and destroys that chain. In a globalised world, supermarkets can buy from countries where labour costs are far lower, meaning that farmers here in Britain today have increasingly less control over what they can charge for their livestock. The buying power of the big supermarkets is so great that they can dictate the prices, with little regard as to how much it has actually cost a farmer to rear a chicken or a cow, and if the farmer can't produce beef (or lamb, or pork or chicken) to meet that price, tough. Until 1990 Brazil produced only enough beef to feed itself. Since then, its cattle herd has grown by some fifty million and one region is responsible for 80 per cent of the growth in beef production: the Amazon rainforest. In 2004, 26,000 square kilometres of rainforest were burned to clear ground to grow animal feed, primarily destined to feed cows in North America.

But, more sinisterly, no one quite knows where in the UK the beef is being sold or how hygienic it is. The big supermarkets profess not to stock it, or only in minuscule quantities. George Monbiot wrote recently in the *Guardian* that the high levels of corruption in Brazil, where he reckons some 25,000 workers are employed on the beef-producing ranches, mean that farm hygiene standards are lax. Foot and mouth is now endemic in the Brazilian Amazon, yet certificates can be easily bought from officials caught up in the gravy train. When the disease hit Britain in February 2001, the government blamed it on meat imported by Chinese restaurants. But Monbiot's investigation revealed that the farm where the outbreak started, Heddon-on-the-Wall in Northumberland, had been taking slops for its pigs from the Whitburn army training camp near Sunderland. And some of their beef had come from Brazil and Uruguay.

I can't really understand just why we became so fixated on meat. I know how and when we did, but the why still puzzles me. When I was a child, we ate meat on Sundays and at celebrations. The leftovers were recycled into meals on Monday, Tuesday and, in the case of a good fat chicken, through to the back end of the week, when chicken stock would form the basis for soups and my mother's version of risotto. Nowadays, in the UK, we expect to eat meat every day, and our consumption has increased five-fold in fifty years. In the last forty years America has increased its per capita consumption of meat from 80 kilos to 184 a year. European consumption has risen from 56 to 89 kilos. If we go on increasing our consumption at the same rate, in the next fifty years we'll have to produce five times as much again.

Our increased consumption of red meat has led to an increase in heart disease, certain cancers and obesity: our bodies just weren't built to absorb such huge amounts of saturated fat. The consumer desire for skinless chicken and non-fatty cuts of red meat means that the inevitable waste products are used for mass-produced food like turkey twizzlers, burgers and chicken nuggets, which, as Jamie Oliver revealed in *Jamie's School Dinners*, are being dished up daily to our children. Some nuggets contain as little as 16 per cent meat and much of that is waste skin. The single, most astonishing fact for me in Oliver's series was that hospitals in Durham have had to set up special clinics to deal with chronic constipation among children who sometimes don't go to the lavatory for up to six weeks. An excess of sugar and salt in these products promotes behavioural disorders. Chicken flu, salmonella and e-coli all result from the dirty and over-crowded conditions in which factory-farmed chickens are raised. A factory-farmed bird is allotted the space of an A4 piece of paper in which to spend its entire, sorry little life. Force-fed from the day it hatches to slaughter in just six weeks, its body weight increases faster than its bone strength, with the result that the chicken's legs give out and it spends its brief life sitting in muck and dirty feathers.

As a nation we have a very strange relationship with meat: we make a big fuss about additives and the importance of good, clear labelling on food products, but we never want to know how an animal has lived and died in order to get to our plates. We are a nation of supposed animal lovers which has recently spent over fifteen parliamentary hours discussing whether or not we should hunt foxes. I read a 2004 report from Churchill insurers which calculated that we spend an average of £5,000 on our dogs in the course of their lifetimes. Our two dogs, Bingo and Dylan, are very spoilt and over-indulged, but I doubt that we will spend a quarter of that on the two of them together; even so, if at all true, it is a startling statistic. As a society we feel abhorrence when we hear of needless cruelty to animals and we stock the coffers of the RSPCA accordingly. Yet we conveniently glaze over the details when it comes to the animals we eat.

When I'm standing next to our pigs, watching them go about their business, rooting and snuffling in the grass, I'm often reminded of a story my aunt Val told me when I was a child. Val had a friend who kept pigs in her orchard in Buckinghamshire. Every year, in the autumn, she'd take the three pigs, which she'd reared over the summer on her apples, kitchen leftovers, rejected vegetables and generous helpings of full cream milk, to the local abattoir. They'd travel in a straw-filled trailer, towed behind her car. It was a short, four-mile journey to the abattoir in Thame and, provided that she threw in a final bucket of food, it always passed peacefully. But one year, just as she was rounding a bend, a car roared out of a side turning. She skidded into the verge and the trailer ended up on its back in the ditch. Trapped inside, the pigs were in an uproar of fear and confusion. It took a few more hours to get the show back on the road and the pigs to their final destination. When Val's friend came to eat the pork, she found it had a slightly bitter taste. The vet explained that animals in fear release adrenalin into their bloodstream which affects the meat and its subsequent flavour.

I've no doubt that Bramble and Guinness's piglets will grow up to become fantastically tasty pork roast and sausages, and I will eat them with enjoyment and the knowledge that they had a good life and as humane a death as possible. We'll eat every bit of them too. At his home in Great Tew, my old friend John Mitchinson keeps pigs. He well remembers the night he took his first two pigs to slaughter. They spent their final night sleeping in a comfy trailer and John went with them on their journey to the abattoir. Over the coming weekend, they processed every scrap of meat from the pigs. 'They had done a good job for us, and I wanted to do right by the pigs,' he says. 'That means not letting anything go to waste. We made stock out of the bones, brawn from the head, pâté from the liver; we ate brains on toast, grilled ears, and we kept the fat for lard. We also made chorizo, salami and hams which will be ready to eat in three months' time at Christmas. Rearing animals should be based on respect, not exploitation. I liked our pigs – if you gave them a football they'd play ball with you.'

Luckily for us, David's other skill, apart from gardening and animal husbandry, is as a butcher. On the site where the small Ilminster cheese shop, Sarah's Dairy, now operates there, used to stand Bellew's Butchers, owned and operated by David's uncle. When David left Holyrood Comprehensive in Chard in 1984, aged sixteen and armed with seven O levels, he went to work in the family business. He didn't last long: in late 1985 he chopped off his finger while slicing up a ham into bacon rashers. It took the doctors in Taunton's Musgrove Hospital five hours to stitch it back on. He moved on to a job boning pigs at Hygrade Meats in Chard. Pigs would arrive as carcasses, ready to be turned into tinned and packet ham. Once boned, the meat was shovelled into great big tumblers made of stainless steel. Water and brine would be added and the whole lot churned up into what David describes as a 'load of pink mush'. The mush is then fed into square metal moulds, cooked, carved and sealed in plastic bags. 'I never ate processed ham or meat again,' he told me, as we stood watching Boris practise having sex with his male chums. 'I could bone out forty-five legs of pork in an hour. I'd start at five in the morning and work until two. We were meant to get through seventeen in an hour, but if you could do more, it meant you could go home early. Most weeks, I'd take home three hundred quid, although you earn more on piecework. Sometimes I'd work on quarters of beef. We were paid six quid for each one and I could do four in an hour. But you need to have a good steady input of cows to make that profitable.' David grew up with animals – chickens, geese and sheep – and before long he couldn't take Hygrade Meats any more. He left to become a gardener: now he's part-owner of his own farm, where all the animals have a life.

Hygrade Meats processes pork and beef for Tesco. If there isn't enough local meat they buy it, frozen, from Holland. The big frozen slabs have to be chucked in water to thaw out. Given the way the majority of pigs are kept, it is possible that Hygrade's pigs have been born in farrowing crates (designed so the mothers cannot move during pregnancy) and kept indoors throughout their lives, in temperature-controlled, permanently lit units, so that the pigs eat solidly, twenty-four hours a day. The babies are weaned from their mothers at three days old, at which point the mothers are put back to the boar. A modern farm-reared pig can have forty piglets a year, an amazingly proficient baby machine. She can keep this up for four years, after which she is slaughtered before productivity declines.

The piglets have their tails docked and their teeth broken with pliers when they're two days old. Even so, cannibalism breaks out in overcrowded pig pens and pigs have been known partially to eat each other in the crazed desperation that results from living in such unnatural conditions.

In the autumn, we connect the duck pond up to the spring which flows under the farm, so the water is now clear and moving freely. The ducks instantly appreciate the change, wagging their tail feathers in glee as they glide on the water's surface, black feathers turning blue and green in the changing light. Even the chickens seem to enjoy the pond, tip-toeing down the wooden ramp to drink instead of using their water containers. The geese continue making their enthusiastic racket, screeching and hissing whenever anyone comes through the gate and keeping up the din as you walk alongside their wire fence. Once you are inside the chicken run, they waddle quickly towards you, beaks ajar, blue eyes steady. If you turn round and walk away, they come up behind and peck at the backs of your legs. But at heart they're just bullies and cowards: swing back to them and start walking forwards and the retreat is rapid.

The only one who is really scared of the geese is our black Labrador, Dylan. He's actually frightened of the low-lying, green electric wire which encircles the coop, but he pretends it's the geese that cause him to tremble. One afternoon in the summer, when the wire was being redirected to go round an extra section of cage, it was lying only a couple of inches above ground. In his eagerness to annoy the pigs, he went too close to the fence and sat down bang on the wire, only to leap up immediately, yelping, after being zapped by a powerful electric charge. Now he flattens his ears as we approach the gate and will walk up the gravel track that separates the chicken coop from the vegetable garden only if he's safely on a lead. But, once at the other end, he more than makes up for his attack of the jitters, rushing frantically towards the gate into the ladies' pen, barking furiously and making attacks and feints at the curious sows that seem to look scornfully on his manic behaviour. I'd trust Dylan to defend any child, or grandchild, of ours to the point of death, and his huge anxiety about the fence is both touching and endearing.

3

The Luck of the Tailor of Gloucester

It's a very clear, still day in the middle of November. Last night there was frost and the water is still frozen in the puddles at three in the afternoon. From inside the Dairy House it looks as though the day should be warm: the trees still have most of their leaves and the sky is a deep blue, not yet the watery thinness of winter. In the nursery, the vegetables look limp and defeated after three nights of hard frost, but there's no frost for a full metre inside the north wall of the garden. The bricks retain sufficient heat to keep it at bay, which is good news for the newly planted fruit trees, espaliered against the wall. Dillington House has been ordering thirty kilos of sprouts a week and soon we won't be able to keep up with the demand. One big patch of carrots is useless because of ringworms eating away at their surface, leaving little thread-like black lines running through the orange flesh. They're unsightly and we won't be able to sell any of them, so the pigs are getting a treat and we're all going to be eating carrots at every meal. David has just learned that the worms stay away if you plant onions in between the rows of carrots: great information, just much too late for this year's harvest. But, to date, November has been a good month: by the 18th we've sold £504.02 worth of produce to Dillington House.

The chickens, however, have not been doing so well. We have two breeds as layers, born a couple of months apart, so that as one age group enters its brief, non-laying period, the other will take over. Theoretically, this should mean that we have 140 chickens laying between five and six eggs each every week. Our first group of 140 Silver and Brown Neros started laying in September, but now, two months later, they're producing only twenty to thirty eggs a day. They peaked at forty. We don't know whether it is the food, the cold, or what. David has installed lights in the chicken shed as the long hours of darkness mean the birds sleep much of the time. A friendly egg producer, plus information gleaned from a chicken-keeping manual, suggested extending the chicken's day with lights. Now, a light switches on at 5 a.m. and another turns on just after 4 p.m., when the birds return of their own accord to their shed as darkness falls. It hasn't made any difference. Now we're wondering whether we ought to change their food. Their eggs are delicious and we have plenty of orders – not just the 750 that Dillington House will consume every week, but orders from colleagues of David's brother Julian at his office in Taunton and orders from neighbours in the village. As with the vegetables, we could sell far more than we are managing to produce.

Bluebell has been moved out of the all-girls' enclosure and in with the boys. The oldest boys, who arrived before Boris and his brothers, are now over three months old, the age at which pigs reach sexual maturity. Female pigs come on heat for a few days every three weeks and so the plan is to leave her in there for six weeks and hope that she gets pregnant, if not at the first opportunity then at the second. Afterwards, it will be Bramble's turn. Bluebell isn't at all happy about the move. The first two days she hardly left the gate, nuzzling up to David, making sad little snuffles and noises. When I walk over to see her this afternoon, I find her standing on her own near the entrance to her run. She comes over immediately I call, and leans against the fence to have her ears scratched. She seems a very subdued version of her normal bumptious self, her head held low and her eyes downcast. The moment I turn to go, she squeals softly and follows me along the fence. One of Boris's unnamed brothers appears from the undergrowth and makes a beeline for Bluebell's rear end. I stop and resume scratching her ears while the little fellow clambers up her back, his muddy cloven hooves just tall enough to reach on to her back, his eager little face pointing skywards above her tail. With a determined expression, he rocks backwards and forwards, mimicking having sex. Bluebell pays no attention at all. She doesn't move away or swish her hips to knock him sideways and rid herself of the irritating presence he surely must be. Instead, she leans more fully into the fence and thus closer to me, eager for more pats and scratches. The off-white hairs of her coat feel thicker than normal and I wonder if she is growing a winter coat. Poor Bluebell, she seems lonely in with the boys, desirous of her sisters and fellow females for company. I feel an enormous wave of affection for her and want to take her back to her own run. David says she is more cheerful than she was a couple of days ago; nevertheless, she seems a shadow of her former self.

Tonight I'm judging the Christmas windows in the town. It's been an extraordinary autumn, the warmest on record, with bulbs shooting up in November when they should be sleeping quietly for at least another month or two. In our wood, primroses have been flowering since the end of October. But today, although it's sunny, it's very cold; under the trees on the far side of the park the grass is still white with last night's frost. At four o'clock the sky is pale blue, fading into white, but perfectly clear. There is no wind, and as the light disappears the cold starts to bite. Perhaps winter is really coming at last.

I meet my fellow judges at the Meeting House, a converted

chapel at the top of the town which now houses the Ilminster arts centre, of which I'm a trustee. I was brought on board by Di Gallagher, who until a few weeks ago was the centre's efficient and committed manager. Since she gave up the job, Di's been to Ladak, one of the most inaccessible of India's northern states, and now she's raising money for an orphanage out there that she is passionate to help. Di is already in the tea room, along with Bryan Ferris, who, with his wife Elizabeth, owns Lane's Garden Shop in Silver Street. As head of the Chamber of Commerce, Bryan is responsible for organising the Christmas Shopping Evening. He's also the most vociferous town campaigner against the proposed supermarket and the one-way system that the planners are demanding so that supermarket traffic doesn't snarl up the small town streets. Di and I are to be judges, along with Wayne Bennett from Dillington House.

By the time we set out, it's dark and freezing. Wayne is wearing a blue hat with long ear flaps and has remembered to bring his gloves. But even though Di and I, hatless and gloveless, are cold, we're all cheerful as we walk off down East Street towards the market square. Bob from the *Chard and Ilminster Gazette*, or the *Chard and Illy* as it is known locally, is with us to make sure that we judge the windows correctly and to ensure that his paper is first with the results.

In previous years, the theme for the windows has been something along the lines of an old Victorian Christmas, but Bryan has changed that this year to classical children's storybook characters. The first shop we encounter is the Sue Ryder charity shop, which has an arrangement of yellow teddy bears in its window and a banner saying 'Pooh and Friends say Happy Christmas'. A few doors along and we're outside the Ile Dental Centre. There's a narrow inside hall between the front door and the main door to the surgery and this has been transformed into an underwater scene: Ursula the Octopus sits on a chair (all long black floppy legs with a cardboard top half), stuffed fluffy fish swing from nylon wires, a mermaid smirks from the corner, sand and shells cover the floor, and over it all a small machine emits translucent bubbles which hover in the air before bursting away into the ether. We all agree that it's great: full marks for effort and imagination, something that kids will stare at and go, 'Wow, look at *this*!'

I know my daughter Daisy would have liked this window and for a moment I imagine her standing there, an eager six-year-old, wearing her grey school coat and dark red hat with its long tail and a bobble on the end. She would have had her nose pressed against the glass. Maybe we would have just read *Snuggle Pot and Cuddle Pie*, the fantastic Australian children's story which features two fishy heroes – John Dory and Ann Chovy – and she would have been telling me of their exploits, wondering if they could have fitted in alongside Ursula and the colourful stuffed fish. But she's twenty-two now, studying for an MA in International Relations at Johns Hopkins University which entails spending a year in Bologna followed by one in Washington; as I stand there feeling the cold seep through to my skin, my sadness for time passed is momentarily overwhelming.

I separated from her father when she was six and I worked every day from then until the beginning of 2001. Daisy had a succession of nannies, some brilliant, but others too young and self-obsessed to care adequately for a growing child. Working wasn't an option for me – I had to, in order for us to survive – but I know that I also worked to fulfil myself, rattling up the career ladder as though my life depended on it, while the most precious thing in my life laughed, cried, learned, discovered and grew, much of the time when my back was turned. There's nothing unique in this story: women of my age were seduced into believing that they could have it all and do it all too, and even if I could put the clock back I wonder how differently I would have lived as a mother. But I mourn those lost times of my daughter's childhood and, as I turn to leave the fishy world behind the plate-glass window, I wish she was with me, laughing and eager, bouncing with delight, the red woollen bobble of her hat swinging jauntily across her back.

Twenty-one shops have entered the competition, almost all the small shops along the three main streets which branch off from the market square. The main street, Silver Street, which is home to the pharmacy, the hardware store, the cheese shop, Mr Rendell the greengrocer, Mr Bonner the butcher and Aaron Driver at the wine shop, runs alongside the wall of the minster. Roughly halfway along Silver Street, you come to the minster, set back behind a wall on a slope above the road. In the fifteenth century, when the minster was built, there were four resident priests, under the patronage of William Wadham, whose descendants founded Wadham College, Oxford. Six hundred years ago, the church was part of the diocese of Wells, and the builders of the minster apparently wanted to create a microcosm of the magnificent cathedral. It doesn't look much like Wells, but it is a beautiful church, built out of the honey-coloured local Ham stone, with a stately central tower which tonight is hung with a Christmas star.

Harriman's, the men's outfitters, has erected a tiny but near-perfect display, sandwiched between men's Sloggi underpants, a couple of tartan shirts and pairs of brushed-cotton pyjamas. A silver backdrop shows off a small mouse made of a brown woolly material, perched cross-legged on an outsize reel of thread. He's reading a book and sports a pair of fine wire glasses. Behind him, a giant pair of scissors proclaims his trade: *The Tailor of Gloucester*. In front of the mouse, leaning against a large silver thimble, is a white card with the words: 'And from then began the luck of the Tailor of Gloucester: he grew quite stout and he grew quite rich. He made the most wonderful waistcoats for all the rich merchants of Gloucester and for all the gentlemen of the country round.'

Next door, Town and Country Hardware has gone for an elaborate Winnie the Pooh display, complete with a house and

Pooh himself, stuck by his bum midway out of the window. A home-made Christopher Robin is tugging on his arms, Eeyore is tugging on Robin, Tigger on Eeyore. It's brilliant.

Walking onwards, we pass Snow White, Cinderella, the Queen of Hearts, a depiction of *The Secret Garden,* Puss in Boots and a fabulous set for *Treasure Island* which has been erected in the windows of the St Margaret's Hospice shop. John and Mary Rendell have set up a Paddington Bear display in the front window of their greengrocer's. Paddington has a jar of fine-cut Chivers marmalade beside him, but no sandwiches. As we pass by the first time, John tells us not to judge the window until Paddington has been equipped with supplies. Sure enough, on our way back, there's a plate of buttered brown bread triangles, liberally covered with marmalade, right by the bear's left paw.

Back at the Meeting House, we count up the points and decide that the *Little Mermaid* display at the dentist's is the winner. *Winnie the Pooh* is second and *Treasure Island* third. *The Tailor of Gloucester* and an excellent *Alice in Wonderland* window in the RNLI charity shop both receive highly commended certificates. Wayne points out that in a small market town like Ilminster, the windows actually serve a different function from displays in larger towns or cities. 'Everyone knows exactly where they're going, don't they,' he says. 'I mean, you know where the butcher is, the baker and the greengrocer are. The window doesn't make that much difference.'

True, but tonight, and tomorrow – when over four thousand people are expected to cram into Ilminster's three small streets and watch the age-old lights splutter into life at 7 p.m. sharp and then shop and eat mince pies and drink mulled wine, courtesy of the local shopkeepers – they're important. They're important because they're a real sign that Ilminster is still a thriving market town, with small retailers and a community which is prepared to put itself out to give everyone a bit of fun. They're also a sign of pride, in the shops and in the town. And it is all now at risk if a supermarket is built in the car park off Ditton Street.

Bryan Ferris has been in the vanguard of the war against the supermarket for three years now. He's lent me the enormous Lever-Arch file that he has painstakingly compiled, recording every letter between the planners, the town council, the chamber of commerce and other interested parties. It's gobsmackingly complex, the letters and reports tedious and full of long-winded gobbledegook. There are arguments about whether the proposed superstore will be sited in the centre of the town or to the west, how big will it be, where the car park will be built, how much townspeople spend in the town versus how much they already spend outside it. Fifty per cent of the district council think it is a good idea; it is, they believe, what people 'need'. The highways department says that they cannot support the application unless the traffic system is altered, but the proposal will mean that it will be very easy for drivers to find and use the supermarket but much, much harder for them to reach Silver Street. The contents of the pile of documents are so turgid and convoluted that I can see why most people just cave in when confronted by planning departments.

Here's small sample from a document issued by the South Somerset District Council. The meeting was held on 8 June 2005 in the ballroom of the Shrubbery Hotel and its prime purpose was to try to resolve the deadlock about the one-way system. One of the councillors is reported as having suggested that 'perhaps the store could be located in the centre of the site' as he did 'not feel that siting it to the west was friendly to linked trips to the town centre and that better linkages would be achieved by the store being located to the east of the site and the car park to the west'. Councillor Kim Turner, in referring to 'a location for the store to the site, commented that English Nature may object, as such a siting would be against planning policy, it would have to be referred to the Regulation Committee and may be called in by the Office of the Deputy Prime Minister'. Later on in what was obviously a tortured meeting, 'The Planning Team Leader advised that this application could not be deferred on the basis of the location of the store within the site as such a change would need a new application to be submitted.' In the end, after almost four hours of talking, it was decided to defer the decision for two months, pending further reports into the effects of the one-way system and proposals for alternative traffic schemes.

One thing that puzzles me the most is the fact that the entire lengthy process has been conducted by developers acting on behalf of the supermarkets. No one yet knows which one is coming to Ilminster. Waitrose? Sainsbury's? Tesco?

We have a Co-op in the centre of Ilminster, a very modest-sized shop as supermarkets go, but in Ilminster terms it is big – the biggest shop in the town. Everyone grumbles about the Co-op: it doesn't stock this or that, it's always a bit muddled and it's not cheap enough. One day in the summer of 2005, Charlie was standing in front of the dairy counter, choosing some cartons of Yeo Valley yoghurt. A woman standing next to him told him he shouldn't buy it here, better to drive five miles to Chard where he could buy it for far less in Sainsbury's.

In the 1950s, traditional Co-ops and small shops accounted for almost 80 per cent of the nation's grocery trade. Supermarkets only had 20 per cent. Today that is reversed and it is easy to see why. Supermarkets brought a huge range of affordable food to everyone. They were a boon to busy mothers with their one-stop philosophy which provided you with everything you needed for your home and larder. The rows of neat, orderly displays were enticing after the chaos of many small shops. And they were smart, baking bread on the premises to seduce shoppers with mouth-watering smells, arranging flowers and vegetables near the entrance to convince us of the healthy nature of their produce. Sainsbury's even has Jamie Oliver, guardian of our children's healthy eating, advertising its food on TV. But as supermarkets grew and grew and their market share increased, their impact on local towns and communities became anything but benign. In 1998 the Department of the Environment, Transport and the Regions (DETR) undertook a nationwide project to try to assess the effect that supermarkets have on regional towns and the results were shocking. 'Large food stores can and have had an adverse impact on market towns and district centres . . . smaller centres which are dependent to a large extent on convenience retailing to underpin their function are most vulnerable to the effects of larger food store development in edge of town and out of centre locations.'

The study looked at specific examples: when Tesco opened a store on the outskirts of Cirencester, the market share of town centre food shops went down by 38 per cent. In Warminster, the decline was 75 per cent: in Fakenham, 64 per cent. In Hove in 2003, the impact of a new 37,000-square-foot Tesco was felt by the local food shops within days of opening. The greengrocer's sales fell almost 30 per cent and the post office lost 25 per cent of its turnover.

The effect of a huge supermarket on a small town is not simply on the local shops. The New Economics Foundation examined the phenomenon they called 'Ghost Town Britain' and concluded the following:

Suppose a supermarket opens on the outskirts of a town and half the residents start to do one-third of their shopping there. These people still do two-thirds of their shopping in the town centre, while the other half still continues to do all its shopping in the centre. Although all the residents continue to patronise the town centre, its retail revenue drops about 16.7 per cent – enough to start killing off the shops. This is a perverse market dynamic: a loss to the entire community that not a single person would have wanted. It is also self-reinforcing: once the down town starts to shut down, the people who might have preferred to shop there have no choice but to switch to the supermarket. What begins as a harmless ripple becomes a powerful and destructive wave.

Bryan and Elizabeth couldn't cope with a loss in revenue of 16.7 per cent. And neither, I suspect, could John and Mary Rendell, or Aaron Driver in the wine shop. The fate of the baker is also vulnerable as would be the Ilminster Pharmacy, which sells a fabulous range of attractive soaps and smelly things to buy for presents, as well as carrying out all a chemist's expected functions. Attached to the chemist is a small health-food centre, run with engaging directness by Peter Green, who always has an answer to your problems and good advice as to what remedy might be suitable. They also have a small therapy unit in the back where a team of excellent local therapists, trained in sports massage and reiki, offer treatments. According to the New Economics Foundation's report on the effects of supermarkets on local pharmacies, they don't stand a prayer when the big boys come to town.

The judging is now over and Bryan and I are standing outside Lane's Garden Shop early on the Friday night, waiting for the festivities to begin. We've each got a mug of coffee in our hands and we're looking at the window that Elizabeth has created depicting *The Secret Garden*. She's used a mirror to represent a pond which reflects the multicoloured kingfisher perched on a branch above and it is obvious that it must have taken hours to make. Tonight is important for the Ferrises:

they need to sell well to get the Christmas season off to a good start, their cash tills ringing before the inevitable slump in January and February. I've spent much of my working life reading statistics and noting their often gloomy outcomes. But now the numbers have names and faces on them. They're where I go on a Saturday morning to stock up on food, vegetables, bread, toothpaste, soap, a new book, a locally reared chicken, the morning newspaper, light bulbs, potting soil and so on. I can buy pretty much everything I need along Ilminster's high street and there's always the Co-op for loo paper, bleach, diet tonic and fizzy water. I'm well aware that I am in a minority: I'm middle-class and reasonably affluent and I don't have to watch every penny. For so many, supermarkets have revolutionised the way they shop and the ease with which they can. But they come at a very high price to local communities, all too often eradicating a way of life in their wake.

I don't know quite what the tipping point would be for our town – just how many shops would have to close before it would become a pointless exercise to shop in the high street because you just couldn't get all you needed. But if the greengrocer, the baker and the pharmacy were forced out of business, that would probably be enough to persuade Charlie and me to drive over to Chard (or Yeovil, or Crewkerne) and load up the car from Tesco or Sainsbury's. But the loss of the small shops doesn't just drive shoppers like us out of the town; it also has an enormous impact on the economy of the local area.

It has been calculated that every £10 spent on a local food initiative – a shop, or a farm shop, even a direct-to-your-door vegetable box scheme – is worth £25 to the local economy. Small businesses use other small local businesses – the local locksmith, photocopier, accountant, and lawyer – and this keeps the money spinning round. Ten pounds spent in a supermarket produces only £14 of benefits to the wider local community. Supermarkets literally vacuum the money away from the local area: they stock almost no local products, so small vegetable growers are left without outlets. When small shops close down there is obviously a loss of jobs, and although some will find work at the supermarket, by no means all do. The National Retail Planning Forum researched the effect supermarkets have on local employment in the retail sector. In a 1998 report they said that the opening of every superstore resulted in the loss of 276 full-time local jobs.

In the autumn of 2005, there was a flurry of newspaper reports saying that the Cornish WI had told its members to boycott the supermarkets. The WI were concerned about the closures of village shops and small retailers and at their meeting on 18 October in Truro, Nan Collier, the local president, had announced this initiative. It seemed extreme for the WI to be calling for an outright ban and indeed, so it was. What Nan had in fact asked was that members take positive steps to support local retailers, not actually stop shopping in the megastores. But such is the charged state of the supermarket in country minds that a sub-editor on the *Western Morning News* headlined the story 'WI Orders Boycott' and it was enough to guarantee national coverage.

Supermarkets are one of the twenty-first century's bogeymen. They break so many rules that they've become the target for environmentalists, foodies, animal lovers and anyone who cares and is concerned about the plight of the countryside, the farmers, food miles, agri-business and globalisation. There's been a great deal of research on what happens to market towns when supermarkets open, but a new study undertaken in East Suffolk between 1997 and 2004 shows what can happen if, as rarely occurs, local protesters have their way and a megastore is stopped in its tracks.

In 1997, one of the big chains applied for permission to build a store outside Saxmundham. To discover what effect this might have on local food producers and the local economy, eighty-one food shops in seven market towns and nineteen villages in the immediate area were asked to take part in a survey organised by the Campaign to Protect Rural England (CPRE). The shops were sourcing food from 300 local or regional food producers: sixty-seven of the eighty-one shops said they thought they would be forced to close if the superstore opened. All the producers who were interviewed said they had started small and depended on other small outlets for their survival. The producers and the retailers also supported a wide range of other businesses, such as builders, electricians, banks and accountants. After planning permission was refused, the local food economy continued to flourish.

Seven years later, the CPRE went back to see what had happened to Saxmundham in its years without a megastore. They found that fourteen of the eighty-one shops had closed, but fourteen new ones had opened, including five with post offices. All the market towns still had their butchers, bakers, fish shops and greengrocers. There were more farm shops and more farmers' markets. Local and regional food suppliers had increased from 300 to 370. All the butchers had taken on more staff. In every area the rural food economy had flourished, providing greater choice and diversity. This diversity had attracted tourists who were fed up with the cloning of our towns, so restaurants, pubs and B&Bs were thriving. A local meat market meant more cattle and sheep grazing in fields, which also attracted tourists. Additionally, the local food economy had provided a seed bed for new businesses, and local shops continued to provide a meeting place for the elderly, the infirm and the young who can't drive.

One of the most significant findings of the survey was the increasing demand for local and regional food. If there's a TV programme exposing illegal practices in the chicken industry, local butchers are always overwhelmed by demands for local birds. The more food is identified by its region, the greater confidence it inspires. Knowing that our vegetables and, in time, our pigs will wind up on tables within a few miles of our farm brings a real sense of responsibility. Supermarkets source only 5 per cent of their food locally (though recent surveys suggest that 70 per cent of buyers would like to buy locally), and I can't imagine that the bosses in the southeast of England lose much sleep if there's an outbreak of salmonella in the northwest.

Just as darkness falls, the Ilminster shopping evening gets under way. Up at the Meeting House, Bryan is organising and judging the children's fancy dress parade. In the market square, a children's orchestra is playing carols. A brightly lit teacup roundabout is parked outside the Co-op and hamburgers are cooking on a huge open barbecue. At 6.30, the Dazzling Sapphires, a cheerleader group of local schoolgirls, brave the cold in tutus and tights to pirouette down the street. They are followed by Santa Claus, who is followed by the fancy dress brigade. There are Red Riding Hoods and Captain Hooks, Oliver Twists and dashing White Knights. Mr B, dressed in top hat, grey waistcoat and pinstriped trousers, calls the crowd to order to present the prizes. Local MP David Laws congratulates the winners of the windows competition and then the vicar, Alistair Wallace, wearing full black robes, a wide-brimmed black felt hat and wire-framed glasses, and looking as though he has stepped straight out of the pages of Trollope, awards prizes to the children. The winner is five-year-old Callum Elsworth, splendidly dressed as Aslan, with a cat's mask and plenty of yellow ribbons for his lion's mane. Down below the small stage, his parents, grandparents and an apparently endless stream of cousins and aunts clap their delight.

It's easy in our current climate to romanticise a town like Ilminster. Locally, it is reckoned to be a 'nice' place, unlike nearby Chard and Yeovil, which both have problems with binge-drinking and drugs. Certainly in a time when the home news agendas are dominated by stories of binge-drinking teenagers throwing up in gutters, violence on inner-city estates, failing schools and fractured communities, the cosiness of a small market town getting together to celebrate Christmas on a Thursday night is wholly seductive. But it is naïve to think that everything in Ilminster conforms to an idealised image of community life, embedded in families and annual festivals which mark the regular turning of the seasons, connecting us to nature's cycles. There's unemployment, illness, divorce and every other pitfall that is so much a part of the human lot. For a few short moments that evening, however, I get a sense of something else which all too often seems to be missing, certainly from my own life in the hustle of the city: a community which hangs together, bound through geography and common purpose, one which knows how to celebrate small but pivotal achievements.

But I find myself wondering as I walk up the hill back home towards the Dairy House: if the supermarket came and the shops started closing, if Lane's Garden Shop went bust and the baker and the chemist, would there be a Christmas shopping evening? No one's going to bother to come if there aren't any mince pies or glasses of steaming mulled wine being handed out for free to anyone who asks. Who on earth will be interested in a Tesco Christmas window?

I also realise that, in concentrating on the town, I've been ignoring all the reports I've read on farming, in particular on small farms. They're closing at a steady rate, right across the country, and why should I assume that somehow we can avoid becoming yet another statistic, a casualty of the war of the countryside, every bit as much as Bryan might well become a casualty in the town? It wouldn't bankrupt Charlie and me if our farm collapsed, but I find it hard to contemplate just how much failure would hurt. For David it would be a disaster. There are so many things that could go wrong: what happens if the chickens carry on laying only twenty eggs a day? We've already had one sick pig: Guinness's foot got infected and required antibiotics and visits from the vet. The bills soon topped the amount she had cost us as an eight-week-old weaner. What will happen if chicken flu strikes? Or if Dillington House stops taking our vegetables, because they run out of patience at our inability to supply all they need on a regular and reliable basis (as happens to small producers who attempt to supply the supermarkets)? Our friends all too often refer to our farm as a hobby, but I realise that has changed. It's not just a hobby any more, it's something that matters very much to Charlie and me and our life together. Somehow it has to succeed.

I keep my fingers crossed that the luck of the Tailor of Gloucester won't desert this town – or our farm.

4

Trees Are Excellent Listeners

Bluebell's departure from the north wood changes the balance of power among the females. In her absence, sister Bramble takes over as top pig, pushing Babe firmly into second place. There's no doubt that Bramble is the biggest pig – she stands about thirty inches tall and is getting fatter every day. She probably has another three inches to grow in height and many inches to grow round her girth, but she now seems to have the psychological clout. All the pigs seem calmer, especially Babe. Now she comes to the fence at a walk, instead of her usual pushy jostle, standing politely beside Bramble to have her head scratched. In recent weeks, Babe has always thundered up to the gate, hurling herself upwards, feet balanced on the top row of wire, lungeing forward to grab anything she can – a proffered vegetable or my sleeve. Today the mood is much more restrained, with all the pigs standing in line, waiting for a stroke. Bramble makes sure she is at the head of the queue, gently sniffing my hand, reminiscent of a dog ascertaining whether you are friend or foe.

One of the gardeners from Dillington House, Adrian, has been helping out on Mondays with the vegetables. This week, the last in November, he'd walked into the pig pen while David was putting down fresh straw in the hut. The pigs love this moment: they kick at the clean dry straw, tossing it into the air with their noses and burying themselves in the soft piles. Bramble heard Adrian coming and rushed out of the shelter, her head on one side (which for a pig is the position they need to adopt if they are preparing to bite) and charged up to Adrian, emitting loud squeals. He didn't wait to discover her intent and beat a quick retreat to the gate. David told me that he reckoned Bramble was defending the house, and possibly him, against a stranger that she didn't know.

David and Adrian have cleared up much of the wood in the last few days and we light a bonfire with the debris. The pigs cluster round, sitting incredibly close to the flames, their bottoms almost in the burning embers. Bramble is so close that I think that her long sandy eyelashes will start to burn. They love the heat and the sight of the flames seems to mesmerise them. When the fire dies down the pigs lie on the hot ashes, their thick hairy coats starting to singe in the heat. When I tell Charlie about this later on in the day, he makes a joke about the crackling we're soon going to be eating. He's not as sentimental as I am about the pigs, but then as a lawyer who has spent so many years of his life working in the field of child abuse, sentiment is not an emotion he can easily afford.

A few days later, I'm in Hay-on-Wye for the winter book festival and I find myself sitting next to gardening guru Monty Don at dinner, telling him about the pigs and the bonfire. Monty has recently set up a small farm where people from Hereford with serious drug problems come for two days a week to learn how to grow vegetables and care for animals. Monty is a great believer in the therapeutic powers of nature, as a cure for depression and as a way to help restore confidence and a will to live in anyone prepared to open themselves a little to the process. They'd also had a bonfire and his pigs, four Tamworth siblings, had behaved in exactly the same way.

While I am in Hay, there is an attempt to steal the pigs. Two things happen over the night of Friday, 2 December 2005. First, a gate that shuts off the road through Dillington Park is rammed sometime between one and seven o'clock in the morning. Second, when David arrives to feed the pigs just after eight on Saturday, he finds the male pigs locked into their small shelter. When he'd left them the night before, they were still outside the corrugated iron structure, rootling around in the incredibly muddy ground. Who had locked them in? We can only assume that someone had rammed the gate, driven down through the park towards the walled garden and then, for whatever reason, changed their minds about actually nicking the seven little pigs. David reckons it is the local gypsies, but Charlie and I are reluctant to buy automatically into the prevalent Somerset belief. Everything, we are always told, is the fault of the gypsies. Over in Charlton Mackrell, the village where Charlie spent his early childhood, a dog was recently kidnapped from the rich new owners of the biggest house in the area and a ransom note for £1,000 posted through their letter-box. Negotiations through intermediaries in the pub reduced the sum by half and the dog came home. Closer to us, a statue of two Labradors cast in bronze and commissioned as a fiftieth birthday present was stolen from some friends' locked barn the night it was delivered from London. There had clearly been some inside tip-off. The police had suspicions but no definite leads. Then a message was received outlining details of a reward for the return of the gambolling dogs. The ransom was paid and the dogs are now firmly fixed in a concrete base on our friends' lawn.

But would anyone want to kidnap the pigs? They're not fully grown, but they stand two feet high, they're heavy and they wriggle like mad if you pick them up. Would someone really want to keep seven noisy little pigs hostage, hoping to cash in a ransom demand? It must have been straight theft with a view to fattening them up for sale or eating. Right now, they'd probably fetch about £90 a pig. There's not much we can do to make the pig pens safe from thieves. The fence posts have been sunk in concrete and extra padlocks put on the gates, but if a thief is really determined, then I guess the pigs are history. Geese might be a good alarm system, but in the middle of the night who is going to hear?

I like Monty Don's idea about healing through nature. Without a doubt it's what helped me through the bleak months after my car accident in May 2003. My right leg took the force of the collision, shattering the lower inches of my tibia into shards. My surgeon later said that it was as though someone had taken a sledgehammer to the bottom of my heel. My leg was pinned together in a metal fixator, known as an X-fix. Two months after the accident, I was back in hospital having a bone graft. They took the bone out of my left hip, mixed it with red jelly-like cells extracted from my blood and squished it around the broken bones. The scar went septic and three weeks later I was back in hospital, hooked up to antibiotic drips. The summer of 2003 was mercilessly hot and I fretted from a chair in the garden. In the autumn, my surgeon at Salisbury Hospital said that the bone graft wasn't working and I was sent home with an electric gadget that I wrapped round my leg at night, so that pulses might be delivered to the fracture site to encourage growth. To make it work, I had to leave it on for eight-hour stretches. I slept like that every night until just before Christmas, when I returned to Salisbury for another x-ray. The doctor was gloomy. It wasn't healing. He wrote me a letter of referral to a surgeon at St Peter's Hospital, Chertsey, and wished me good luck. I was seriously frightened that I was going to lose my right leg.

My new doctor wasn't optimistic. In time, I got to realise that he never was. He always erred on the side of caution. Bob Simonis is something of a genius. His surgery is the last resort for a generation of young men who've piled their motorbikes into walls, suffering fractures which, only a decade or two ago, would have resulted in amputation. Like me, their primary doctors had despaired and referred them to Simonis to see if he could succeed where they had failed. In the late 1980s, Bob started working with Ilizerof frames, a complex, Meccano-like system of wires, rings, nuts and bolts invented by a Russian doctor of the same name. Dr Ilizerof founded a huge institution in Russia, which, until the fall of Communism, no Western doctors were allowed to visit. Bob went out there in the early 1990s, his visit recorded by a BBC crew. Until that moment, he'd been fitting the frames using his own skills and the information contained in a textbook.

As I sat in the waiting room at our first meeting, I couldn't take my eyes off my fellow patients. The frames were simply terrible. Mediaeval torture instruments, heavy, clumsy, with wires going straight through the skin and bone and twisted tightly in place into heavy circular rings. The skin round the entry holes was red, sometimes bleeding, always angry. When he told me that I was also going to need wires through my foot, four of them, I wanted to scream. Instead I asked him my chances – '40/60,' he replied, and right up to the moment that he took the frame off he never altered that verdict.

It had been a long autumn, hobbling around on crutches, getting exhausted when I walked any further than a couple of hundred yards. None of my clothes fitted, partly because I was putting on weight, but also because no trousers would fit over the X-fix and I looked and felt like a bag lady. I was also in a deep depression which had been living inside me like a malignant storm for almost two years. After I left the *Express* at the start of 2001, my sense of self seemed to curl up and wither. The paper had been sold to Richard Desmond, multi-millionaire pornographer who made his fortune out of titles like *Asian Babes* and *Big Ones*. His every other word was 'fuck'. From the moment details of the sale were confirmed, I knew my days as the paper's editor were numbered. Even so, I wasn't remotely prepared for the shock. I'd been going to work every day for the last fifteen years; for the last ten of them I'd been an editor. Work, I realised, had meant a great deal more to me than simply a way of paying the bills. It defined the way I spent my time, the structure of my days, the mood of my evenings and weekends. To a large extent it provided the subjects of conversation. On a deeper level, it defined who I was, to the world at large and, all too often, to myself. I hated to admit just how much I had become attached to labels to define me, but it was the truth.

There were mornings when I'd wake up in tears, unsure how to get through the day, unsure of who I was. I was furious with myself for being less than fine. The last few months at the *Express* had been a nightmare and much of it had been played out in a very public arena. I had a terrific husband, a great daughter, four wonderful stepchildren and a lovely house to enjoy. Plus I'd been given a chunky golden handshake and was able to depart the *Express* with my head held high. To confess that I was less than fine felt self-indulgent and ridiculous. The inner resources that had stood me in good stead through difficult years had evaporated and, after twenty years of mostly continual sobriety, I began to drink again. I knew as I picked up the bottle that it was a form of insanity. I'm an alcoholic and drink is as dangerous to me as sugar is to a diabetic but, in my gathering depression, the brief oblivion that it offered seemed preferable to the chilly reality of my life. Inevitably, it only caused more chaos, not just for me, but for Charlie and Daisy and my family as well. I was drunk when I had my car accident, which was reported in the papers under a picture of me looking wild-eyed and crazy after a court case in Salisbury. It was as though everywhere I turned there were nails punching holes through my shattered self-esteem.

The only moments of peace I could find were in the garden, particularly in the wood. In September 2003, when I could still convince myself that I was going to walk freely again by the end of the year, I'd decided to create a garden in the overgrown wood which joins our land. The wood had been planted twenty-five years earlier, mainly with oaks, but it had been neglected over the years and now the trees were growing too close together, slender trunks rising up to a canopy of leaves. We began by cutting down some fifteen of them, opening up spaces and allowing sunlight on to the leafy floor. In the centre we carved out a pond which was lined with old carpets, some donated by friends in the village. Paths were laid and some huge lengths of oak dragged into the wood to create chairs and a sofa, which we positioned by the fence, overlooking the park in a southwesterly direction. On those autumn weekends I'd balance on my crutches on the leaf mould, watching Charlie planting bluebell, aconite and snowdrop bulbs and think that when the bulbs started to grow, pushing their sweet young green leaves up to feel the sunlight, then my leg would be better. It was extraordinarily calming to align myself with the rhythms of nature, which cannot be hurried. All you can do as a gardener is prepare and feed the soil, provide the water, see that the light can get in and then wait. For the brief moments that I felt at one with the natural world, the panic that seemed to beat incessantly inside me would subside.

Nine months after my accident, I went into hospital for the five-hour operation. When I came round I was in agony, not just from the wires that had been drilled through my bones. There was no guarantee that this would work. No miracles had occurred on the operating table to alter Bob

Simonis's original verdict. All that was certain was that there was no certainty and I had no inner resources to deal with it.

When I was in my twenties, I studied Buddhism under a Tibetan teacher called Chogyam Trungpa Rinpoche. With my then boyfriend John Steinbeck, the author's youngest son, I'd lived in Boulder, Colorado, where Trungpa had set up a university and spiritual teaching centre. I'd wrestled then with the notion of impermanence, which the Buddhists understand as the only guaranteed condition of our lives. All sadness, they maintain, comes from failed expectation, from regretting what has happened and waiting for circum-stances to change and make you feel better. By living with one foot in the past and another in a fantasy of how things might be, we fail to live in the present. And that way a sort of madness lies. I knew intellectually that everything in life is impermanent and that all we truly have is the moment in which we live, right here and right now. And that it is within our gift to live in that place and thus to feel and see all that is fine and right in our universe. But there is a huge divide between understanding something intellectually and finding a way to live it. I found it almost impossible to accept what had happened; I wanted to rewrite my story, to make it more palatable. Charlie is much more realistic than me, good at coping with consequences and facing reality. Thirty years of being a lawyer, of listening to people say, 'If only this hadn't happened,' have bred in him a rare ability to face the music fair and square. Now his once determined and focused wife was wallowing in egotistical self-pity, turning his own life into a nightmare not of his making.

The dull winter of 2004 turned into spring and the days were drifting past, like flotsam in the tide. I had no connection with them. My life just seemed to be a matter of getting through from dawn till night, lumbering around on my frame, eating too much, sleeping too much . . . waiting, waiting, waiting, sentenced to a kind of limbo which would only, I believed, be altered by external events. I was still occasionally drinking and I couldn't see how to stop. The long years that I'd spent sober felt like a foreign country for which I'd lost the visa. So at the end of May I went to get some help.

Mr Simonis, who I saw regularly every month, had told me that the only thing I could do for my leg was walk on it. I needed to walk a mile a day, preferably without crutches, though using one would be acceptable. The fact that the wires made my feet bleed when I walked couldn't be helped; bones need weight on them to encourage healing, the more weight the better. As he explained, animal bones mend fast because they continue to stand up and move despite the fractures. The lumps and bumps that you see on a sheep's leg are the result of their bodies forming calcium deposits around the breaks. Not pretty, but wholly functional.

I went to get help at a therapy centre in Woking, run by Americans who I instantly trusted. There was a red-brick path running through the garden and every day I'd aim to walk up and down it twenty times. The bricks were laid in a herring-bone fashion and halfway along the path there was a huge copper beech, its branches providing shade from the sun and shelter from the rain. The path was to become my own little road to Damascus. Walking along it one day, I saw how much I needed to change. Not the world, not other people; I could do nothing about them. All I could change was myself and my reactions. The walking hurt, but I was doing it and so, I reasoned, I wanted to get better. I was physically and spiritually sick. I'd stopped seeing the trees, stopped seeing the way the sunlight made patterns on the bricks beneath my feet, stopped hearing the sounds of the birds or watching them fly. I remember sitting down on the bench under the beech tree, its generous silvery branches reaching away above me. I have always found that trees are excellent listeners. They've been here so long that there isn't much they haven't seen. In the past trees have been worshipped and wars have been won and lost on the ready availability of timber. In the dining-room of my late parents' home there was a huge, curved oak beam holding up one wall. It had been cut from local Shropshire oak, used in a ship which sailed against the Armada and then, as had been agreed, returned to its place of origin for use in house-building. When I was little I used to daydream about that beam and the places it had been. Sitting under that copper beech I found myself thinking: the tree breathes out what I breathe in and I breathe out what the tree breathes in. That interdependence is part of my equation for living on the planet. I began to get better.

In our wood there's an old oak tree. It's dying and when in full leaf in the summer its dead branches stand out from the crown of greenness, like gnarled bony arms reaching up towards the sky. The oak is probably about three hundred years old and it stands next to the pond, casting its long shadows across the water. I like leaning against its trunk. The knobbly bark reminds me of an elephant's skin. It's a tough tree, resilient, able to keep on living proudly even while it's dying. Right now, up in a crack just where the main boughs grow away from the trunk, two hornets hover at the entrance to their large nest. By standing back, you can see the papery structure, balanced in a gap in the rough bark. Hornets always keep two guards in place in front of a nest, checking for intruders, allowing only their friends to enter. Last summer wasps made a nest further up the tree. Its branches are home to birds, the cracks and crevices in the bark shelter a myriad of insects.

We're all tenants of this land and when we garden we plough something back. It's a way of saying thanks. If gardening were just growing a row of pretty flowers then it would be meaningless. But it's not. Planting and sowing and digging are the ways in which muddled people connect their lives to something bigger, to all our joys and sorrows, because when you push a bulb deep into soft wet earth it is always a symbol of hope. Hope that nature will not fail; hope that you will still be alive to see the bulb burst out of the ground and unfurl its delicate leaves, opening the way for the miraculous flower. It is always about the future, but about a future which you can only hope for. Maybe you won't see the flower in all its glory, but someone will. Gardening connects us to a bigger picture, in which we are small, but crucial, players. It also offers a solace against much that is tough today. Many of us have little control over our working environments: we're hostages to the mortgage, the boss, the kids. Gardening is something private, with its own triumphs and disasters, and our gardens are our retreat from those problems. When we step out under the sky and into our own space we can leave behind some of the pressing clutter which makes modern life so stressful.

It's late 2005 and in three weeks' time we're going to kill our first animals. We've got an order for ten geese from Charlie's old friend Rowley Leigh, who is the chef at Kensington Place restaurant. Rowley and Charlie were at Cambridge together and in the last few years they've become good friends. We're lucky to be able to sell our geese to him. Kensington Place is fantastically successful and last year Rowley opened a fish shop, housed in a glass-fronted annexe on the side of the restaurant. Half of the geese will be sold whole through the fish shop and the others will appear on the menu, accompanied by braised red cabbage. Rowley is a brilliant cook and KP's ever-changing and always interesting menu has ensured packed tables for over twenty years, no mean feat in London's febrile restaurant world. We'll get better money from Rowley than from Mr Bonner, but while that's important, it is not just a financial matter. Rowley has huge clout in the restaurant world and if he likes our geese – and in time, our pigs and vegetables – then it will be easier to find other outlets.

'How do you feel about shooting the geese?' I ask David as he sits in our kitchen, nursing a cup of coffee and rolling a cigarette of Woodbine tobacco in licorice-flavoured Rizla.

It is a Saturday morning in early December and last night there was a sharp frost. The weather has been topsy-turvy. It's been raining and it's been freezing but the trees with small leaves, like the oaks and the apples, remain resplendently green. Temperatures in October were about 2.5°C above the thirty-year average, and in November the hours of sunshine were 50 per cent above the norm. Most years the fall in temperature through the autumn is the catalyst for trees to start slowing down, drawing the chlorophyll out of the leaves and exposing the carotene pigment, which produces their vivid reds, yellows and oranges. The mild autumn, followed by the sharp frosts of early December, further confused the trees. Those with big leaves – like walnuts and horse chestnuts – have shed their big, fleshy leaves, but smaller, tougher leaves – like the birch, oak and apple – are still clinging on. The mild weather meant there was poor colour this autumn: trees need cold nights to bring about the change.

But already, according to David's reckoning, there have been as many frosts in ten days as there were in the whole of last winter. The brugmansia, which grew all summer in a large, heavy pot on the terrace, is dead. In the vegetable garden, the leaves of the parsley plants and the spinach have wilted, as though struck by lightning. This time last year we still had roses in the garden and we mowed the lawn in mid-December, but now the garden lies dormant.

'This is what it's all about, isn't it?' he says. 'If you can't kill animals and do it quickly and cleanly, then you can't do *it*.' I know he's pleased with the geese. They've been a success, easy to look after, fattening quickly and well. We're keeping two ganders and six females to breed from next year and David wants to add some turkeys to our mix of fowl.

'I want to buy two girls and a stag,' he says. 'They'll cost £80.'

'What do you call a lady turkey?' I ask.

'I dunno. Mrs?' he replies. David's been over-working and he's lost weight. The doctor has told him he's putting in too many hours and not getting enough time off. Charlie has suggested that we approach the prison in Shepton Mallet and see if they would be prepared to let someone near the end of their sentence come and work on the farm. His long years in the law have led him to believe that prison rarely helps to rehabilitate its inmates; working on the farm would mean gaining a trade as well as hopefully discovering some of the therapeutic benefits of rearing animals and growing vegetables. I like the idea and we clearly need some extra help.

The chickens have laid a little better this last week, though we're still only getting about two dozen eggs a day when it should be almost four dozen. Apparently it is better to have your chickens reach point of lay in the spring as they'll get into their laying routine while the days are long. If they mature in the winter, it is hard for them to establish a good routine, even with lights coming on in their hut at five in the morning. Wet feet may be another problem. Chickens hate being damp, and the big-footed geese have churned up the ground, killing off most of the grass. After Christmas we're going to have to move them to another run, along with the ducks. The spring that feeds their pond will have to be run through a pipe into their new pen.

Ten days before Christmas David kills eight of the geese. I'd asked him to leave two to kill until I arrived, so that I could see for myself what it was like to kill an animal that you'd reared. He was reluctant. Despite his confident words that morning in the kitchen, killing the geese has made him feel 'tight' and he's upset that the geese now regard him as an enemy, not a friend. When I go over to the farm on the last Saturday morning before the holidays, the remaining eleven birds are clustered at the far end of the chicken run, completely silent, an unheard-of state for a gaggle of geese. Even when we walk in to feed the chickens, they still hang back. 'They know,' David says, as he flings handfuls of corn towards them. Their egg-laying has improved a little and is now back to about thirty a day. As there is no chance of the rare breeds getting pregnant in the deep winter, they are all out of their pens: magnificent Brahmas, speckled Sussexes, bantams with wildly feathery legs, all clustering round the pond, choosing to drink there rather than from the relative safety of their water trough.

Killing a goose isn't that easy, certainly not as easy as killing a chicken. Holding each head in his left hand, David fired his 2.2 air rifle into the back of each downy white skull, then quickly made an incision through the neck to allow the blood to pump out. Plucking takes almost two hours per bird: first the outer, big feathers, then the downy layer beneath, and finally an all-over singe with a blowtorch to remove the last feathery bits. The huge naked birds are then hung up by their feet, their heads enclosed in plastic bags which collect the last of the blood. That morning David and I are in the shed, looking at the ungainly, naked birds hanging from the ceiling. We take them down one by one. David chops off their heads then severs the neck close to the body, keeping the bony tube as part of the giblets. He makes a further cut to remove the rear end, through which he pulls out the gut, gizzard, heart, kidneys and liver. I take each bird outside and clean it inside and out with a high-pressure hose, washing away any remaining bits of blood, singed feathers and loose fat. They are heavy, between twelve and twenty pounds, and their breasts are plump with flesh and thick, yellow fat. I tie the feet together and, with the same bit of string, pull the wings close into the body. Then I stuff the finished birds into plastic bags which we've been given by Mr Bonner. They look good: eight fat geese lined up on the shelf in the shed, ready for Christmas tables.

Financially, they are useless. Each bird has cost £4.50 as a day-old gosling. Even if we charge the plucking costs at the minimum wage, each goose costs over £10 to prepare. Add into that each bird's share of fencing, food, man-hours for feeding, watering, checks by the vet and I think you must add about a tenner. Then there is the price of driving the birds to Kensington Place restaurant in London. That's roughly £20 in petrol, or £2 per bird, plus the cost of labour, which comes to another £2 per bird. Total cost per bird: £28.50. Sale price to Rowley: £35.

David has cut down a big old spruce that had been threatening to fall on to the fence along the north side of the girls' wood. After the geese are safely in their bags, we light another bonfire to clear away more wood, ivy and undergrowth so that there's clear space to plant some cooking apple trees. The pigs cluster excitedly round the fire as it leaps into life, but then stand still, their eyes caught by the flickering lights. David sits on Bramble and I perch on Bluebell, who has returned from her stay among the boys, hopefully pregnant. Both pigs move close to the fire, their noses just inches from the flames. They stand still and solid and I feel touched that a semi-wild animal lets me sit peacefully on her back. David has news about the pig rustlers. According to local gossip, on the basis of no evidence, a gypsy family has been on a mad stealing spree. The most

astonishing theft concerned a Range Rover which was discovered by Rodney, Ewen's gamekeeper, hidden in a nearby
field of maize. But the gypsies themselves have been in serious
trouble. The weekend before, one of them had been hit on the
head in a pub fight in Broadway. He'd recently had a heart
attack and was on prescribed blood-thinning drugs and the
blow had killed him. Now a local man was being held on a
manslaughter charge.

If there were truffles growing under the ground in Somerset,
then it would be understandable why someone might want to
steal a pig. One of nature's more extraordinary symbiotic
meetings connects a pig's snout to certain fungi. Truffles live
underground, below broad-leafed trees which lack phosphorus. The trees need the fungi to supply them with this
vital trace element, so the parasitic fungus lives on their roots
well below the surface. The best known of these is the *Tuber
melanosporum*, which unites with the hair-like rootlets of the
European oaks and develops tiny organs called mycorrhizae.
These allow the fungus to access carbohydrates, produced up
above in the leafy canopy, and they return the favour by
spreading out in webs throughout the soil, collecting moisture
and minerals which they share with the tree.

Root-bound and down in the dark, the fungus had a
problem. The oak tree could reproduce via its acorns, but
how was the fungus going to spread its spore? The famous
black truffles of Périgord hit on an ingenious solution: the nose
of the wild pig. The fungus somehow synthesised a perfect
chemical copy of 5-alpha-antrostol, the active testosterone
normally found in the salivary glands of boars in the mating
season. So, in the dead of winter, the truffle emits a smell
strong enough to attract the nostrils of passing female pigs,
who dig down in glee, hopeful of finding a randy boar under
the soil.

It's an extraordinary, though mostly one-sided, bargain.
The fungus gets to spread but the sow is left disappointed. For

humans, though, it's something of a bonanza. They follow the pig and push her away before she can reduce the truffle to a cloud of dust, selling the prized fungi for up to £700 a pound. I pat Bluebell on her bristly rump. I'm sure that, given half a chance, she'd be a great and determined truffle pig, rootling her way through the undergrowth in search of the buried treasure. Even so, she will more than earn her keep: over her breeding lifetime she will give us at least forty piglets.

We decide that next year we're going to rear at least fifty geese and fifty turkeys and we're going to either rent a machine that will pluck them or take them somewhere that will do it for us. Mr Bonner has sold ninety geese this year, forty up from Christmas 2004, so hopefully we can make a deal with him early on in the year. Of our twelve remaining geese two are ganders. Assuming the ten females lay ten eggs each and successfully hatch half of them, we'll have fifty of our own goslings. As ever, these things look good on paper but go awry somewhere in the actual process of growing and selling. We're still subsidising the farm to the tune of some £1,500 a month, and even though we're selling all we grow there's a vast gap between outgoings and income. In January we're taking on another four acres, specifically to grow vegetables. That will cost £1,000 a year, plus fencing, plus the extra labour that will be needed to keep rows of organic vegetables weed-free. It's no wonder that organic vegetables cost more. Before he began working full-time on the farm, David helped set up an organic vineyard for a Londoner who wanted to go into wine production. The vineyard consisted of some five miles of vines, all of which had to be weeded by hand. David reckoned the wine would have to cost £30 a bottle.

5

A Christmas Market

The Empress died on Christmas Eve, 2005. When David went to feed the pigs early in the morning, the usual stampede was light one animal. The little black pig was lying on her side in the shed, partially covered by straw. There were no marks on her body. The vet said that she had died of suffocation, probably after being slept on by the bigger pigs. It seems sad and pointless. Although I'm not at all sure that I would have done anything different myself, I am somehow aggrieved that David hasn't eaten her: she might have tasted delicious and my sense of waste would have been partially mitigated. But he says that while he did think of it, the fact that she hadn't been correctly slaughtered stopped him and he buried her three feet down, under a laurel tree. But I think he's too much of a softie to butcher her himself and I wonder how the two of us are going to cope when we set off to Snells the abattoir in the middle of March with the first two boys.

The Empress's demise hastens the planned relocation of the pigs. When they're born, the first piglet, generally the biggest, latches on to the best teat nearest the sow's head and, unless forcibly moved, stays there throughout. Pigs have a very acute sense of smell. Get a pig to select a playing card from a washable pack, wash the pack and then ask it to find its original choice, and it will do so unerringly. It is bizarre to imagine some hapless researcher attempting this experiment, but it explains how they always know which teat – among twenty – is theirs. The same rigid pecking order carries on into young adulthood, with the biggest pigs getting bigger and the small ones lagging behind. They need to be kept in similar sized groups, something that might well have saved the Empress's life. We divide the girl and the boy groups, leaving Babe, Bluebell, Bramble and Guinness to roam around their large wood, with the bigger boys in the other heavily wooded region. The unnamed boys-to-be-eaten are all now in a smaller run, next door to Hyacinth, Blossom and Lobelia.

The moves meant some new houses being built and, for the larger boys, a house with a difference in the form of a very old, clapped-out caravan that David had been given last summer. It seemed like a good idea at the time, somewhere Josh might want to spend the night with his chums, but as the months went by the old white, grubby heap had sat in the corner of the walled garden, steadily falling to pieces. We drag it into a clearing in the wood, remove the wheels, rip out the cupboards, the seats and the small sink and park it on a bed of pine needles. A mountain of sweet-smelling straw fills up one half. The pigs are delighted and immediately start zipping in and out of the open door, looking through the low picture window at their leafy environment.

When my father left the army in his late forties, we moved to Ludlow in Shropshire where he worked for a company that manufactured agricultural machinery. Dad didn't much like the job but he liked his country life, especially the fishing. Along with his good friend, Joe Attlee, a local GP, he rented a stretch of river in North Wales, where the sea trout leaped in their thousands, flashing their silvery scales in the moonlight as they swam upriver from the sea. A caravan was required, occasionally for sleep but mostly for cooking up a vast breakfast of kidneys, bacon, eggs, tomatoes, fried bread and sausages, which Dad and Joe would eat at five o'clock on a summer's morning, before starting their three-hour journey back to Ludlow, driving too fast along the windy Welsh roads, hoping to get home in time for work. The caravan lived with us for almost a quarter of a century; when Daisy was little, she loved going off with her granddad for picnics, the caravan bouncing along behind his car. We'd park in woods, or on hilltops and cram ourselves into the tiny home on wheels to watch Dad cook up one of his legendary fry-ups. After my mother died of bowel cancer at the age of sixty-three, Dad took a cooking course and became a dab hand at chicken breasts in wine and lemon sauce and rich beef stews. But fry-ups were his *pièce de résistance* and they never tasted as good as when eaten round the fold-away yellow formica table, the windows foggy with our breath and the smoke from the frying pan. The day came when Dad was too old to go night fishing for sea trout and, anyway, by then the river was fished out, its clear waters wholly devoid of the magical creatures and we advertised the caravan for sale in the local Ludlow paper. It was priced at fifty quid, but really Dad just wanted someone to come and take it away as it was clogging up space in the driveway. I was there the day a man drew up in a battered blue Cortina to buy it. 'What are you going to use it for?' Dad asked as we helped position his towing cup over the caravan's steel ball. 'Well,' he replied, 'I've got nine children and I reckon that four of them can sleep in here.'

Bluebell isn't looking that fat, but her teats are bigger. The first sign we'll have that she is pregnant is that her stomach will drop: she'll get bigger downwards before she starts getting bigger outwards. But at least she puts up with her nuptial sojourn with the boars. Big sister Bramble doesn't take to it at all. David shoves her through the gate, where the mud is deep and gluey, clinging and sucking at your boots. Bramble squeals madly, thoroughly miffed at this turn of events on an otherwise peaceful morning. She takes one look at the four eager little guys who started clustering round her and makes an immediate bid for freedom, forcing her considerable bulk through the wire fence between the wooden gate and one side of the chicken coop. The wire doesn't stand a chance and Bramble is out on the track, huffing and puffing after her exertions. Consequently Plan B has been adopted. The area of the girls' wood where their original big house stands was partially enclosed. Now we gate it off and build a new wooden house deeper into the trees, down near a muddy wallow. As David quips, if the mountain won't come to Mohammed then Mohammed will come to the mountain: Boris is stepping up to the mark and has been sent to live with her. Secretly, I think we're all impressed by Bramble's independent streak. And we did need another, separate area with its own shelter for when Bluebell's piglets finally emerge.

It's now mid-January 2006 and I hope that Charlie and I have signed the last cheque for capital costs for the farm. We've rented an extra five acres on which we plan to grow just vegetables. No animals, no plants, just rows and rows of sprouts, carrots, onions, cabbages, cauliflowers, courgettes, beans, peas, beets, turnips, swedes and spinach. There seems to be no feasible way of fulfilling our contract with Dillington House unless we do. But the new field has meant new fences, new gates and the purchase of fifty poplar trees to provide shelter from the north wind along one side of the field. I walk across it on a bitingly cold day, crunching through the stubble left over from last year's crop and shiver. Just this time a year ago, we were still hauling old fridges out of the area where the chickens now live. I know how much work it has been and how much it has cost, but although I can see that, on paper at least, we need to expand in order to produce enough to supply not only Dillington but everything that the Popp Inn (with which we have arranged a small, regular supply contract) needs, as well as some other local restaurants. I'm worried. Bob, who used to be a council worker in Yeovil, mowing the roundabouts and tidying up the town's public spaces, is now with us full-time. Clearly we needed an extra pair of hands, but that means another salary to pay.

The original budget is way out of kilter. Last night Charlie and I decided that we needed to have a serious financial conversation with David, but we're both rather dreading it. The farm has grown in lopsided ways with little formal structure and hope has generally triumphed over more serious considerations of profit and loss. Charlie is good with figures: his VAT returns go in on time and he compiles them himself. I bundle all my receipts, bills, invoices and cheque stubs into an envelope and send them to my accountant with only days to go before the quarterly deadlines. In our marriage, Charlie looks after our joint finances, but I'm meant to be in charge of the farm business and I've been ducking the need to sit down with David to hammer out just where our investments are going and, more importantly, when and what money will be coming in. But I'm cheered when David tells me that the chickens laid seventy-five eggs yesterday, 17 January, their record production to date. We've laid four-inch-wide bendy blue plastic perforated pipes through their run and the ground is now dry, despite the heavy rains. It may be fanciful, but I think they look happier, standing around in peaceful groups and pecking the ground for grubs, their eyes bright, their feathers glossy.

Since we started the farm, I've been reading copiously about food, farming, the countryside, the environment and animals. One of the best books I've read is Felicity Lawrence's *Not on the Label*. This searing indictment of supermarket practices lifts the lid on chicken production, food miles, additives and more. I met Felicity at the beginning of January at the Soil Association's annual conference in London. When she learned that our smallholding was just outside Ilminster, she told me she'd recently written about the situation in Chard, a small Somerset town five miles away, where Portuguese immigrants have been brought in to work for Oscar Mayer, a firm which manufactures ready meals for Sainsbury's.

There are, she told me, enormous problems with the Portuguese immigrants and they are directly linked to the cheap food available in our supermarkets. Oscar Mayer, which employs 900 people, was also once the owner of Hygrade Meats, where David spent his dismal years processing pork into ham and stuffing it into packets. Supermarkets keep firms such as Oscar Mayer on a tight financial string. Their contracts are never assured and can be cancelled at a moment's notice. Like many companies that have contributed to the UK's economic success in the last decade, Oscar Mayer has invested in all the latest technology to keep up with the demands of the supermarkets, their main employers. When Tesco opened up their 'metro' stores in the middle of busy high streets, they ripped out the storerooms in the back to create extra retail space. Computers linked to cash registers signal when supplies of product are running low; these messages are fed to trucks which restock the shelves, sometimes several times a day. This technique, where nothing is kept in stock and food is constantly on the move in trucks, is known as 'just in time'. For the supermarkets, it means prices are kept down because food is never idling in storage, but supplying this market means that firms like Oscar Mayer have to cope with huge and often last-minute fluctuations in orders. The retailer's risk of under- or over-supplying is kept to a minimum by transferring the risks down the line. Meeting this unpredictable demand requires plenty of casual labour, which firms like these achieve by hiring workers from countries with high unemployment and rudimentary labour rights. Between 2000 and 2001, Oscar Mayer in Chard found itself unable to recruit a sufficiently large, flexible workforce locally. So they looked abroad, especially to some of Europe's poorer countries.

Employment agencies were quick to exploit the need, placing advertisements in newspapers in European countries with areas of high unemployment, offering jobs in Great Britain. In the case of Oscar Mayer's Chard operation, the spotlight fell on Portugal. In return for employment, migrant Portuguese toiling on the conveyer belts in Oscar Mayer's chilly factory in Chard receive the minimum wage of £5.05. While in the UK, the foreign workers are the sole responsibility of the employment agencies. This means that though the workers' wages are indirectly paid by supermarkets, they can conveniently distance themselves from the realities through this complex chain of out-sourcing.

I tracked down the local boss of the GMB for the West Country, Tony Dowling, who had been agitating on behalf of the Portuguese, and we arranged to meet in the Phoenix pub in Chard's once-grand high street, which now looks down-at-heel and scruffy, with charity shops vying for space next to cheap clothes shops. Chard was once a town of some significance, a major cloth-making centre in the Middle Ages and a prosperous lace-making town until the early 1900s. Set in the heart of rich farmland, it was a centre for small farmers until the post-war years, when farms consolidated and smaller players were forced out of business. Ilminster folk visit Chard to shop in Tesco or Lidl, the German supermarket chain which sells products in bulk for very low prices.

Tony is a friendly, engaging man with a black beard and bright, humorous eyes. In the late 1980s he worked at the Oscar Mayer factory on the spice machines. His job was to assemble the specific bags of spices that were needed in each ready meal. He'd weigh and measure, weigh and measure for eight long hours, day in, day out. To preserve the food, the temperature in the factory is kept very low, making the air chilly and damp, like living in the cold food section of a supermarket freezer. Over a pint of West Country bitter, Tony explains how the system works.

The Portuguese workers arrive in Chard unable to speak English; most have no money to their name. They live eight to ten in small, rented two- and three-bedroom houses and are picked up by truck each day for their twelve-hour factory shifts. The agency extracts rent, the cost of cleaning, transport, laundry directly from their pay packets. Tony suggested that there were some migrant workers who pay £65 a week in rent alone, which, as the houses themselves rent out at only about £450 a month, means hefty profits for the agencies. Added into their profit is the charge to Oscar Mayer: for each worker they claim just over £7 per hour, so earning themselves a tidy £2 every hour, right round the clock, as Oscar Mayer operates twenty-four hours a day.

Broke and unable to speak the language, the Portuguese are dependent on the agencies for their wellbeing. But their presence effects the town. Locals who find themselves living next to a house full of disgruntled foreign workers with whom they can't communicate turn into low-level racists. For Oscar Mayer, the immigrant workers are the perfect employees: they can't complain, they don't belong to unions and they can be chucked out whenever the bosses want. And because the agencies don't subscribe to British union rules, they don't have to pay overtime rates. The Portuguese put in extra hours, all on the minimum wage, so the local employees no longer get the right to do extra hours at time-and-a-half when they need extra cash. Tony sees the treatment of immigrant labour as an assault on all workers' rights. 'If you can employ them and pay them the minimum then why bother to employ English people who demand more?'

I used to think that it was only the chickens and livestock who suffered in our never-ending quest for cheaper food, but it is people too. The carpets in the Phoenix are frayed and there are cigarette marks on the wooden table we're sitting round. At night the pub employs bouncers to kick out troublemakers. Chard isn't a wealthy town and Oscar Mayer is its largest employer; the firm's continued success is crucial to the town's economic prosperity. Tony points out that the supermarkets operate by comparing profits, and thus fixing prices among each other, not by considering what is fair and reasonable. Our cash-rich, time-poor society has provided the platform on which the supermarkets have built the business of ready meals and convenience foods.

Thirty-five years ago, all you could buy in the ready-meals line were Vesta curries, a dried concoction sold in an exotic-looking box which, every so often, my mother would dish up for dinner. I remember always being delighted by Vesta suppers, particularly because we often ate them in front of the television. They were an alternative to my mother's rather monotonous meals. She didn't like to cook, and I don't think she much enjoyed the business of eating. Her portions were always small, she didn't like meat and she hated encountering something new and possibly strange. I have a vivid memory of my mother, father and me going out to lunch in Denmark with some friends of my sister Collette's new Danish husband. The meal was long and lots of small courses were served: cold pork, salamis, liver paste, stuffed rolled beef and at least five varieties of pickled herring. Not a vegetable in sight. My mother kept refusing the various plates as they were offered. Then came a large flat dish on which were arranged what looked like two or three packets of Birds Eye fish fingers, deep-fried, golden-coloured breaded rectangles, garnished with lemon wedges and crisp lettuce leaves. She brightened and helped herself to three. I watched my mother trying to cut off a bite-sized piece, her enthusiasm giving way to horror as she realised that these breaded rectangles weren't the same as those she so often dished up to her children, accompanied by frozen green peas and a dollop of ketchup. Our host spotted her consternation. 'Fried whale skin, a great delicacy,' he said, smiling happily as he speared a hefty chunk on to his fork. I could see her glancing around, clearly wondering where she might hide these fishy horrors. As our host launched into an involved story about whale hunting in Greenland, I watched her slide two of the breaded rectangles off the plate, into her hand, and from there into the leather bag at her feet.

I don't remember her ever saying that something was delicious, or licking her fingers after scraping something tasty from the bottom of the pan. No effort was made to teach my sister or me to cook. Maybe she thought that school would take care of such matters, but all the domestic science I learned at Cheltenham Ladies' College involved making a blue-and-white shift dress and a grey shirt for my boyfriend when I was fourteen. At home we ate our way through a limited repertoire of dishes: chops with two veg, baked fillets of sole smothered in breadcrumbs and Heinz tomato ketchup, the occasional roast chicken. For dinner parties she became more adventurous: an egg mousse with a brilliant tomato-based hot sauce, a delicious coffee meringue pudding and, for the main course, a boned shoulder of lamb in garlic, red wine and coriander, which she served with green beans and mashed potato. It proved that Mum could cook and cook well when occasion demanded. This meal was a big hit with Dad and their friends and in my memory it seemed that she always produced it whenever we had guests.

Over the winter months, Oscar Mayer manufactures 900,000 ready meals a week, and I think my mother would have loved them: chicken à la king, beef bourguignon, Lancashire hotpot. They would have expanded her repertoire without the bother and mess of handling raw meat. My mother was unusual among her peers in her dislike of things domestic, though in 1956, when Constance Spry published her 1,200-page magnum opus of recipes and cooking tips, she noted that:

'Since it would seem to be the simple duty of any woman with a home to run, of those with any civic conscience, to understand about food and cooking, it is strange how low the subject ranks in the estimation of many academically minded people. The influence of good food in the bringing up of children, its importance in the building-up of a strong people, the contribution it may make to the harmonious running of a home, may be acknowledged theoretically, but there is still a tendency to consider the subject suitable primarily either for girls who cannot make the grade for a university or for those who intend to become teachers.'

My mother, university-educated but frustrated by her subsequent life as a housewife, was clearly one of those who ranked cooking as a lowly pursuit and she passed her lack of interest on to me. In my turn, I furthered the belief that cooking was a demeaning pursuit for women who wanted to get on in a man's world. In 1972, when I was twenty-one, I co-founded *Spare Rib* magazine with an Australian friend, Marsha Rowe. The newly emerging feminist movement wanted to get women out of the typing pools and away from the kitchen sinks and into the boardrooms of the land. I remember being particularly adamant in my belief that the way to get ahead was to refuse to learn to type and to spend as little time as possible in the kitchen. As a subscription offer for the magazine we printed a purple dishcloth, which, though tattered and a bit torn, is still in use in our home today. Written on it are the words: 'First you sink into his arms, then your arms end up in his sink.'

By the mid-1970s, when *Spare Rib* was three years old, more than half of all UK households were equipped with the first wave of labour-saving electrical appliances: fridge-freezers, Kenwood mixers, non-stick pans and dishwashers. Ours was an exception: till the end of her life my mother always refused to have a dishwasher on the grounds that it was a waste of money. She would often start washing up a meal before everyone had finished eating, a habit which I sadly, on occasion, find myself repeating.

Supermarkets such as Sainsbury's, with their efficient cold-storage distribution, fulfilled the demand for convenience frozen foods, peas, pastry, pies and complete packaged meals. Liberated from domestic slavery by these modern miracles, women were, in theory, no longer required to devote all their time to household chores. My generation of women whole-heartedly embraced the workplace and it was just as well, since when it came to generating the necessary purchasing power to keep up with the technological revolution, two incomes were certainly better than one. Influenced by American prosperity, the boom in advertising, the arrival of credit cards (Barclaycard arrived in the UK in 1966) and built-in obsolescence in the gadgetry, the latest fashionable must-haves were essential to maintain and improve a rising standard of living. With no one at home in the kitchen, modern families willingly embraced the cultural revolution of oven-ready pre-prepared meals eaten not in the kitchen but in the sitting-room, in front of the TV. By the 1980s – the decade of the super-woman who could work full-time, bring up children, run a home and knock up a mid-week dinner party for eight – about a third of households owned microwaves, the ultimate gadget to minimise cooking time. Kitchens equipped with a large fridge-freezer as well as a microwave ushered in the era of the true 'ready meal', and the untimely demise of the great tradition of domestic cookery in British homes. Sales of convenience foods ballooned to £11 billion in 2001, and are projected to grow by 33 per cent over the next ten years. In 2005, the *Guardian* analysed the contents of some of Britain's best-selling ready meals: Sainsbury's Taste the Difference Luxury Shepherd's Pie, 'based on the Ivy restaurant's recipe', and sold to the public as a healthy meal that you could have made at home if you'd only had the time, contained sixty-nine separate ingredients, including a large range of chemical flavourings, preservatives, hardened fats and laboratory-made additions like wheat gluten and dextrin. When I make shepherd's pie, I use just six: mince, onions, tomatoes, potatoes, Worcester sauce and beef stock. Britain has the uneasy distinction of eating 49 per cent of all the ready meals consumed in Europe. For companies like Oscar Mayer, this trend is nothing less than a licence to make ever-increasing profits.

We didn't devote much space in *Spare Rib* to food, although in the first year we ran articles entitled 'Greedy Picnics' and 'Edible Presents'. Neither involved cooking and we certainly never thought that it was important to tell women how to feed their families. Within a year of its birth, food vanished entirely from the magazine's pages. Today, cook books dominate the best-seller lists: in 2005 their sales grew by 22 per cent, while fiction increased by 5 per cent. When Charlie and I merged our respective households in 1999, we ended up with well over a hundred cook books between us. We actually use fewer than ten of them. They're a kind of harmless porn, allowing you to fantasise about what you might, one day, get round to cooking. Of the two of us, Charlie is by far the better cook, and at weekends he dishes up an endlessly varied selection of meals, made, whenever possible, from the contents of our garden. So far we haven't eaten any of our own meat, but our eggs have yellow yolks the colour of sunflowers and taste delicious.

Just after Christmas 2005 two new characters joined our bird flock: the turkeys, George and Mildred. George is unpleasant, though very exotic. If I'd met him in a swamp in Botswana I'd have immediately started taking photos of this mad-looking creature. He's huge, heavy, with scrappy feathers and a piece of blue and red flesh that hangs down from his nose, completely covering his beak, a fleshy extension so long that it swings to and fro when he walks. Round his neck there's an ungainly pile of folded layers of red skin which he can puff up to emit furious gobbling noises. Even the wonderful Galapagos frigate birds, their red necks blown up and out into huge balloons as they soar above the drabber females, hoping that their colours will prove the most attractive, have nothing on George's tools of attraction. When he's sexually excited his neck swells up to the size of a large grapefruit, a bright, pillar-box red which contrasts weirdly with the blue of the skin on his head. The fleshy tube that hangs down from his beak swells and stiffens, like a virtual reality erection. His big, round body, perched atop sturdy legs with big-clawed feet, is covered in long feathers, black, brown, grey, yellowish, lots of shades of colour, which shimmer in the sunlight, turning shades of green and orange. Mildred, by contrast, is a sad, dull-looking creature. She is almost bald, her small head covered with very short, grey hairs, as though she's had a bad haircut. Her feathers are grey and brown, not that short, not that long, just boring. She always seems to be looking down at the ground, as though life has defeated her.

George spends most of his time attempting to mate with Mildred. As a preliminary she flattens herself on to the earth, wings spread. George lumbers around her, periodically clamping his big heavy claw on her neck to keep her pinned down. He lurches his full forty pounds at her rear end, wobbles a bit and falls off. Then he starts all over again, seemingly getting crosser and crosser as though his failure is somehow Mildred's fault. I bought a new book on keeping fowl and it says that 'natural' mating can be very hard for turkeys: basically the male grows too fat and ungainly to manage it and you usually have to resort to artificial insemination. David is firmly rooting for George's masculine rights and assures me that Mildred will be producing eggs by the beginning of February. I remain to be convinced. His antics seem tantamount to harassment.

I wrote an article about the smallholding for *Country Life* and one weekend in January the magazine sends photographer

Brian Moody down to take some shots. He takes pictures of George, of chickens being fed, of winter cabbages and strawberries on bales of straw out of reach of the slugs, as well as of Bramble, Bluebell, Guinness and Babe eating nuts in the wood. Finally, he takes a picture of me sitting in a wooden hut, holding a very muddy Hyacinth in my arms. She's still a very little pig, far smaller than others of her age and even though she's fattening up a bit now that she's away from the older pigs, she's well below size. In early January, she developed a cold and had to be kept under the heating lamp, which is generally used for rearing tiny chicks, until her body temperature returned to normal. Brian works quickly, and Hyacinth stays reasonably still, seeming to quite enjoy the fuss. But half an hour later, when I walk past her pen, I notice that she's disappeared. She's retired to the warm bed of straw in her hut, her venture into show biz clearly overwhelming. The Greta Garbo of the pig world is, as Charlie jokes, just a pig that wants to be a-loin.

The first pig I ever saw was a saddleback sow who was living in one of a row of three Cotswold stone pigsties, which faced outwards on to the cow yard at my aunt and uncle's Oxfordshire farm. My father had been in the army when I was born and my sister Collette and I spent the first years of our childhood in army HQs in Germany, Vienna, Tripoli and Bury St Edmunds. In contrast, my mother's sister, Giogia, had met and married an English farmer at the start of the war and settled down on a 350-acre farm outside the village of Great Tew. To this day, their farm remains the most constant physical presence in my life, a place my sister and I relished in our peripatetic childhood. We both loved our aunt's big-hearted warmth and the fact that in spring there'd always be an ailing lamb or two, wrapped in old towels, their heads peeking out of the bottom drawer of the Aga. We loved going off with her and our two cousins, Ander and Richard, to collect fresh eggs or pull up carrots from the vegetable garden.

Uncle Ben let us ride on the tractor with him and, if we were lucky enough to be spending Christmas there, the Christmas Eve trip to cut down a fir tree from the heart of Conegrey Wood was, to me, almost the most exciting event of the year. I loved the fact that all the fields had names: the Oxpen, the Hangings, Limekiln Quarry, Three Gates, Porbridge Bank, the Skills, the Wallet; that a sheep called Esther whom Giogia had hand-reared would return to the farmhouse bringing her two lambs with her to steal a drink from the lavatory off the corridor from the front door; that there was always a big saucepan on the stove, full of delicious soup made from potatoes, onions and carrots. My mother, Betty, and Giogia were Jersey born and bred. Their father, my grandfather, was the island's first fully qualified vet. Giogia studied agriculture at Reading University in the thirties and, when the Germans occupied Jersey in 1940, she left the island for a job near Oxford, looking after a herd of Jersey cows. My mother was already in London, working as a military driver, and Granny, by then a widow, left her island home and joined Giogia in Oxfordshire to sit out the occupation.

While taking care of the Jerseys, Giogia met and married my uncle Ben, and when a Mr Evans – the tenant of Beaconsfield Farm, Great Tew – was kicked out by the Ministry of Agriculture for not achieving high enough production levels, Ben and Giogia moved in. There had been a farm there for centuries. They took a lease on the main farmhouse, a lovely Cotswold stone building dating from about 1720, which faces south down a long valley where the soft green folds of the hills seem to embrace the small stream that runs down alongside the rough track. They also acquired three cottages for workers (with the instruction that they were not to be fed salmon more than three times a week) and a set of farm buildings, also built of Cotswold stone. The roofs of the farm buildings, one over fifty metres in length, are made from Stonesfield slate, which comes from a quarry near Woodstock. It was hewn out of the ground in metre-square chunks and then, over the winter, doused with water so that the frost would work its way into the crevices and break the stone into the half-inch-thin tiles that make up the roof. As my cousin Ander says, that would be impossible now, there's just not enough frost.

In the 1970s, a tractor suddenly capsized while crossing the top yard. It had fallen into a perfectly preserved Roman culvert. Excavations revealed an entire villa, complete with the skeleton of an adult male with an eight-inch knife stuck through his thigh, which is now in the Woodstock Museum.

My aunt Giogia, a natural born organiser, was soon in charge of the hastily assembled 'land army' for the region, responsible for visiting local farms and seeing that they were maximising production. They were allocated four POWs to help out: two Germans called Kurt and Hendrik, an Italian named Aldo and a Serbian called Pieter Vaser, whose mother somehow became the farm cook. Kurt was nicknamed Booby, and for many years after the war he would return to Beaconsfield to visit Giogia and Ben, seeing them as surrogate family.

In addition to the pigs, who lived in some style in their Cotswold stone sties while they were nursing their piglets, the farm then consisted of 150 sheep, 28 milking cattle, 600 Rhode Island Red chickens who produced fertile eggs which would be sold, as well as wheat, barley, swedes, kale and mangel-wurzels. All the food that the animals needed was grown on the farm. During the war, War Ag – as Ben and Giogia called Lord Woolton's Ministry of Agriculture – insisted that every possible fertile square foot be ploughed up and put to use. In the 1930s, Britain was importing 70 per cent of all its food, but once war broke out importing food became impossible. Making Britain self-sufficient in food was a government priority, a goal which persisted after the war ended.

In 1947 the National Farmers' Union persuaded the government to offer a guarantee to British farmers for the price of beef. So much beef was being imported cheaply from Argentina, that the price guarantee was, in effect, the first 'subsidy' or, as it was initially called, 'a deficiency payment'. At the same time, the Milk Marketing Board also extended a guaranteed market for milk. It was a huge incentive for British farmers to produce more and it was vital for the government, who didn't want to return to the pre-war position of being so dependent on imports. In 1947, the government held out a further incentive to farmers by giving farming tenants lifetime security of tenure. That security, coupled with the guarantee and regular income from the Milk Marketing Board, gave farmers a new ability to borrow money to buy machinery and modernise. Other subsidies followed: for ploughing up the ground, for liming and for adding phosphate and potash. The Ministry of Agriculture sent advisers round to all the farms, who were on tap for free advice. Giogia and Ben's advisers were called Mr Eddie and Mr Stanforth, and they worked out of a pre-fab office in Oxford opposite what is now the Islamic centre.

For my cousin Ander, who was born in 1942 and started working on the farm when he was nineteen, farming really changed in the 1960s when technology moved on to the land. Once you'd invested in a combine harvester you felt obliged to use it to the maximum, to get value for money, and so fields that were once used for grazing went under the plough. Uncle Ben's first combine was a Ford, called an Alice Chambers, and he travelled to Ireland to buy it. The machine arrived at the farm in bits, and reps from Ford assembled it in the farmyard. Its span was two metres – a midget compared to today's giants, which can stretch up to ten metres – but it could process twenty-five tonnes of grain in a day. Ben and Giogia gave up the pigs first, then the cows and finally the sheep. By 1970 the farm was entirely arable: wheat, barley, grass seed and twenty acres of spuds. By then I was living my own life in London and I visited the farm less often. But I remember that every time I did the farmyard would have grown, the new

Dutch barns, built of corrugated iron and painted green, towering over the old stone buildings. The small buildings with their relatively narrow doorways were useless in this new world of automation and bigger and bigger machines, which are effectively factories on wheels. Once they were home to horses and carts, which in 1939 still outnumbered tractors by 1.5 million to 600,000. By 1960, only 20,000 were left and the word 'horsepower' is now used by people who wouldn't know the difference between a snaffle and a snafu. The old cow yards, flanked on all sides by beautiful stone walls and arches where the cows once bellowed as they waited their turn for the milking machines, stood empty. The other buildings slowly turned into storerooms. Perhaps if Giogia and Ben had owned the farm they might have embarked on an ambitious conversion into flats and offices which, across the farming communities of Britain, became the fate of farm buildings towards the end of the century, but it wasn't to be.

Today, they're home to swallows and barn owls and, as they're now rearing industrial quantities of pigs again, to sick piglets and young beef cattle. But the main business is in the huge grain stores, where underfloor aeration helps dry the grain. At the start of the twentieth century the weight of grain from the harvest was an average of 0.95 tonnes per acre. In the year the war ended it was 1.05 tonnes. Now, farmers are expected to produce 3.24 tonnes per acre, in a mechanised system of production that has more in common with a factory floor than with a natural relationship between the farmer, the soil and the crop. Not many people are needed on the farm these days: from a high of ten in the immediate post-war years, it is now just my cousins Ander and Richard, Richard's son Mark and one full-time employee who look after the twenty-first-century Beaconsfield. And it is bigger too: today they rent 500 acres, and in the 1970s they bought a neighbouring farm of 150 acres. When Alistair Cooke started writing and broadcasting from America in 1942 he noted that in Kansas, with its high-powered machines, it took between one and two man-hours of labour to grow an acre of wheat; in China it took 243 hours. In some ways, this change is clearly a good thing. Much of the traditional work on farms was backbreaking and ghastly, but it has also altered beyond recognition the life in the village of Great Tew. Ander can remember when there was a blacksmith and a butcher, as well as the school, the village store and post office. Almost all those that lived in the village worked on the main estate. Now these tiny cottages, clustered picture-postcard fashion around the village green where the Falkland Arms pub attracts Sunday lunchtime crowds in their hundreds, change hands for well over £350,000. The only cottages to sell in the twenty-first century have been to Londoners like us who visit at weekends.

At the bottom of the farm, where the buildings peter out and the rough track leading down to the Hangings begins, is a wooden lean-to shed with a heavy wooden door with a padlock. I remember being about six or seven years old, standing in the yard with Giogia firmly grasping my hand and telling me never to go inside this shed. I remember that every so often there'd be a pool of evil-looking black liquid collected in the dips in the concrete outside the shed and that inside there were white plastic drums with a skull and cross-bones stamped on the side. Soon after the war, the first industrial chemical, MCPA, replaced sulphuric acid as a basic weedkiller. It instantly increased crop production. It wasn't dangerous to humans and it worked on cereal crops because it stayed on the flat leaves of the weeds but ran off the upright stalks of the cereal. Poking around in the shed today, I found Stacato – which warns against contact with eyes – Starine and Opus, a collection of fungicides, pesticides and weedkillers, an alchemical arsenal without which no modern farm can hope to compete. Ander is realistic about chemicals: they increase production, but they come at a price. Natural soil fertility is depleted, the balance of nature disrupted, and many, such as the pesticide DDT, have caused enormous harm to wildlife. DDT is soluble in body fat, which means that once it has been ingested it is not easy to eliminate and remains in the body, becoming increasingly concentrated as it moves up the food chain. Thus it passes from plankton to fish and into water birds. Its accumulation in the bodies of birds of prey such as peregrine falcons and eagles causes them to lay eggs with thin shells which break during incubation, leading Rachel Carson to title her influential 1960s book on the coming environmental crisis *Silent Spring*.

In the 1960s, the government, anxious to encourage beef production, instructed British farmers to use one-third more than the recommended dose of organophosphate (OP) to kill warble flies, which lay their eggs subcutaneously along a cow's back. When the grubs form they crawl out through the skin, leaving holes in the hide which reduce its value as industrial leather. The organophosphate was used simultaneously across Europe and Southern Ireland, but only in Britain was the dose increased above the recommended safety level. Ander is now firmly of the unproven belief that the drug upset the chemical balance in the cows' brains, leading, years later, to the BSE outbreak. OPs were originally designed as a nerve agent for use in combat and, despite clear evidence of their dangerous side effects, the military used them in the Gulf War to spray the insides of tents against flies. They have been cited as causing mental health problems in Gulf War vets.

Ander and Richard are good custodians of the land. Since the war, they've ploughed up only one hedge to make bigger fields to accommodate today's gigantic machines. There are 4,500 pigs on the farm these days and they rotate the pigs and the grain crops, thus dramatically reducing the need for fertilisers. The pigs have good lives, living in large fields with corrugated-iron pig arcs as homes. They sell each animal, at six months old, for around £75, and in 2005 the pigs made them £70,000. Supermarket buyers drive hard bargains: if a pig has arthritis in one of its legs, they'll hack it off and chuck it away. Even though the meat itself is edible, arthritis causes discolouring. They're also fussy about fat, wanting it less than twelve millimetres deep and reducing payments for every extra millimetre on the animal.

Ander and Richard have two hundred beef cattle which sell for £2.09 a kilo. Each year they slaughter half of these, earning about £700 per animal. The remaining income comes from the cereal crops. It doesn't sound that bad, but the farm supports three families, one full-time employee and the costs of machinery, drills, building maintenance, chemicals, antibiotics and feed for the animals. My cousins could never be described as the sort of farmers – so despised by rural-phobic city folk – with grand lifestyles, supported by EU subsidies. My cousins still belong to a community which modern life has done so much to traduce. Farming in the past might have been a miserable affair for many, but living closely with the land did provide a network that was sustainable through good times and bad. A community is like a coral reef in its multiple layers of dependency and in its relationships. I see it now in Ilminster and I see the way that politicians, always keen to stress its importance, are also so willing to chuck it all aside in the relentless pursuit of profit.

One bright, wintry Saturday morning, Charlie and I set off to the farmers' market in the old stables at Montacute House, seven miles away in the small village of Montacute, nestled under the easterly side of Ham Hill, from where all the mellow local stone originates. Montacute is a perfect Elizabethan house which Lord Curzon once rented as a love nest with his mistress, the infamous Elinor Glyn, with whom he was said to have committed sin on a tiger's skin. Curzon installed

Montacute's first bathroom, a tiny chamber built in one corner of his bedroom, less than one hundred years ago.

We're meeting our friend, the food and cookery writer Rose Prince, who is signing copies of her just published book, *The New English Kitchen: Changing the Way You Shop, Cook and Eat*, from a rickety table under the roof of the open-sided barn. The market is jostling with people: business is clearly terrific for the stallholders with their cheeses, vegetables, meats, ciders, jams and chutneys. Food here is about history, culture and ritual, and shopping here is probably the only time that buying food can be described as retail therapy. The rich local cheddar has been made this way for hundreds of years, and the flour for the bread has been ground between stones, not squeezed between two rollers to extract the wheatgerm from the grain, which modern millers then sell to the health-food industry to sell back to us as expensive wheatgerm oil.

There's a stall selling salt marsh lamb, the sheep fed on the wild grasses found only in estuaries. I go over to introduce myself to the man running the stall. Until 2003, Andrew Moore worked as an international stockbroker in the City, but after a series of take-overs and rationalisations, he found himself with a decent pay-off and the chance to change his life. 'My passion was food,' he tells me from behind the table where the joints of lamb are laid out in cold boxes. 'I'd always gone shooting and to start with I dealt game, smoked it, made pies out of it, made sausages. It was OK, and the margins are good, but if you're talking about a 20p margin on an 80p product, you've got to sell a lot of product to make any money.' He is so earnest, I start to laugh: clearly it takes a lot to get the City out of a man. I hadn't thought of our business in terms of margins, but it makes sense. 'I had a friend in London who was looking for lamb for a restaurant,' he says. 'We went into business with a farm near Bridgwater. I supply the sheep and they've got the estuary grazing. It's not only the taste that improves when they eat grass grown there;

the salt water of the spring tides floods the marshes, naturally killing off harmful parasitic worms and bacteria. We sell at markets and through box schemes. We send half or whole lambs all over the country.' I choose a plump-looking shoulder and start counting out the money: it isn't cheap, Andrew's lamb averages £7–£8 a kilo, but I am sure it will be delicious. As he wraps it up, he tells me that what he likes most about the markets is the chance to talk to people and get feedback on his food. 'Although some people do come up with the most amazing things,' he says with a grin. 'One man spent ages staring at some smoked pheasant breasts. Finally he asked me if they were fish as they didn't look like the sort of meat he was familiar with. I told him they were breasts. He cheered up immediately, saying, "Oh, I see, they're from the females." '

There's farmhouse cider, handmade chocolates and stone-ground flour from Burcott Mill. Next to the archway, there's delicious bread from the Thomas Bakery and Patisserie of Wells. Tina Thomas, a Pakistani who's lived in England for twenty-seven years, started the bakery three years ago after quitting her job in telecoms. Following a stint in Paris studying pastry cooking at the Ritz, she took a lease on an old hair-dresser's shop in Wells. It is now her bakery, where she specialises in producing bread that has been fermented for between sixteen and twenty hours, which allows the yeast to metabolise fully. Tina's husband Paul helps with deliveries, but she sells most of her bread, croissants, Bath buns, smooth macaroons and saffron loaves through farmers' markets. 'I started baking at 1 a.m. this morning,' she says with a yawn, 'I finished by 8 a.m. Got here by nine. Market days are tough. But I'm doing well, I love having my own business, I love making food that's just how I want it to be.' Under the long open barn, there's a stall selling ewes' milk cheese. Their leaflet tells me that sheep's milk is both nutritious and delicious, containing twice the level of important minerals such as calcium, phosphorus and zinc, and B vitamins. By now I've collected a handful of leaflets, colourful and informative about the food and the process of making it: a great alternative to reading the contents on the back of a ready meal. Rose is doing good business too, signing copies of her book while Dominic, her husband, pockets the money. And there are lots of delicious things to eat: little bits of brown bread and butter, slithers of cheese, slices of sausages fried on small stoves and skewered with toothpicks, small glasses of cider and fresh apple juice, biscuits to dunk into homemade raspberry jam.

In their modern incarnation, farmers' markets are barely a decade old. The phenomenon emerged in 1997 with a single fledgling market in Bath. Now 550 markets are thriving across the UK, generating a total of 8,000 market days. More than fifteen million people visit these markets each year, with 60 per cent of customers going back regularly. There are no big advertising campaigns: farmers' markets rely on word of mouth, leaflets, temporary road signs, local media, tourist information and returning customers. There are few regulations, apart from a stipulation that all stall-holders actively farm or manufacture in the locality, and that everything they sell must have been home-grown, reared, cooked, brewed or baked. In 2002, farmers' markets earned producers a total of £166 million and for some stallholders it can mean an extra £20,000 worth of business. One unexpected boon from this remarkable growth is that up to 80 per cent of neighbouring businesses have seen a boost in trade following the establishment of a market nearby. And they're not expensive, I realise as Charlie and I tour the stalls, sampling bits of cheese and sausage. As well as Andrew's salt marsh lamb, which we'll eat for dinner, we buy a circular goats' cheese called a Little Ryding, which weighs 220 grams and will last us for a week at least, a loaf of Tina's bread, a bottle of cider and one of cloudy apple juice, half a kilo of pork and apple sausages, and several jars of jam and local honey. In the nearby West Country town of Wincanton, a survey revealed that the seasonal purple sprouting broccoli on sale at the local Safeway was selling for £7.10 per kilo, nearly four times more expensive than the local organic farmers' market broccoli at £1.90 per kilo. In the same survey, imported Spanish carrots at the Stroud Tesco superstore were selling at 99p per bunch compared to 80p per bunch for the local carrots selling at Stroud farmers' market.

The setting gives the market an old-fashioned feel, but there's nothing either old or exclusively middle-class about the shoppers. Many of them are having their lunch on the move at the same time as filling their baskets with weekend food. When the rural poor began moving into the cities in large numbers in the first half of the nineteenth century, many of them had no option but to eat on the street, as their homes had no cooking facilities. Street eating must have been a little similar to being at a farmers' market, and in London, which in the mid-1800s was home to 15 per cent of the population, street food grew in popularity as choice and availability expanded. Strolling the city streets in the Victorian era you could have found hot eels, whelks, oysters, sheep's trotters, pea soup, fried fish, ham sandwiches, hot green beans, kidney puddings and baked potatoes. Sweet biscuits, gingernuts, fruit tarts, Chelsea buns, muffins and crumpets rounded off the meal, and drinks such as tea, coffee, cocoa, lemonade, peppermint water, rice milk and sherbets washed it all down.

Here in Montacute the money is changing hands briskly. Before we leave, I track down the organiser, Elaine Spencer-White, to ask if we can have a stall in 2006. All the stallholders live and work on the Somerset Levels, the region of flatland between the Quantocks and the Mendips, with Glastonbury Tor standing proudly at its heart. Ilminster is on the extreme southern edge of the Levels, but Elaine reckons that we just qualify. However, the only slot left is for a stall to sell herbs. The rental will be £25 a day, or £120 for all six dates. So far we haven't pursued a speciality, but herbs seem like a good idea so we sign up straight away.

Now it is mid-January 2006, under three months till the date of the first market, and we are sowing vast quantities of herb seeds: parsley, rosemary, thyme, basil, chervil, oregano, chives, mint and sorrel. I've found some research on the net which tells me that sales of fresh herbs have soared by 124 per cent in the last five years to the value of £38 million. Despite the demand, the home market is lagging well behind. Most of us are buying our herbs from the supermarkets, in neat little plastic packets and grown in Israel, Spain and North Africa. And they're expensive: right now, a 10g pack of rosemary costs 75p in Tesco, which translates to an incredible £75 a kilo. Maybe we're on to a good thing, but how well they'll sell at Montacute is anyone's guess. Charlie thinks we probably need at least fifty of each, but that's pure guesswork. I like the idea of having a brochure for the nursery, so I've asked my friend Yseult Hughes to help write and design a booklet explaining how to grow each herb and including a recipe. We can sell them for £1 each and they'll be a good advertisement for the nursery.

6

The Nature of Soil

We hold our first board meeting on 22 January 2006, sitting round our dining-room table after lunch. Charlie and I have now invested £70,000 in the farm, far more than we had intended a year ago, but then the farm is bigger and more diversified than we planned. It is clear that David's energies are scattering in different directions and we're worried that we're neglecting our core business. Our income is still incredibly small: a few hundred pounds from Dillington House, the same from the nearby Popp Inn, which buys our vegetables, and just over £300 that Kensington Place owe us for the eight geese before Christmas. Our outgoings are shooting up. On top of David's wages of £250 a week, we're now employing Bob on a month's trial for a possible full-time job at £180 a week. Adrian works a day and a half a week for £70, and David's mum, Anne, does six hours for £36. That makes the total wage bill £536 a week. On top of that, our monthly outgoing on animal food is £42.50 for pigs and the same for chickens, plus £21 on turkey food. Corn, which we buy in bulk from Dillington Farms, is an extra £20 every month. We also have bills for seeds (£350 for the year), compost (£500), sawdust (£150), plus all the extra capital costs that have been needed to build a second chicken shed, fence, gate, and prepare the new land, lay drainage pipes under the chicken run and the extremely muddy parts of the pig pens, and buy a computer. Most of these are one-off costs, but, even so, January turned into an expensive month, with Charlie writing a cheque for almost £6,500.

The immediate financial returns don't look good. We have very few vegetables to sell, the pigs aren't yet fat enough to go to slaughter and the rare-breed chickens will not start laying till February. We've spent close to £1,000 on fruit trees. Some have been planted round the walls, others are positioned to grow on to wires stretched between eight-foot-high posts, standing in lines running north to south in the main garden. In years to come they will look beautiful, espaliered against the wires, with vegetables growing in between. Right now, they're thin and weedy-looking and it will be three years before there is any fruit to sell and any chance of a financial return. Our plant stock is growing too, small cuttings of box, bay, hydrangeas, pitto-sporum and ivy, arranged in neat rows against the south wall. But, like the fruit trees, there's not going to be much to sell this year and, as yet, we don't have an outlet which will take our plants. I phoned the local organic farm shop to ask if they would be interested and they didn't even bother to return the call. It's clear that, certainly until the spring, we will have to underwrite the wages. But David is still confident that we'll be breaking even by June and possibly making a small profit. On paper at least, this certainly looks like a real possibility. But I can tell that Charlie is feeling a little gloomy. The economy Mercedes has now become a top-of-the-range model and we're adding extras all the time. Between ourselves we've agreed a limit of £80,000 as a total investment, but I also know that we will go on forking out money beyond that. But till when? It is impossible to imagine not paying the wages one month, but the finances need to turn a corner soon.

The best news at the start of the year is that the chickens have gone from laying thirty-five eggs a day to seventy-five and then over a hundred. It happened in a matter of days and the only explanation we can come up with is that the blue drainage pipes which we've installed under the yard are doing their job and the chickens now have dry feet. I think they look happier, but this is probably wishful thinking and more connected to the fact that I no longer see them as just a mass of feathers, each bird indistinguishable from the other, but more as individuals. All animals are like that: the longer you watch them, the more they emerge as themselves. Like the supposed silence of the countryside which you come to realise is always full of the sounds of animals and birds or wind rustling through trees, or like the signs of spring, so absent from London but all around us in January: the shoots of leaves, the pushing of bulbs and the first lambs standing in the chill January air.

Josh discovered that the chickens are keen on sprouts, of which we currently have plenty of rejects. Chuck one into a group of birds and their heads bob up and down trying to find the small green ball. Then you notice that one bird has crouched down and is running as hard as it can, pushing through the mass of legs and feathers towards the outside of the scrum. Bursting into the open with the sprout firmly in its beak, it puts it down and takes a huge peck of leaves. By that time, the other chickens have noticed and the scrum formation is reassembled round the lucky bird. The game starts all over again.

Along the back wall of the chicken coop, nesting boxes open on to lidded metal trays attached to the outside of the hut. It makes for easy collecting. The mostly clean, sometimes still-warm eggs roll on to the trays, where it is a simple process to collect them. In the last few days, I've picked up over fifty eggs in one go. Inside the coop, a few chickens still seem to prefer sitting on the sawdust in the corner and laying there. Their black eyes study you fiercely when you go in to see whether any eggs are rolling around on the ground. But it does seem to be the case that happy chickens are productive chickens: not much different from human beings.

After the war, when servicemen were struggling to re-enter civvy street, one of their options was starting a smallholding. I have a copy of a splendid book called *Livings from the Land*, written in 1947 by S. A. Maycock. Mr Maycock was the proud owner of a smallholding and he writes with affection about his vegetables and birds. Even on his Sunday afternoons off he chooses to spend his time with his chickens. 'Having eaten our modest meal of rationed meat, we don't rush around too much, but take an extra look at the baby pullets. Now, as we sit on the floor on the peat-moss litter, my wife smoking her cigarette and I my pipe, the chickens jump all over us, and we are all friends together – and this is the state of affairs when you get the very best results, for it is surely work for love's sake.'

I am sure that the chickens would not appreciate having me in their midst smoking a cigarette, but at the end of the middle week of January the eggs are piling up and we are suddenly confronted with a new problem: we have an excess. Dillington House has over-estimated its egg demand. Instead of the 750 a week we thought they wanted, they have announced that they can take only 300. So, on Saturday morning, I go to ask Mr Bonner if he wants the surplus. He doesn't: he already has an egg supplier and it would upset the delicate status quo between producer and supplier if he started taking ours. I mill around in the busy Saturday morning queue while he calls his friend at the Shrubbery Hotel, but it turns out that he has just done a new deal with a local supplier and is happy with his arrangement. Feeling more than a little crazy, I go down the street to John Rendell, the greengrocer. He doesn't want any either. I catch sight of my reflection in a store window: I look like a mad middle-aged woman, in a muddy coat, having a bad hair day. What on earth am I doing? This is a pathetic way to run a business. We need proper contracts: wandering around town like a travelling salesman trying to flog bibles is a good joke, but it isn't solving the problem.

Rescue comes from Rowley Leigh, our friend who is chef at Kensington Place restaurant. He will have 300 and, if he likes them, maybe this could become a regular order. So, on Sunday night, Charlie and I load 300 eggs on to the back seat of the Land Rover and deliver them to the storeroom at the back of the restaurant on our way to our London home. I attach an invoice for £40, deciding that I can write off the delivery costs as we are going that way anyway.

In early February some of the chickens fall ill. First one, then another, develops runny eyes and becomes weak and lethargic. They stand around in the coop, heads down or under their wings, their feathers limp and dusty. Over three days, six die. David isolates the sick ones, sixteen of them, in a separate shed and adds a broad-based antibiotic to their water supply. The vet says we need to take one of the dead chickens to DEFRA at Langford House in Bristol for autopsy. We all have only one thought: bird flu.

Avian flu had been making its way from Asia, to Turkey and into Africa. It seemed a distant problem, but then, in the middle of February, the potentially deadly strain of H5N1 was detected in four European countries, carried by swans who had been driven south by the freezing weather in northern Europe. Over one weekend infected swans are found in Italy, Bulgaria, Greece and Slovenia. So far, the disease is confined to swans and has not crossed over to domestic fowl. The Italian minister of health, Francesco Storace, says that the strain of flu that has been responsible for more than ninety deaths in Asia has been found in dead swans in Sicily. Twenty-one swans were infected by the virus, five of them with a virulent form. The Italians establish two-mile protection zones round each of the outbreaks and all poultry within the zones must be kept indoors and moved only to travel to a slaughter-house. The Italians say they are not worried about human health, but avian flu is spread by migrating birds and we are just approaching the start of the major migrations. Although February is early for birds to be taking to the skies, it is possible. I have a vision of our little farm being screened off from the world, of men in white coats, with masks on their faces, wearing white wellingtons, cramming our chickens into incinerators.

DEFRA takes three days to pronounce on the chicken: not avian flu, just a bronchial virus, which has most likely been caused by the recent long stretch of sustained very cold weather. The nights have been freezing for almost six weeks now, with the temperatures going down to minus 6°C on occasions. Mr Rendell the greengrocer says that he can't remember such sustained cold since the winter of '63 and, before that, the winter of '47, when his father's car had frozen to the road.

The DEFRA vet prescribes a course of Tylan Soluble for the remaining sick chickens, but by the time the virus is under control we have lost twenty-four birds and twenty-two are on medication. Even though they start laying again before reaching the end of the antibiotic course, the eggs cannot be eaten as it is against the law to sell an egg laid by a chicken on medication.

The rare breeds are well into their laying season and our smart new incubator arrives just in time to hatch the newly fertile eggs. It can hold eighty eggs at a time, keeping them at exactly 37.2°C and 45 per cent humidity. It takes five days for the incubator to reach the right temperature, where it will now stay, apparently ad infinitum, provided there isn't a power cut. There are sixteen eggs – Leghorns, New Hollands and Barn-velders – in the small incubator that are due to hatch on 16 February. David made a mistake with our last batch because he removed the chicks immediately they had hatched, thus minutely, but crucially, changing the temperature for those still inside their eggs and, more importantly, altering nature's ordered progress. Chicks live for their first twenty-four hours on the remaining yolk sac, which provides essential minerals and vitamins to the baby bird. Once they drink on their own, this process is fatally disrupted.

The first goose lays an egg on 8 February and now they are appearing every day. Goose eggs are big – about three and a half inches long – white and a more oval shape than a chicken's egg. Mildred lays four eggs: also white, but con-siderably smaller. All of these go into the new incubator when it reaches the right temperature, though we will leave some goose eggs out in the coop for the female geese to hatch.

Eggs are extraordinary things. It takes twenty-five hours for an egg to form inside the chicken's oviduct. The oviduct is more than two feet long and is lined with glands that secrete the materials for the albumen, shell membranes and shell. Strong muscles keep the eggs spinning round, making ten to twelve rotations every hour, like a potter's wheel. The spin gives the tiny embryo its early sense of orientation. As the yolk spins, the cells at the leading edge of the small disc of dividing cells will become the head. Egg formation is a physiological process that can be triggered by light conditions and produc-tion of yolks in readiness for breeding. The yolks aren't formed after mating – the delay would be too great – so ripe yolks are released from the ovaries and undergo the process of egg formation even if the male is absent. That's how our domestic chickens manage to lay their five or six eggs each week. In the wild, though, it works differently. Wild birds synchronise egg formation and mating to the time of year, giving us the wonder of birds' nests in springtime hedges, filled with colourful speckled eggs.

When I was a child, our garden in Ludlow would boast at least ten nests in the garden hedges every year. My father was keen on birds and allowed me to collect two or three eggs a season: bright blue hedge sparrows', speckled thrushes' and the blue blackbirds' eggs. If there was a tit's nest, it was well out of bounds, which seems ironical now as our garden is full of tits – long-tailed tits, great tits, blue tits and coal tits – but it is rare to see any thrushes, and even the blackbirds, which I remember as being classed as common birds when I was a child, are infrequent visitors. Using a needle, I'd make a tiny hole in either end and then gently blow out the yolk and the white, adding the hopefully intact egg to my collection, stored on cotton wool artfully tricked up with old bits of moss, in a drawer of my bedside cabinet. The question of why eggs are coloured and speckled has engaged scientists for over a hundred years. Many believed that it was for camouflage, useful for concealing eggs from predators, but if you think about it, this theory doesn't stack up at all. Why leave a bright blue egg in a dusty brown nest, signalling its presence to any passing predator? Many eggs, like the white and reddish brown speckled eggs of the great tit, are so distinctive that a blind weasel could find them in the dark.

Recently a better theory has emerged. Speckling may be a unique solution to the engineering problem of how to strengthen unusually fragile eggs. The pigment chemicals that create the speckles may act as a kind of glue, supporting thin areas of shell and protecting them from breakage during incubation in the nest. Ornithologists studied great tits living in woods near Oxford where the soil is low in calcium. Their eggs are very heavily speckled. Calcium carbonate is the main construction material for shells and birds get their calcium from eating snails, which in turn extract their calcium from the soil to make their shells. The speckled areas, which have less calcium, gain reinforcement from strong, flexible compounds called protoporphyrins. This suggests that speckling, far from being a beauty or camouflage aid, actually has an engineering function. But no one has yet explained why robins' eggs are blue.

Boris has pneumonia and his coat is ragged due to a fungal infection. He's looking very miserable and is off his food. I know David is worried that the little pig might not pull through, but I refuse to believe that another one of our herd might die. Although he is meant to be the breeding boar, he is clearly not up to it so one of the other boys has been moved in with Bramble in the hope of successful mating. Their initial meeting wasn't promising as they tore into each other, squealing aggressively and biting each other's ears.

A few hours afterwards, Charlie and I are walking back to the nursery to spend the afternoon planting seeds when we notice the male pig standing in the middle of the sprouts in the vegetable garden. He's making his way towards an open gate, so while Charlie goes off to find some pig nuts I stand in the gateway to stop him getting out. But Number One Pig, as I'd christened this unnamed porker, isn't that serious about making a bid for freedom. He stands quite still in the gateway while I scratch him behind his ears and rub the wrinkly skin above his snout, which pigs seem to like. He leans against my knee and moves his weight forward on to his front legs, his back ones stretched out behind so that he looks like he's getting ready to do press-ups. We stay like this for quite some time as I forgot the key to the feed shed and Charlie has had to go home to collect it. But Number One's attention snaps back when he hears the rattle of the nuts in the bucket, so I tie my grubby white pashmina shawl round his neck like a lead and walk him back to his run. As soon as we turn the corner and he sees Bramble, he breaks into a run, the scarf billowing out behind him. I whip it off his neck just before he scampers through the gate. I think he looked rather debonair in the scarf, a regular pig about town.

In 1842 Charles Dickens was in New York where he met a boar walking along Broadway who inspired him to write: 'He leads a roving, gentlemanly, vagabond kind of life, somewhat answering to that of our club men at home. A free and easy, careless, indifferent kind of pig, having a very large acquaintance among other pigs of the same character. In this respect a republican pig, going where he pleases and mingling with the best society.' In the 1980s the *New York Times* reported seeing two adult pigs trotting through Manhattan in the early hours of the morning. They were later spotted strolling along the shore on Staten Island. William Hedgepeth, author of *The Hog Book*, wondered: 'How in the world did they do that? Hogs can swim well enough, but that would have been stupid. Clearly they got aboard the Staten Island ferry, but how?' We still have no idea how Number One Pig got out of his run. So far, there's no record of a pig figuring out how to unlatch a gate and then close it carefully behind him.

Charlie is growing increasingly concerned that, because of the diversions into pigs and birds, we're neglecting the bread-and-butter of our business, growing vegetables. We started the farm exactly a year ago and its prime purpose was to fulfil all of Dillington Park's orders for vegetables and eggs and we are failing badly in this respect. Right now, in the middle of January, the polytunnels are largely empty, most of the walled garden is empty too and there's now the huge five-acre field, stretching away to the west of the garden, which is still covered in the stubble of last year's wheat. David's energies have been diverted into laying drainage pipes, building a new chicken shed (which will house all our birds if the threat of bird flu means that all free-range fowl have to be moved indoors), planting the fruit trees and fencing off the new land.

All through January, we've been spending several hours every weekend sowing seeds for the first Montacute market of the year. On these cold days, I love being in the potting shed, where it is warm and life springs up all around me. There are heated shelves covered with gravel along two sides of the room, where the newly planted seeds germinate, warmed from below, watered from above by the sprinklers. At the far end, there's a big table where plants in various stages of growth stand in rows. On the remaining wall, another wide bench provides space for planting seeds, potting up seedlings and transferring cuttings into bigger containers. In the open areas underneath the surfaces, black plastic seed trays, pots of different sizes and bags of soil are neatly stacked. Trowels, small forks, scissors, Stanley knives, labels, pens, string and wire are assembled on a shelf above the potting-up bench. Everything you need is within easy reach, including the kettle and the radio. Fat-Boy, as Dylan is nicknamed, likes it too, as the potting shed connects to the room where the eggs are stored and there's usually at least one egg that gets broken, or is cracked and therefore can't be sold, which he then gets to eat, slurping up the yolk and the white, every so often spitting out a bit of shell.

Crumble up the rich, moist potting compost in your hand, pack it into the pots, make a small hole and drop in the seeds.

Marjoram, coriander, green basil, purple basil, flat-leaf parsley, curly parsley, chervil, oregano, peppermint: I have planted
ninety of each this morning. Then cucumbers, peppers and
chillis. Then some flowers: phlox, delphinium, carnations and
pinks. The smallest seed is the peppermint, smaller than a
grain of salt, practically nothing at all. It is almost impossible
to believe that this will turn into a big, leafy, sweet tasting,
powerfully smelling plant in a matter of weeks. Soil is extraordinary stuff. The more I learn about it the more I realise that
it is at the heart of everything on our planet, the substance that
provides us with all life. It is what allows the earth to breathe
and to live, to function.

It even has its own association, the Soil Association, whose
roots go back to the 1940s, to a group of English eccentrics led
by the magnificent Eve Balfour. On her farm in Suffolk, Lady
Eve struggled to grow good vegetables and raise livestock. In
her spare time she wrote detective stories and played in a jazz
band and smoked cheroots. You could find her, it was said,
dressed in tweed trousers, leaning on a fork, a cigar clamped
between her lips, surveying her crops. She described herself as
a flapper-farmer. In 1940 she'd read a book by the explorer
and naturalist Sir Albert Harrison, who had spent the previous
decade studying the lifestyle of the Indian Hunza tribe. The
Hunzas lived well into their hundreds and Sir Albert was
desperate to discover their secret of long life. Farmers worldwide had understood the necessity to rotate crops in order not
to deplete the soil of essential nitrogen. They'd understood
biological control, the process whereby specific pests can be
destroyed by predators and parasites. Conscious biological
control is an ancient concept: the Chinese encouraged ants
into citrus groves to eat caterpillars and boring beetles, even
building bamboo runways to aid their progress from tree to
tree. Sir Albert, I'm sure, would have known to grow a row of
onions between his carrots, to keep the carrot fly at bay and he
would have known the extraordinary benefit to the soil of

regular plantings of clover. The Hunza did all this, but they had an extra secret: they irrigated their terraces with water from glacial streams, a rich source of minerals released from volcanic dust, which meant that their food was enriched with high levels of essential trace elements and it was this, he concluded, that gave them their long life.

Lady Eve was entranced and she set up the association and published her book, *The Living Soil*, which encapsulated her belief that that the health of soil, plant, animal and man is one and indivisible. 'The criteria for a sustainable agriculture,' she wrote, 'can be summed up in one word – permanence, which means adopting techniques that maintain soil fertility indefinitely; that utilise, as far as possible, only renewable resources; that do not grossly pollute the environment; and that foster life energy (or if preferred biological activity) within the soil and throughout the cycles of all the involved food-chains.'

Monty Don once told me that he had a dream when he was a young boy in which he'd been planting some seeds and his hands were buried in the soil, but it wasn't the seeds that began to grow. It was his hands, stretching down into the earth and turning into roots. When he woke up, he knew he wanted to be a gardener. But to most people, and indeed to me until recently, soil is just pretty boring stuff which clogs up the bottom of your wellingtons: it is indeed the dirt beneath our feet. Governments have spent a fortune exploring the potential for life on other planets, but exploring the soil is a fledgling, under-funded and unglamorous industry. Yet the earth in our gardens, our fields, our forests, as well as the sediments at the bottom of every river and stream and marsh, harbour the most diverse life known in our universe. It is nothing short of magical. It is also critical to our survival. Without it, we literally have nothing and would be nothing. Every bit of energy that the world has comes from the sun, and there is only one way that living creatures can obtain it. Only plants can convert the power of the sun into the sustenance that all life on earth needs and it is the soil, in all its marvellous complexity, that allows this intricate exchange of sunlight into digestible energy to take place. Leaves and roots, forged in the reaction between the sun and the soil, have enabled us to create our civilisations and to look outside ourselves towards the distant surfaces of the planets.

Inside every leaf the chloroplast cells are tiny workshops for photosynthesis, the process which traps the sun's energy and converts it into carbohydrates. To do this the plant takes in carbon dioxide from the air and emits oxygen: the exact reverse of the way animals breathe. Using the sunlight for energy, it strips away the carbon and uses it to assemble sugars and other organic compounds needed to fuel life. In the process, the microbes discard the oxygen molecules from the carbon dioxide, creating the most precious waste in the universe. But the plants don't just need sunlight and CO_2. They need water and they need minerals. Both these come from the soil. Soil has been called 'the poor man's rainforest' because a single spadeful of rich garden soil may contain more species than the entire Amazon rainforest nurtures above ground. Think about it: it is, to coin an overused word, awesome. Two-thirds of the world's biological diversity lives in the soil and in underwater sediments. You could call it a micro-menagerie and it includes uncatalogued millions of microbes, mainly bacteria and fungi, single-celled protozoa, and tiny animals such as nematodes, copepods, springtails, mites, beetles, snails, shrimp, termites, pillbugs and earthworms. Crumbling the rich, dark soil through my fingers, I try to get my head round the fact that this neglected substance is actually stuffed full of tiny creatures all performing an essential part of life's essential rhythms. It's the sort of idea that, in 1960s hippy speak, blows your mind away.

The Harvard University ecologist Edward O. Wilson calculated that 93 per cent of the 'dry weight of animal tissue' in a patch of Amazon rainforest belongs to the invertebrates, from

mites and springtails to ants and termites. And that, apparently, doesn't count the microbes. Despite their minute size,
the bacteria in an acre of soil can outweigh a cow or two
grazing above them. Most of the underground creatures live
near the surface but there are some extraordinary beings
known as 'extremeophiles', bacteria and ancient microbes,
which live a mile or more deep in the earth, or in boiling
springs or polar ice. Although most soil organisms are tiny and
short-lived, some are huge and very, very old. American soil
scientists have measured the Armillaria root-rot fungus, a
sprawling underground mass which can exceed the size of a
blue whale. The largest yet discovered stretches under 2,200
acres of Oregon.

Wilson calls the creatures below our feet 'the little things
that run the world'. Soil science is in its infancy, but what we
do know is that, acting together, these little things form the
foundation for all life on earth. They break down organic
matter, store and recycle nutrients vital to plant growth,
generate soil, renew soil fertility, filter and purify water,
detoxify pollutants, control plant pests, yield up our most
important antibiotics, provide us with vitamins and minerals,
and help determine the state of the earth's atmosphere by their
absorption of greenhouse gases.

In prehistoric times, long before we started mucking around
with it, our soils were so rich in vitamins and minerals and
goodness that trees could grow ten metres in a single year, and
in the late Jurassic period, the gigantic thunder lizard was the
size of a swimming pool and weighed twenty-five tonnes. Yet
it was a vegetarian with a mouth the size of a horse. To grow
that big on a purely vegetarian diet, nutritionists estimate that
the plant life must have contained thirty times the mineral
levels that we find today.

Of all the creatures that live in the soil, the nematode is the
most extraordinary. It is the most diverse and abundant
creature on the planet; four out of every five animals are

nematodes and in a single square yard of pasture soil you could expect to find ten million of these tiny worm-like creatures. Throughout the world, 25,000 species of nematode have been named, but there are several million more waiting to be identified. Not all nematodes are benign microbe-eating decomposers: they can also be hookworms, round worms, ring worms and the cause of elephantiasis and river blindness.

Nematodes are so structurally different from us that, in biological classification terms, they are grouped under their own phylum. The phylum that we belong to, called the chordate phylum, also includes all birds, reptiles, amphibians and fish, as well as mammals. Nematodes breathe and reproduce in a unique way: they are characterised by their S-shaped, snaky movements. Some are free-living, some are symbiotic, others are parasitic, but they all play a vital role in the process of breaking down dead and waste matter – plant and animal – and in making it ready for re-absorption by a new plant.

Each earth creature eats waste and excretes it, in the process making everything smaller and smaller. They then mix the organic matter with the minerals in the soil and with fungi and bacteria. They move the dead matter downwards where it gets eaten again by different types of bacteria. Bacteria come in all shapes and sizes: some secrete a sugary gum which binds soil particles together; others break down molecules so that they can be absorbed by the plant roots. The cyanobacteria, single-celled organisms in a kingdom of their own, turn the nitrogen in the air into soluble nitrogen which plants can take up through the soil. Other bacteria change molecules into amino acids which plants translate into vitamin C.

Fungi secrete specific enzymes that chop up molecules into the exact sizes and shapes that plants need. Tiny protozoa roam the soil and feed on the bacteria and fungi. In the process of feeding they release excess nitrogen which the plants take up through their roots. Various organisms, including fungi, help plants take up the minerals they need as well as acting as physical barriers around the roots to stop disease. Others attach themselves to roots, operating like vaccinations which trigger an immune response in the plant. Other organisms directly attack harmful bugs. It's a complete, complex, totally interdependent world which provides the basis for plants to grow, and to harness and pass on the energy of the sun. Every plant has its own diet and knows what to pick out of the vast quantity of minerals, acids, carbohydrates, hydrogen molecules to enable it to perform its genetic inheritance. So a carrot will select what it needs to produce vitamin C, beta carotene and other vitamins. Flowers will take something different. Trees something different again. When the cow comes to graze, it will choose to eat the plant – grass – that tastes good but also enables it to grow and produce beef.

Standing in the potting shed, with my hands buried deep in the mound of rich potting soil, it's weird to imagine all this going on inside this pile of earth. One thing is clear though: somehow or other this rich array of species manages to coexist successfully. It has long puzzled scientists how this is possible and they attribute this peaceful sustainability in part to the tremendous diversity of habitats available, from tiny soil pores to clumps of soil particles to larger patches created by the engineering work of ants or earthworms. Food sources like plant litter, root secretions, dung and dead bodies are patchily distributed throughout the soil. Above ground, competition for resources has limited the number of species that can pack themselves on to the planet: down below, competition is less fierce, possibly because the little creatures cannot move well and because many spend long periods in dormant states. But thinking about the world beneath as like our own with tiny animals bustling along, jostling for space like crowds of shoppers on a Hong Kong street, is inaccurate. From the point of view of the microscopic organs, there is plenty of space and plenty to eat. The typical soil microbe, according to George Kowalchuk at the Netherlands Institute of Ecology, plays a long game: 'They can wait a really long time, perhaps years. Then when a root comes along or a drop of water or whatever, the cell blooms into a colony. Once the plant or the source of riches is gone, the colony dies out and the few remaining microbes go back to waiting.'

At the beginning of the 1990s, I used to play a computer game called SimCity which became incredibly popular amongst journalists, so popular that at the *Daily Telegraph* it was banned as being an addictive time-waster. The principle of SimCity is brilliant: the player is presented with the outlines of a city and a sum of money. As the newly appointed boss of the city you decide how to spend your cash. You can build roads, or hospitals, or art galleries, or parks, or low-cost housing, or yuppie apartments. You can buy buses, or statues, or install a metro. Or you can make provision for people's pensions, or pay council workers higher salaries. The game is endless in its permutations and my daughter Daisy, who was then ten years old, became addicted too. What is abundantly clear from SimCity is how even apparently random acts have knock-on effects: that everything is indeed linked up to everything else. If you build too many parks, there's not enough left for buses to get people to the parks. Too much yuppie housing means that hospital workers have nowhere to live.

It was in the middle of our SimCity craze that Daisy and I went on our first safari, to the Okavanga Swamps in Botswana. At dawn on our first morning, we awoke to the sound of an elephant crashing around outside our tent. We were both too excited to breathe.

One of our guides was an insect specialist who took us on bush walks. After he let us marvel at the magnificence of a termite mound, he instructed us to just stand still, put our heads down and study the ground. After days of watching big, grand animals, it took a few minutes to adjust and get used to looking at the tiny insects. There were hundreds of them, moving this way and that, rustling through the grass, intent on their business. He told us that all of African life depends on these tiny creatures, and that the removal of one species would drastically affect all the others, and that the removal of these termites would result in a dead, useless land where nothing could hope for life. Daisy looked at me and said 'Mum, it's nature's SimCity.'

We were seeing the real interdependence of the natural world but, apart from humans, it is only the insects who have established anything remotely resembling cities. What sets humankind apart from other creatures is our ability to grow food, and our ability to live in large groups which in turn can support great institutions. Cities are the heart of our global world and they need to be subsidised from the outside. That makes them vulnerable. A small town won't possess a museum or a specialist neuro-surgeon, but its inhabitants live closer to sources of food. As cities get bigger so the brilliance of our civilisation becomes increasingly evident: opera houses, metro systems, grand monuments and stately buildings. But as they get bigger they become increasingly dependent on supply chains, electricity grids, water and food that is produced far away. We inhabit our concrete streets and take for granted how it all works but, like the planet we live on, cities walk a tightrope to survive.

When we close down a corner shop, thus making people drive to an out-of-town superstore for their groceries, or dig up a hedge to enable farmers to grow even larger areas of wheat, when we ship apples all the way from South Africa to sell in a Somerset supermarket, and when we rip up great swathes of the Amazon rainforest to grow feed for cattle that live in the

USA – to be turned into hamburgers to keep the dollars flowing through fast-food restaurant tills – we upset the complex balance of the natural world. As I shake a tiny coriander seed out of its packet and drop it on to the soil in the pot, I realise that by growing food organically I am doing something, albeit something very small, to try to redress this balance. I also realise that the process makes me happy. All my life I've lived within a political system which believes that sustained economic growth is always a good thing, leading us towards happier, more fulfilled, more enriched lives. Yet evidence now points to the contrary. Once a country has filled its larder, or a person has met their basic needs, do extra riches bring extra happiness?

Surveys of happiness are both popular and revealing and they show overwhelmingly that industrial nations have not become happier. Random samples of British citizens demonstrate that we are no more satisfied with our lives than our parents were, yet we have two cars, three annual holidays, endless gadgets and gizmos, access to worlds of information – so much stuff that my parents, at least, never even dreamed of. Measures of health, probably more accurate than measuring elusive qualities like happiness, paint the same picture but endorse it with harder facts. Rates of depression have increased while stress levels at work have soared. In the USA, even though real incomes have risen six-fold, the per capita suicide rate remains the same as it was in 1900.

Innovative academics point the finger at the deadly sin of envy. We are creatures of comparison and we want what others have. Research conducted in 2005 showed that happiness levels depend inversely on the earnings level of your neighbour. If they're richer than you, you're dissatisfied. If their child has got into a better school, you're envious. If they drive a better car, take more exotic holidays and buy more expensive shoes, then your own fleeting pleasure is destroyed. We live in an age which is constantly on the hunt for the next new thing. Something that might seem brilliant today – like a pay rise, or moving to a bigger house – quickly becomes routine and ceases to delight. The old empty space opens up inside us, nagging at us with the vexed question of what new material goody might fill the void.

Here on the farm, I am able to step aside from the competitive world I inhabit in the city. Watching the pigs going about their business, seeing the plants grow, and knowing that though what we do might be small, it is also an affirmation of something more solid and tangible. Growing plants and vegetables is something that is nearly free for everyone, even though this particular project is causing us a few sleepless nights as the cash flow steams on in only one direction. Charlie's notion when we set out on this adventure, that it would cost us the same as a Mercedes, now seems more apt than ever. If we had spent £70,000 on a flash car with all the trimmings, within a few months there'd be another one in the window of one those grand car dealers in London's Park Lane, beckoning us with the promise of an even better driving experience and, unsaid but true, a quick way to get one up on the neighbours. I was a hippy in my teens and early twenties and I believed passionately in hippy things like communes and community and the power of nature and the spirit. Now, in my fifties, after a long diversion into the material world, maybe I am reverting, although the prospect of one day entering one of our pigs in a show, and winning, seems a very attractive notion.

We've bought three new saddleback pigs, including a splendid boar who we've called Robinson. After I finish in the potting shed I go to look at them, lying on top of each other against the garden wall, enjoying a rare moment of sunshine in this cold, long lasting winter. Saddlebacks have amazing markings, black at both ends with a white band round their shoulders and front legs, so clearly defined it is as though they've been kitted out to play on the same football team. They have longer snouts than the Gloucesters and, because they arrived with us as grown-up pigs, they're definitely more skittish and less keen on human affection. Bramble is sharing a pen with them and when I arrive she ambles over to get a rub behind her ears. Within seconds, Robinson is heaving himself up on to her hind quarters, something Bramble clearly doesn't have time for. She shrugs him off, so he has a go at one of his own kind, who is also wholly unresponsive to his ardour.

Boris's health is not improving. He is clearly a 'sickly pig'. First pneumonia, then a skin infection, which, despite anti-biotics and daily baths with an iodine solution, is wretched. Most of his hair has fallen out and his skin is red and scabby and itchy. I watch him desperately rubbing his shoulder against a fallen tree-trunk, grunting in his efforts to dig deep into the itchy patch. Two days ago, David moved him into the new chicken runs, where he has sole occupancy of the large wooden hut, built to house the geese and turkeys or, in the event of a lock-up due to bird flu, most of the flock. For now, though, it is Boris's home. Inside the hut, he has a pile of straw and a heating lamp which is normally used for baby chicks. Outside, he has the run of the old vegetable garden, which, when he's not scratching his itchy skin, he clearly enjoys. I'd decided to try tea-tree oil as a cure for his skin complaint, and when he's finished scratching himself on the log I enter the run to catch him, a bucket of tea-tree oil and water in one hand. He runs off towards the purple sprouting, grabbing quick mouthfuls but moving on every time I get close.

I pull off some leaves and hold them out to Boris, who gingerly comes closer. Then his nostrils quiver at the unfami-liar smell coming from the bucket and he's off again, haring back across the rows of old vegetables towards the shelter of his hut. Inside the hut, the sad-looking little pig is shivering in one corner. I offer him the leaves and while he crunches them up he stands still long enough for me to brush his back, sides, stomach, ears and chin with the oil.

The chickens have laid seventy-two fertile eggs, and as I am brushing Boris with tea tree oil an egg cracks open in the incubator and a tiny bird emerges into life. Within half an hour his feathers are dry and he's flopping around, tweeting incessantly, leaning his head against the other eggs, checking for signs of movement inside. Bird flu has crept even closer in the last two weeks. It has now reached France and according to DEFRA it is inevitable that it will arrive in Britain before too long. The failure to vaccinate livestock in the foot and mouth outbreak resulted in the needless slaughter of thousands of herds. I remember reading stories about farmers, heartbroken because their beloved cattle were destroyed. Despite that disaster, we are once again facing a possible pandemic without reserves of vaccination. But this time, for me, the issue is personal and as I watch the tiny new-born chick take its first tentative steps, I realise how much I will mind if we are told that they all have to be killed.

The weather has been freakishly cold this January and February. It reminds me of how cold it always seemed to be when I was a child and we would go skating on shallow ponds every January. My father had a wonky pair of skates, two blades screwed on to the bottom of some old brown army boots. The ankles flopped this way and that, but he was nifty on the ice and worked hard to teach me how to waltz on frozen water. He was well over six foot and we must have made a funny sight. I'd hang on to his hand and practise turns and backwards movements, crashing into his stomach as my balance teetered. But in recent years the winters have been mild, the early spring flowers arriving at the same time as I took down the Christmas cards.

In this cold, Hyacinth has been suffering: she's so little and one night David found her shivering uncontrollably outside her hut. She was, he said, almost frozen to the spot. Two days in the shed, in a warm straw-filled box under the heat lamp, coupled with extra nuts and fresh vegetables, had her back on her feet. Now she's putting on weight at a terrific rate. But I still agonise that she isn't going to make it and wonder what Charlie would say if I were to suggest that Hyacinth spend the night on our bed.

7

The First Slaughter

Four days before the first three boy pigs are due to go 'up the hill', as a trip to Snells is called, I go to visit Mr Bonner to tell him to expect the imminent arrival of our first pork. 'Are they boars?' he asks, as he bags up a string of sausages. 'Oh yes,' I reply, thinking of the discreet though pronounced double bulges under their tails.

He pauses and pushes his white cap back on his head, looking thoughtful. 'Well, I'll take them this time, but the trade doesn't like boar meat.' He puts down the sausages and reaches over the counter to pick up a pork chop. He bends it backwards and forwards, the pale meat chunky under his fingers, the fat well attached to the outside edge. 'Boar meat doesn't set so well – don't know why, something to do with the hormones. The fat falls off and the meat is less solid. It tastes OK,' he adds, looking at my worried face. 'And I will take them.'

'That's true,' David says when I ask him what we are going to do. 'But only when they're more than a year old. Taste goes as well, not just the texture.' Ouch, another example of being a dumb townie, thoroughly ignorant of the art of butchering meat. But I have scored a small but significant triumph. After a week of having tea-tree oil and water brushed on his skin, Boris is on the road to recovery. He's back with his brothers, his skin still scabby and rough but no longer inflamed, and his bristly white hairs are clearly growing again on some of his bald patches. I watch him in delight, chuffed as anything to have made a contribution to animal welfare and relieved that Boris isn't going to be consigned to the group of pigs going 'up the hill'. David's impressed. 'Good stuff – doesn't dry his skin out,' he says.

It is a rare day of warm sun, a spring day sneaking into this long winter when the sun shines brightly and the sky is blue and the early flowers start opening up their petals: crocuses and a few daffodils mixing with the snowdrops which have loved the endless frosty days. In *The Times* this morning there's a report from Kew gardens, where the daffodils are still tightly shut. In recent years springs have been so early that it has been predicted that winter will disappear altogether. We've had the ten hottest years on record in the last eleven years: lawns have been mown in midwinter and bulbs have bloomed in February. This winter, although there's been little snow, has actually been more normal and it feels wonderful to be outside in the soft warmth. In the nursery there's a definite feeling of spring. In the last four days, thirty chickens have hatched in the incubator; now they're in a wooden box, clustered under the heat lamp, chirping and tweeting in high-pitched voices. Some are yellow, looking like chicks on an Easter card, but others are various shades of browns, blacks, stripes, with black or white markings on wings and above eyes. There are eleven different breeds hatching and they're still too small to tell one from the other. Just over a third of the incubating eggs have hatched successfully, and some of those needed human help at the crucial moment. When the membrane has dried too much, it becomes too tough for the tiny bird to break through. The geese have not fared so well: at one point one solitary goose was sitting on twenty eggs, fiercely guarded by the ganders, but she suddenly upped and left her nest, leaving behind a pile of eggs which duly addled. George and Mildred have produced eleven eggs, but so far none has proved a winner. Still, the hen coop is in a tizzy of excitement: George and the ganders patrol the ground near the coop, hissing and gobbling with macho vigour; the rare-breed cock birds crow throughout the day, puffing up their chests and strutting in majestic circles in front of the females who look fat and full of purpose. There's loads of testosterone in the air.

Fat-Boy the Labrador has woken me up at dawn: he too is beside himself with energy and vim and the reason soon becomes clear. Charlie turned fifty-five this week and he'd been given a box of truffles, well sealed in a wooden box which was nailed shut. The box had been left overnight in the bottom of a carrier bag full of books. Fattie has taken out the books, ripped off the wooden lid and devoured the lot. I go downstairs with him and we watch the huge red sun rising through the bare trees of the wood to the east of our house and listen to the birds going crazy outside the window.

There's an order to the dawn chorus: first the blackbirds break into song, starting about forty minutes before sunrise, closely followed by the song thrushes; then the wood pigeons, robins, mistle thrushes, turtle doves, pheasants and willow warblers join in one by one, until finally the tiny wrens start singing too. I've learned this week that there is a reason why birds choose dawn as the time of day to make so much noise: the sudden inversion of temperature from the cold of night to the first warmth of day creates a reflective layer on which sound waves can travel further. It's why noise carries further across the cold surface of a lake and campers can hear each other talking on the other side. The birds discovered this several million years ago but we've only just figured it out.

I learned about it at a lecture on climate change which I'd

been to earlier in the week. Standing in front of an audience of almost two thousand people in St Paul's Cathedral, Sir David Attenborough asked whether it was God's will that we should bring nature under human control. Were we more important than any other creatures? The answer, he feared, was yes, this is what humanity has always thought. We need, he said, to change our perceptions if we are to save our planet, we need to learn how to tread lightly upon the earth, as guests rather than owners. We are all in too much of a hurry both to conquer and control. There can be no doubt, he said, leaning his elbows on the makeshift lectern, his clothes crumpled, his authority unquestionable, that the planet is changing. Twenty years ago scientists warned of climate change. He had been sceptical, but he is no longer. The graphs of CO_2 emissions in the last hundred years rose slowly, then more steeply. Now they travel off the page in a vertical line. The lines mirror the rise in population; there is no doubt that what we are experiencing is not a climate change caused by natural forces, but by us. He said how hard it was to find remote places any more, and that forests like Borneo, once the richest in the world, had been hacked down to grow oil palms, then abandoned, leaving depleted soil which is so poor it can't support life. In just a few years, natural abundance has given way to a wasteland.

He paused and shook his head: he'd just heard that grass had been found growing in Antarctica. We need a change in the way we live our lives, he said. Small acts like switching off the TV and taking fewer plane trips will add up to fewer carbon emissions but, more importantly, they will alter the way we look at our world. In the war, he continued, there was a morality about waste. People were careful with their resources because that was the way they knew it had to be. Now we need a change of moral attitude. We need to understand that the world has finite resources and that it is sinful to be wasteful. Sitting beneath the vast, ornate dome of St Paul's, I found myself thinking of my mother's brother, my uncle

Francis. Francis lived in a tiny bungalow on a beach in Jersey. He had been a member of the resistance during the war, captured by the Nazis after leaping from a window while trying to escape and breaking all the bones in his left foot. He mostly ate fish, which he caught from the beach or crabs and prawns from the plentiful rock pools of La Rocque bay. Whenever we went to have a meal with him, the one thing we all knew was that we must finish everything on our plates. As an eight-year-old girl, I remember thinking that he was a bit bonkers to be so obsessed but I never forgot those meals or his passion.

Two days before the first four pigs are due to go up the hill to Snells, we move them out of the caravan wood and into the pen nearest the gate. It's hard not to make gloomy comparisons between prisoners being transferred to cells nearer their execution chamber and, once in mind of that, I decide that I will take them a huge last vegetable supper. Pigs can, in fact, eat anything. It's one of the reasons they're so bright: any animal that doesn't have to spend most of its life searching for food has had time to develop its brain power. Mammals can be roughly divided into insectivores, carnivores and herbivores, but there's flexibility between the divisions. Foxes eat meat, but they'll also forage for wild fruit. Antelopes are herbivores, but occasionally they've been known to eat birds. The mice that live in our house probably like cheese the best if given a choice, but they eat meat and paper as well as bird food, which they steal from the big plastic sack of the stuff stored in the downstairs loo. They also seem to eat the plastic, since they make a hole but leave no trace of the bits. This ability to eat a wide range of food makes mice successful and – certainly in our house – prolific.

Most carnivores, like cats, are pure meat-eaters, but there

are exceptions among the group, most famously the panda, which survives on bamboo shoots, a food so low in essential elements and minerals that the panda can never hibernate and, unlike his meat-eating bear relatives, has to eat all year round to stay alive. Herbivores graze, browse or pick fruit. Cattle eat grass. Elephants eat leaves and twigs, monkeys and apes live off fruit. There's only one group of herbivores which eats everything regularly and that's the omnivorous pig. Their teeth are as generalised and non-specialist as our own.

Being omnivorous not only increases the pigs' chances of survival; it means survival almost anywhere, as they are curious and dexterous. Like us, they can be described as being neophilic, or fond of things which are new. Their brains are bigger than those of animals of equivalent size and, according to studies conducted at Bristol University, they're able to remember places where food can be found, even after long intervals.

On the last morning of the four boys' lives, I watch them happily rooting around underneath the wild rhododendron bushes and I find myself remembering the fantastic story of the Tamworth Two. At the time that those two little pigs made their gutsy escape in 1998 I was editing the *Independent on Sunday* and we published a story by Dick King Smith, West Country author of *Babe*, the children's classic about a pig who escapes the knacker's yard to become a skilled sheep-pig, winner of medals and prizes. *Babe* had just been adapted as an enormously successful film and we were all chuffed to be able to include a story honouring the Tamworths' free spirit by its author. But, as I read the papers in the days following the escape, it was clear that this story really belonged to the tabloids, who had thrown themselves into the fray with verve and open cheque-books.

The Tamworth Two escaped from Newman's abattoir in Malmesbury, swam across the River Avon and holed up on a wooded hill which looked out over Malmesbury's historic abbey. This small fact was recorded by the local paper and, on a quiet news day in the middle of a dreary, grey January, a reporter for *The Times* picked up the story and filed it to his news desk. *The Times* ran a graphic that illustrated how the pigs escaped, and plotted their route across the river and into the trees. Next day, the *Daily Mail* jumped in. *Mail* readers are never slow to respond to stories about animals, and as letters and calls flooded in from readers anxious to know where the pigs were and how they were doing, news editor Ian MacGregor saw the potential. This could be much more than a good heartstring-tugging story, it could become a world-class event, devouring as much space in the *Mail*'s pages as any diplomatic incident, political upheaval or death of a statesman.

The pigs had to be found, saved and then provided with a fairy-tale environment where they could live out their natural lives. MacGregor despatched a young reporter, Barbara Davies, to Wiltshire, with the instruction to find the pigs and bring home the story. But Fleet Street is a competitive place, and news of the *Mail*'s movements soon reached the ears of the *Daily Express*, the paper I was to edit just over a year later. The *Express* news team saw that the *Mail* meant business; their problem was how to get their own story without the huge financial and manpower resources that the *Mail* had at its command. Gerard Greaves, with whom I worked closely in the coming years, recalls the air of panic round the news desk when it became clear that two small pigs were going to set the news agenda for Britain in the coming days. 'The *Mail* had vets, snappers, tractors; they'd hired the only loader suitable for moving the pigs in the area. And as usual, the *Express* was miles behind.'

As a first move, the *Express* despatched Sean Rayment, ex-officer in the paras, to Wiltshire. 'Sean was being screamed at to get a pig, or a pig story, at any cost. He was wading around in the mud, carrying a bucket of nuts and yelling "pigs".'

The hunt was on. Other papers muscled in: the *Sun* and the

Mirror sent reporters, TV news crews rented helicopters to trace the piggy footprints. Even the broadsheets joined in. Within a couple of days, the pigs had captured the country's imagination: they were brave, they were smart, they were two little guys getting one over on the evil forces of big business. As they roamed around the winter woods, comparisons were made to war heroes escaping from Colditz. A Japanese TV truck arrived in Malmesbury, and NBC sent a veteran of the Gulf War and the Rwandan genocide, Donatella Lorch, to make sense of it all for an American audience.

News stories come in many categories. Some are clearly big stories which all papers must cover; others, like that of the Tamworth Two, acquire their importance and magnitude solely through media hype. The more that is written, the more important it becomes. From being a simple tale of two pigs who broke out of their pen, it blew up to be the biggest story in Britain that week. It was talked of in pubs and opined about in broadsheet editorials which saw true British guts in the pigs' escape. The *Mail* called them Butch and Sundance, further cementing the general belief that these outlaw animals were actually on the side of the angels.

Down in Wiltshire, Barbara Davies enlisted the help of Kevin and Debbie Stinchcombe, owners of an animal sanctuary. As a boy, Kevin had appeared in a musical version of *Dr Dolittle*, so he was well placed to 'talk to the animals'. The three of them set off to the woods, armed with buckets of nuts and metal hurdles and ropes. Barbara told them she would lose her job if she failed to capture the pigs, something the Stinchcombes took very seriously, and by dawn one pig was in captivity. They tried to keep it a secret while they searched for his companion but a nosy neighbour, alerted by the squealing, rang the local radio station, which was running a 'pig hot line'. Desperate to preserve its lead over the pack, the *Mail* then sent Steve Morris to buy the pigs from their last known owner, Arnaldo Diiulo. Diiulo was a road cleaner who had reared the pigs as a sideline on his three-acre smallholding. His pigs, probably worth no more than £65 each, were now being fought over like rough-cut diamonds. The problem for Morris was that Gerard Greaves had already made an offer which Diiulo felt honour-bound to accept. As Morris was explaining that this was problematic, as his paper already had custody of one pig, the back door of Diiulo's cottage burst open to reveal a gaggle of other reporters, waving cameras and microphones and offering huge sums of money. Diiulo barricaded the door and signed up with the *Mail*. Gerard was part of the pack pushing at the farmhouse door. 'It was mayhem,' he recalls, 'but what I clearly remember is that a reporter from the *People* passed her card through the door. On it she'd written, "£50,000 for the pigs".'

Meanwhile, the *Mail* despatched yet another journalist to Malmesbury to interview the pig. Star writer Paul Harris reported Butch as saying, 'I caught a glimpse of the *Daily Mail* girl, a redhead like me, and I knew I was in safe hands.' Paul and Butch appeared on TV that night, after Paul had been styled by the *Daily Mail*'s fashion team to ensure he looked suitably 'country casual'. The hunt was on for Sundance, who kept being 'spotted' in various gardens. Rumours flew that rival papers were preparing to parachute a 'fake' pig into the fray. Harris called one of the UK's leading DNA experts to find out if it would be possible to prove such skulduggery, then bought a set of pig's trotters to lay false trails. Steve Morris was put to work on the pigs' family tree, discovering that they were not pure breeds but the progeny of a Tamworth called Miss Piggy and a wild boar called Amadeus. The *Daily Mail* were delighted when it transpired that they had been bred at Bolehyde Manor, where Prince Charles had wooed Diana.

Sundance was finally spotted in the large garden of a nearby farm. There were two entrances. Gerard and Sean, still without a pig-exclusive, parked their respective cars in the two driveways, where they spent the night, in the hope that they

might capture the pig if it came past. But their efforts were to
no avail. The following morning, Sundance was finally captured, tranquilised and secured in a bunker next to the vet's
surgery in Malmesbury town square. The world's media
congregated outside as NBC's Miss Lorch pointed out that
250 million people worldwide were waiting for a first glimpse
of the pig. At that moment, Sundance let out an almighty
squeal and her cover was blown. The world's media glimpsed
the groggy pig for the first time. In a final attempt to recapture
the headlines, an exhausted Gerard flung himself towards the
pig and photographer Jonathan Buckmaster got to work.
Throwing his arms round Sundance's neck, Gerard turned
to face the lens. In a split second, the *Express* had their
exclusive photo for the following day: a snap of Gerard
and his pig, under the headline, 'The *Express* Brings Home
the Bacon . . . from Gerard Greaves in the thicket of it'.

'It had become such a big story that PRs from different
companies had rushed to Malmesbury, trying to catch some
of the media spotlight. There were girls handing out sweets and
offering bystanders samples of washing-up liquid,' he recalled.
The following morning, Gerard received a herogram from
Express editor, Richard Addis: his paper's 'exclusive' had cost
virtually nothing and the paper's honour was intact. Later that
day, the pigs were reunited. The *Mail* wanted a picture of them
peeking over a stable door, but as they were too small to manage
this a carpenter had to be hastily called in to build a platform.
The mayhem was over: as quickly as it had arisen, the story
fluttered and died, the world moved on and the two pigs were
sent to a rare-breed centre near Ashford in Kent where they've
grown old and fat, their days of stardom firmly behind them.

Eight years later, on an equally cold late-winter morning,
Dennis and I load up the pigs just after seven o'clock: a keen

east wind is gusting under grey skies and the four boys zip into the trailer in pursuit of the bucket of nuts. We shut the gate: from inside is the healthy sound of munching interspersed with squeals. The trailer rocks as the pigs bustle about after the food, then there's silence. We're hooked up to Dennis's B-reg gold Mercedes and I keep remembering my aunt's story about the trailer full of pigs that turned over on the road, but Dennis is a good driver and the trailer rides easily behind us. Just where we turn on to the main road, there is a big clump of snowdrops, still in full flower.

'I saw a squirrel there on my way in – he had a whole snowdrop bulb in his mouth, the flowers still attached. Maybe he was taking them home for Mother's Day,' Dennis jokes.

We arrive at Snells well before eight, the time of our appointment. A sharp turn off the Axminster road out of Chard and up a steep track brings us to a jumbled collection of tatty-looking buildings perched on the top of a hill. The view is fantastic, rolling wooded hills that lead southwards towards the sea at Lyme Regis, but the north-east wind is blowing strongly and it is bitterly cold. Already there is a small queue. Immediately in front of us is Darren Riggs, a designer who keeps pigs, sheep and two beef cows on his smallholding near Taunton. Darren's two pigs are Duroc Gloucester crosses, blackish with huge spots, far fatter than our four. They are fast asleep on the straw in the back of his trailer, and when the time comes for them to move he has to prod them awake and chivvy them down the ramp. They are not nervous, just lazy. Inside the pens immediately outside the door leading to the slaughter room, there is a pile of multicoloured pigs – a Tamworth, a Berkshire and a Gloucester, apparently asleep in a colourful pig sandwich, the black Berkshire snugly held between the sandy Tamworth and the pink-spotted Glouce-ster. For a minute I think they must be dead; they are so completely still and it seems impossible that any animal could kip while its relatives are meeting their maker in the room next door. Darren sees where I'm looking and laughs. 'It's a good place,' he says, herding his duo towards the heavy metal door. 'The best round here. The animals are never nervous.'

I had expected to be deafened by pig squeals and the racket of animals bashing against clanking bars, but the only sounds are the trailers manoeuvring into position. Then it's our turn. Dennis backs the trailer up to the entrance to the slaughter pens and our four come trotting out. Beside the fat Durocs they look more swimsuit model than WeightWatchers regulars. They amble into the long hallway, looking around curiously. The vet, a Spaniard called Jose who is wearing a black nylon balaclava under a bright yellow hard hat, checks them off on his list and bends down to look them over.

'What are you looking for?' I ask.

'I check zee feet,' he mumbles through the balaclava and puts a tick beside our entry. While the buildings might look jerry-built and untidy, all the important things seem just right: it is clean, there are piles of fresh straw on the ground, it doesn't smell that bad, and the atmosphere is conducive to keeping animals calm in their last moments.

I pat our pigs on their rumps and leave them trying to engage in conversation with the Duroc Gloucesters who are being held in an adjacent pen. The day before I had asked Trevor Symes, the owner of Snells and son-in-law of the founder of the abattoir, Charles Snell, if I could watch the process, so I walk round the back of the white pre-fab building, up some concrete steps and in through the office door. Trevor hands me a white coat and a rolled-up blue hairnet. He is similarly attired, but over his hairnet he wears a white plastic hard hat. On his wrist is a copper bracelet like the one my mother used to wear to help with her arthritis.

Trevor has a warm smile and an easygoing nature. If he'd been a doctor, you'd have said he had a good bedside manner. I follow him through a series of white doors, through a room where the carcasses of pigs and cattle are hanging by one foot from a long rail attached to the ceiling, through another door and into the centre of the slaughterhouse. Pig bodies, in varying stages of dismemberment, hang from rails around the room. The concrete floor is streaked with blood and the noise level, from saws and turning machines, is deafening. We walk past a yellow vat of pale grey intestines, looped and bunched in an undignified heap, past a row of hearts, lungs and livers, still attached to each other by veins and fatty tissue that are slightly steaming in the chilly atmosphere, round a low wall and back into the area where the animals are waiting. Our pigs are nowhere in sight, but Trevor opens a gate and now we're looking over the top of a waist-high railing at the four of them as they stand quietly beside a pulley-style hoist, breathing in the last few seconds of their lives. The slaughter man looks young enough to be at school. He is nineteen and his name is Ryan. He quickly sprays the pigs with water from a hosepipe in the wall, then grabs the nearest one by the shoulders, turns him on to the ground and deftly loops a chain, attached to the waiting hoist, around one back leg. The sudden speed is shocking and I step backwards, noticing that the other pigs are making anxious movements and backing away as far as they can, looking for a way out of their enclosed space.

'Why are they being sprayed?'

'To make sure the electricity does its job,' Trevor replies. At that moment, Ryan clamps the two prongs of the stun gun around the head of the pig which is now on the floor, its left back leg attached to the chain. He presses the button, pumping 1.3 amps of electricity through its brain for just over three seconds. The pig squeals once, loudly, its back legs jerking up towards its stomach while its front legs stretch stiffly forwards. It is a horrible, gut-wrenching squeal and, as I watch, the other three rustle nervously round in circles. I wish that all the pigs had been electrocuted at once. Ryan then pulls down a lever on the wall and, with a grinding noise, the hoist cranks into action, swinging the pig up by its leg and moving it to the left, through a grimy plastic door. As it begins its last journey, Ryan reapplies the stun gun, although I'm sure that the first bolt has rendered it completely unconscious. Once it is in the air and over a low wall leading out of the small death chamber, he takes a blue-handled knife from the pouch attached by a metal chain to his waist and deftly and quickly slits the pig's throat. Blood gushes and pumps, pouring down into a concrete well where it is collected and taken to be recycled for biofuels in a factory in Barnstaple. I realise that I've been holding my breath and that my heart is pounding, and I reach out to hold on to Trevor's arm. We follow the twitching carcass, hanging from its chain attached to a circular railing, as it swings round the corner of the blood-collection vat, bumping up against other pigs waiting in line to be dropped into a bath of hot water.

'That's kept at 70 degrees,' Trevor shouts above the roar of the electric saws which are chopping through carcasses further down the production line. 'It loosens the hair.'

With a splash, our pig drops into the steaming metal tank. A slaughter man in the uniform white coat and blue hairnet turns the pale pink body in the grey, murky water. After a couple of minutes he heaves it out and pushes it on to an adjoining metal rack, which then starts moving quickly from side to side, tossing the pig up and down on its shifting paddles in the process, shaving off most of the now-softened bristly hairs. Even though it has been shocking to see a pig that we have fed and reared actually be killed, the process up to now has seemed both humane and somehow dignified, but the sight of our once-lively fat pig twisting and tossing on the bars is strangely affecting. It is as though he is dancing, his feet moving and his ears flapping, his blood-stained mouth opening and shutting as though he is trying to talk, to tell us something. It is almost as though he is still alive, performing the last desperate dance of his life.

From the rack, the pig is laid sideways on a slab and the

remaining bristles are scraped off with a knife. From there, it is hooked back on to the overhead railing, and then a slaughter man wielding a chainsaw makes a neat, straight cut through the sternum and the stomach, opening up the inside of the pig as easily as opening a cupboard, displaying the intimacy of its heart, liver and lungs and the long, pouchy pale purple coils of its intestine which slither down towards the floor. The intestines are pulled out and consigned to a waste bin, the heart, lungs and liver hung up on hooks. All that remains inside the body cavity are the kidneys, nestled neatly against the backbone. Once the hair has been scraped off our pig, it completely ceases to resemble a living animal. Now he's just a carcass, ready to be hacked into chops and legs and loins or minced into sausages or sliced up for bacon, like something you'd see in a butcher's shop.

Every stage is carefully watched by one of the two meat inspectors who work at Snells. Like Jose the vet, they're a mandatory addition to any modern slaughterhouse, employed by the Meat Hygiene Service to monitor the process. The MHS charges Trevor about £2,000 a month, a fee that is based on the number of animals that pass through the abattoir every day. The inspectors are there to ensure that standards are upheld, but, Trevor tells me, if anything goes wrong, he's the one responsible.

It is breathtaking how quick the process is. One minute our pigs were rooting around on the floor of the holding tank; seven or eight minutes later, the meat inspector is slapping a purple stamp bearing the authorised Snells' number UK 8191 on to the carcass, thus ensuring that the meat can always be traced to its source.

Back in the office, I take off my hairnet and white coat, which, to my surprise, is spattered with blood, even though I haven't touched anything, keeping my arms by my side and steering clear of the walls. I presented our DEFRA form entitled 'Report of a Pig Movement Made under the General

Licence for the Movement of Pigs'. David had filled in our DEFRA identification number, the date of transport, our address, the destination address, the time of arrival and departure, and the number of Dennis's car. I ask for two whole pigs to be delivered to Mr Bonner's, one whole pig to be left for us to collect (destined for the kitchen at Kensington Place) and the remaining pig to be butchered into a 'farmer's cut', which means joints, loins, chops and sliced belly. Do I want the belly sliced thinly or not? Thinly, I reply, though I haven't a clue. At the office counter, a ten-year-old girl in pigtails is efficiently carrying out the business on behalf of her dad, the owner of a single Gloucester Old Spot, who is now washing down his trailer with the high-pressure hose which Snells charge their customers 10p for using. 'That one's got her head screwed on well,' says Trevor as she bounds out of the office. He signs off my form and hands me a brightly coloured leaflet entitled 'Sausage and Smashing Recipes', produced by the British Meat Organisation. I'm still too caught up in having just killed a pig to want to learn how to cook pork and Stilton sausages with onion mash and an apple and plum spicy relish, so I thank him and leave, my first voyage into the sharp end of pig-rearing successfully completed.

Dennis and I drive home through the village of Windwhistle, where there's a pretty golf course with wonderful views to the north, across the Levels towards Glastonbury, then on down a winding lane with high verges leading towards Ilminster. I can't get the image of the pig dancing on the rack out of mind. The lane takes us through the tiny village of Cricket Malherbie, where Lord Beaverbrook, press baron, political force and brilliant proprietor of the *Daily Express*, once maintained his country estate.

'I used to work here,' Dennis says, as we passed the high gates leading towards Beaverbrook's old house. 'I was head cowman for twenty-six years.'

As we drive on, leaving the farmyard with its high red-brick walls and archways behind us, Dennis tells me about his job. His working day would start at 4.30 a.m., winter or summer, when he'd bring the pedigree Ayrshire herd in from the fields for milking. There were eight separate herds on the estate, each consisting of forty cows. One cowman was exclusively in charge of each herd, working six days a week. A relief cowman filled in on his one day off. Nothing was automated: Dennis's first task was to wash the mud off the cows' tails so that no impurities could get in the milk. It took him one and a half hours to milk the herd, then he'd pour the milk into churns in the dairy, where it was cooled and bottled. When he'd finished that task, he'd lead the cows back to the field for the day, where they fattened themselves up on the rich pastures. In the evening he'd go through the same procedure all over again. Dennis met Beaverbrook only twice: wearing a heavy overcoat and black hat, he came to inspect his herd and congratulate Dennis on doing a good job. The herd became famous in the cattle world, frequently taking home the top prizes at the Bath and West annual show.

I find it very strange to listen to Dennis's story. The *Express* has played a consistent role in my life, and not just because I became the paper's first female editor at the end of the 1990s. Now I'm learning that our partner, David Bellew, was born while his father worked for the paper's proprietor. But a long time before David's birth in 1968, another life that has closely touched mine had been largely determined by the newspaper. My first husband and the father of my daughter Daisy, David Leitch, was given away as a baby in the advertisement columns of the *Daily Express* in early November 1937. His parents, John and Truda Chester, had decided, with what always seemed to me to be a breathtaking degree of callousness, that they couldn't cope with their newly born son, so they'd offered him for adoption to the Middle England readers of Britain's then greatest newspaper. In the Russell Hotel in Bloomsbury on a cold Sunday afternoon, John and

Truda had handed the eight-day-old baby over to the care of David and Ivy Leitch. Truda never expected to see her son again, but she bargained without his skills and the awesome powers of the media. In 1970, David, then an award-winning reporter and war correspondent for the *Sunday Times*, published a book called *God Stand Up for Bastards*, in which he outlined what he knew of his murky beginnings. He laid down a challenge to Truda to emerge from the shadows where she was lurking, 'as crafty as a trout'. And she did, after being confronted by the sight of her long-lost son talking about his mother on a TV show. David's been dead for over a year now, but I think of him as we negotiate the narrow, winding country lanes, and I know how much he would have loved this strange twist in the tale: he was never a great believer in the randomness of coincidence.

We are four pigs down, but not for long. Back at the farm, Dennis as I pick up David and set off to Devon to collect two new Berkshires and eight saddleback weaners. Our first port of call is Dittisham Farm, set high on a hill above the River Dart. It is even colder when we climb out of the car into a muddy driveway. I can hear loud grunts coming from a parked trailer, and David and I look through the small slits to be faced with two huge, mottled snouts. There is a brief moment of panic – they are far too big to travel in our small trailer – but it turns out they are waiting for another prospective buyer, who is running behind schedule. We're early and the farm's owner, Sue Fielder, hasn't yet brought our pigs down from the field. I look around: it seems a lonely place, marooned on its hillside, just one woman, her black Rottweiler and maybe one hundred pigs of different ages. Sue explains that her husband suddenly died of a brain haemorrhage four weeks earlier and she is selling off half her stock. Two Berkshires have just gone to

Japan, where the pigs are prized for their black skin and can fetch up to £700 each. The others are being sold when and where she can find buyers. Later that day, a sow with eleven four-day-old piglets is leaving; another nursing sow will be on her way tomorrow.

I watch her deftly lower the fork-lift bucket containing our new Empress and her husband Earl to the ground and shudder. In comparison to Sue's, my 'life as a farmer' is middle-class play-acting. It's not only that I can get up and leave it at any time. The reality is that I don't have to stand around in the mud and the freezing wind, selling off my pigs because that's the only source of income I have to support myself and my daughter. I was a single mother from the time Daisy was six and I remember my initial sense of panic as to whether we'd survive financially. I was working at *Harpers & Queen* when David and I split up and, even though my pay cheque arrived regularly every month and my father stepped in to help with the mortgage for the two years it took to sell our Little Venice apartment, my sense of financial insecurity was acute. Six months into single motherhood there was a change of editor and I was, for the duration of one long day and a night, unemployed, until Terry Mansfield, my boss at the National Magazine Company, offered me a job on the newly launched *Esquire* magazine. It turned out brilliantly for me: I joined as features' editor and became editor six months later; slowly, my financial fears began to fade.

In the year leading up to the breakdown of my marriage, my great friend and mentor, the war correspondent and writer Martha Gellhorn, had written to me frequently, a series of encouraging, hopeful letters in which she said, in many different ways, 'There are many things that are terrible in life and one of them is being stuck in a bad marriage. It is far more frightening than being alone with a child.' When I did leave, her words were a comfort, but that first year alone was tough

and I'll never forget how scary it was suddenly to find myself
the sole supporter of a child I loved so much.

Once the pigs are successfully loaded into our trailer, Sue
invites us up to her bungalow for coffee. In her cosy kitchen,
red, yellow and blue rosettes hang on the wall, symbols of
porcine success at local shows. On the draining board, about a
hundred newly laid eggs are waiting to be boxed up and sold.
On a sideboard there are half a dozen jars of bright yellow
honey, solid at the bottom, liquid at the top. A few bees' legs
float around in the liquid and the jars are sticky to the touch.
Dennis and I buy one each. Outside the wind whips through
the trees and a small flurry of snow blows past the window.
We pay Sue £180 for the Empress and £220 for Earl. Earl can
be rented out for £50 a time for stud, making the financial
rewards from a pedigree boar substantial over a five-year
span. Sue fills out the transfer forms and draws us a diagram
explaining the complex ear markings of the Berkshire breed.
Notches on the outside of the right ear represent units, those
on the inside, thousands. On the left side, the inside notches
mean hundreds and the outside ones, tens. The pattern of this
abacus-of-the-ears is particular to Berkshires and any breeder
can immediately determine the origin of a pig from the cuts.
Earl, whose pedigree name is NarmaAbel, is number 687 and
the Empress, an excellent and chubby pig with a shortish nose
who has show qualities, is the daughter of Ambassador and
Excelsior. Her number is 591.

I ask Sue what farmers do about the boars' tusks. She looks
at me sceptically. 'Do you really want to know?' she asks,
clearly aware that I am not, in any true sense, a farmer. I nod.

'Well, boars' teeth don't come through till they're over a
year, so sometime between twelve and fifteen months, some
people put them in a head clamp, push a piece of wood
between their teeth and then file off the four teeth with an
angle drill.' She pauses. 'It takes about two minutes if they
know what they're doing. Then they give them a whole bucket

of food and the boars seem to forget it. They could,' she adds, hastily, 'get the vet to give them an anaesthetic, but some people don't want the expense.'

Our next port of call is a small farm at the bottom of a steep valley. Richard Fox's farmyard looks old and scruffy, with pigs living in sheds around the four walls. The little weaners we've come to buy are clustered together for warmth on a deep bed of straw inside a stable. We pick them up one by one, carrying them by their back legs to the trailer. We'd asked for eight, at £20 each, but Richard throws in the other four for an extra £20. After filling out the purchase forms and handing over the money, he shows us his prize boar, Little Richard, who stands about three feet six inches tall and eight feet long. 'That's what Robinson will look like in a few months' time,' David says cheerfully, stepping neatly out of the way as Little Richard lunges towards the open door. I wonder how on earth we're going to contain a pig that big on our farm.

I fall asleep in the back of Dennis's warm car on the drive home and when I wake up we are bumping down the track to the nursery. Even though it is still freezing and the sky is stony grey and bleak, our farm looks extraordinarily chipper. David is an incredibly tidy man. Our fences aren't falling down, our gates are neat, the pathways, even in winter, are level and dry. Even the recycled two-litre plastic milk bottles which hang from the wire fences, doubling as water troughs and feeders for the rare-breed chickens, look efficient and useful. We carry the little pigs down to the big shed which has been divided in half by a two-foot-high wooden wall. They're sharing the space with Robinson and one of the grown saddleback gilts, as well as Guinness. They settle in quickly on to deep, clean straw, noses immediately in the trough which had been filled with nuts. Earl and the Empress move into the pen vacated earlier that morning by the four now-deceased Gloucesters. Sue had told us that the Empress, while an excellent pig in every respect, has a funny habit of sticking her tongue out when she isn't actively engaged in eating or rootling. I watch her investigate her new home, looking inside the small house, checking out the water supply and, seemingly finding it all satisfactory, she again looks about, her little pink tongue protruding from her mouth, every inch a curious young woman who's quite pleased with life.

The following morning, Mildred falls into the duck pond and can't get out. When we find her she is perched precariously on a stone, wet, cold and miserable. George waddles around proprietorially as David carries the bedraggled turkey into one of the chicken sheds where she settles down in the straw, next to a goose sitting on her eggs. David has seen an advert in a local free paper offering grown chickens for just 75p each. They are a year old and have been living as deep litter birds in a huge group of some six thousand squashed together in one enormous barn. Reared like this, chickens will produce almost one egg a day for the first year of their lives; then production tails off to about four or five a week, at which point most birds are converted into soup or stock or turned into filling for cheap pies. But 75p for a full-grown chicken, even one that doesn't lay to her full potential, is incredibly cheap and, since we lost some of our birds to the viral infection, David decides to buy one hundred.

They are a sorry bunch when they arrive: their feathers are falling out, their eyes runny and their combs floppy and dull. But they quickly improve, venturing further and further from their coop, setting off in groups of four or five to explore the rows of old vegetables at the bottom of their run, digging out a central dust bath in which they take turns to dig, scratching up the earth and sending it in showers over their feathers which keeps them both clean and healthy. Within ten days, they are laying sixty eggs a day, their feathers are fluffing out, and their eyes are distinctly brighter.

Twelve years ago, when Daisy and I had moved out of the home we'd shared with her father and into our own house, we'd gone to Battersea Dogs' Home to get a dog. We walked through the rows and rows of cages, assailed by barks and whines and pleading eyes, until Daisy suddenly decided on a small, thin, uninspiring white mutt with brown patches. I wasn't that keen, but she was determined, so we filled out the forms, paid our £50 and left with a little bitch we called Bingo. We were warned not to let her off the lead for at least two weeks, but our first stop was Hyde Park, the sun was out, and we decided to let Bingo have a good run. She never left our side and she's never left it since, turning from a shy little runt into an incredibly sweet and loyal dog, who has blossomed on a diet of cuddles and new-found security. Looking at our rescue hens, I am reminded of Bingo's inauspicious beginnings: she'd been abandoned on a south London street and had already been waiting in Battersea for over four months before she caught Daisy's eye. I always feel that Bingo somehow knows that she's been lucky and I wonder if the hens have a similar feeling.

By the middle of March the lateness of the spring is generating newspaper headlines such as 'where have all the flowers gone'. Down in Cornwall the annual daffodil festival at Cotehele Manor has been postponed until April. The average mean temperature for March has been just 2.4°C, about 4°C below recent years and that's meant that many early-flowering flowers such as crocuses, daffodils and hyacinths are still keeping their buds firmly closed. Only the snowdrops have flourished, flowering for far longer and growing far larger than anyone seems to remember. I know that we're not alone, but as the days creep by and the ground in the market garden refuses to warm up, nothing can be planted. Seed potatoes, onion sets, carrots, cabbages, beans, parsnips are all waiting to go into the ground, but without a sustained period of warmth when the temperature stays above 6°C for a number of days, there's no point in sowing anything.

Charlie and I write cheques for wages, pigs, animal feed, telephone bills: by the first official day of spring on 21 March, our investment totalled £86,540, much more than our first 'limit', more than our second one too. Our bank in Yeovil, the NatWest, has been a lousy partner in our small business venture. At Christmas, they bounced three cheques, charging us £37 every time. I negotiated a small business loan of £1,000, explaining to the manager that we often had a short-fall between paying necessary bills and new investment. Charlie and I bank with NatWest in London and our main accounts act as surety for any loans. The manager, Lee Chapman, agreed, but two months later, he bounced another three cheques, charging us again for the privilege. My normally mild-mannered husband hit the roof. I went to ask David if he knew what was going on. He told me that when he and his wife Tracey split up, the bank wanted David to clear the debt on their loan. He had asked to renegotiate the repayments but the bank hadn't got round to doing so, and now the banking system at the nursery was being penalised. It was an explanation of sorts, but Charlie and I were still furious with the bank and argued to have the bounced cheque charges refunded.

Our income stream remains tiny: 800 eggs a week, a small amount of vegetables and now four pigs, which will make us about £500. There's not much chance of having many vegetables to sell before June, and I know that it is only Wayne Bennett's patience and belief in the project that is making him keep faith with us as suppliers of all Dillington's vegetables. Charlie and I have stopped talking about what our limit is in terms of investment: neither of us would pull the plug on the project, but I'm worried. The cold weather has put our earning potential back a good few weeks. Bluebell is definitely not pregnant, and that's another financial setback. The newly hatched rare-breed chickens won't be big enough to sell till May, and if bird flu is found in Britain then not only will the bird markets be cancelled, private sales will be impossible as well.

But the cold weather isn't deterring the birds from mating. All the females are laying and the incubator in the office is full to bursting with seventy-two eggs in various shades of brown and white. Unlike that of the pigs, who mate for a full half-hour, chicken sex is fast and furious: they just need to position themselves correctly so that the sperm can enter the female vagina. All animal copulation takes place in full view of the other animals and zoologists have learned that the sight of others having sex can work as a powerful aphrodisiac.

The most bizarre experiment I ever heard about took place in Japan. Researchers put two female and two male quails in a pen together. The female birds showed a definite preference for one of the males, so the rejected male was removed, filmed having sex with a third female and then the resulting video showed to the two lady quails, who immediately developed an overwhelming interest in the porn star. The Japanese researchers had no idea why the film helped the birds to change their minds, but concluded that female quails are, like humans, affected by watching sex and seem to prefer males that have demonstrated their sexual dexterity.

I had begun to wonder if the fear about a supermarket opening in Ilminster was just that. Time had passed and there'd been no signs of movement from the developers and no firm announcements as to which of the Big Four would be moving into the site on Shuddrick Lane. But now in early March there is a report from the Office of Fair Trading that shoots the whole issue into the headlines. In 2005, the OFT had ruled that there were no grounds for probing the power of the supermarkets; now that decision has been reversed. A report from the Association of Convenience Stores said that they were stealing the identity of our towns and cities. In the year leading up to May 2005, 2,157 unaffiliated independent retailers had shut down, compared with only 1,079 the year before. MPs expressed fears over this unchecked expansion, which they warned could lead to the closure of 40 per cent of small shops by 2015. The 2003 decision to allow Tesco to buy up high-street convenience chains has further strengthened their market share of Britain's grocery business and the report recommends that the issue should be re-opened by the Competition Commission. For the first time in my memory, supermarkets led the evening news on the BBC. One morning shortly after the report's publication I am in Lane's Garden Shop, talking to Bryan Ferris. We express our optimism that this might mean that Ilminster will be spared. But on 16 March the *Chard and Ilminster Gazette* tells a different story. A colour picture of the Shuddrick Lane site reveals a barren stretch of land, scored by the deep marks of tractor wheels. The trees have all been felled and bulldozers have flattened out the bumps. As reporter Laura Thorpe notes, 'The face of Ilminster is set to change for good as work begins on a controversial supermarket development.'

'No one had any idea this was going to happen. The workmen just arrived.' Bryan has come round to the Dairy House for tea, with his friend Mike Fry-Foley who, with his wife Patricia, runs a small hotel in Beaverbrook's old village of Cricket Malherbie. Bryan and Mike have just sent a letter to our local MP David Laws, asking him to attend a meeting to protest about the one-way system. 'I know we've lost the battle over the store, but we can at least keep fighting about the one-way system,' they wrote.

The new one-way system was authorised by the council

following the decision to build the supermarket. It will divert traffic around the town and away from Silver Street, where all the independent shops are located: Bryan's garden shop, Mr Bonner's butcher's shop, the greengrocer's, the chemist, the cheese shop, the bookstore, all the shops that give Ilminster its character and vitality. A further blow to the town traders is the council decision to allow the supermarket to build on the site of the existing car park which means moving the car park out eastwards into an area which, at the moment, is a field. 'To get to Mr Bonner's,' says Mike, 'you're going to have to walk over half a mile.' The new road system, which the road department are insisting on for reasons of safety, will turn a journey that at the moment is about two hundred yards, into one of over a mile. For Bryan and Elizabeth, Aaron Driver, Mr B, John and Mary Rendell and others along Silver Street, it's like having a heart by-pass.

'Of course, there's another alternative road scheme,' says Bryan. 'We've proposed it and this is what we need David Laws to help us with.'

'Three thousand people in Ilminster have signed a petition objecting to the traffic scheme,' added Mike, who knows that Ilminster's market town diversity is so attractive to his guests. 'This is like using a sledgehammer to crack a nut.'

Bryan has another worry. While building works are going on, spaces in the existing car park will be reduced from 160 to sixty. He's been checking the car park every few hours, counting the actual number of cars parked there at any time. It's rarely under ninety. In their memo to David Laws, Mike and Bryan write that 'there can be no doubt that the road plans and proposed car park layout are designed exclusively for the benefit of the superstore and to the detriment of the rest of the town. A look at the plans and time spent "walking the job" will demonstrate this. We see no malice here, only lack of detailed thought: no consultation; incompetence and an "it's not important" attitude.'

'We know the superstore is coming: we just want a level playing field to fight it from,' Brian says, adding that he's recently heard from a retailer in Tiverton who has told him that, since major traffic deployment schemes following the opening of a Tesco superstore, his turnover has declined to the point that the outlet is no longer profitable and remains open only because it can – for the moment – be bailed out by his other outlets. If you have only one outlet, like Bryan and Elizabeth, this option is not available.

Bryan and Elizabeth used to have another shop in Wellington, which Bryan looked after while Elizabeth took care of the Silver Street store. But a couple of years ago they had to close it down and consolidate their resources in the one shop. The development of the superstore might bring more people into the town, but they will be dedicated supermarket shoppers who, after spending one and a half hours filling up their trolleys with frozen meals and chilled food and then pushing their groceries back to their cars to unload, won't then set off back past the store and into town. Bryan's right: the way the scheme is planned, it will mean only loss of business for the existing shops.

Fat-Boy's constant quest for food often goes badly wrong. We left a bag of rice out on the table in the kitchen overnight. It was half full and I'd rolled down the cellophane and secured the bag with an elastic band. Fattie nicked it off the kitchen counter, his teeth puncturing the thin transparent bag. When I come down in the morning there's a trail of rice leading out of the kitchen, along the corridor and into the sitting-room, where he's abandoned what's left of the bag beside the fireplace. He's really been after the leftover pheasant bones, which had been boiling on the stove the previous evening, but the saucepan, with the lid firmly on, had been placed well out of his reach so he's settled for stealing the rice. It's the end of the shooting season and Mr B is selling a brace of pheasants for as little as £2.50. There are so many round here that I realise I take their exotic gorgeousness for granted. Their lives, though, are tragic. Deliberately introduced here from a faraway habitat, they're mostly raised in captivity then released into the wild, knowing nothing about how to survive, only to be shot or squashed under car wheels after wandering unwittingly on to the road. Pheasants were first brought to Britain by the Romans, but these early birds were kept in pens and never went native. A thousand years later, the Normans brought in a new strain, with the white neck ring. These adaptable birds naturalised well in the woods and grasslands of Britain. At my cousins' farm, many of hedges were planted as 'doubles' in Victorian times: two hedges separated by a gap of some fifteen feet, where trees and brambles were allowed to grow wild. Doubles were designed with pheasants in mind, providing safe corridors for them to live and nest in. Victorian gamekeepers would be under instruction to shoot anything that might eat pheasant eggs, young chicks or the birds themselves: badgers, foxes, weasels, stoats. But in the 1920s, when the Depression began, money ran out and the pheasant population, quite unable to fend for themselves, was decimated. Wartime followed and, after the war, estates were too expensive to keep up, which further reduced pheasant numbers. It wasn't until the financial boom of the 1980s that estates began intensive breeding programmes again, rearing the birds in coops and releasing them on demand into the line of the guns. In the name of sport, twenty million pheasants are bred every year across the English countryside. As Ander says, it's a heartless business. They don't like to fly and they often get winged by city gents who don't shoot straight; then they're left as prey for the foxes and badgers.

My father used to shoot, primarily, he always said, because he liked the walking and the company. But after he turned seventy-five he stopped, saying that he no longer wanted to kill anything. As he aged he grew more vociferous about his love of the countryside, and his view of what human beings were doing to it became increasingly savage. His main anxiety was population growth, and as Alzheimer's slowly ate into his brain this turned into an obsession. When I became the editor of the *Daily Express*, Dad's first suggestion was that I should publish a whole page every day showing on a graph how much the world's population had grown in the previous twenty-four hours. When I pointed out that this would be an extravagant use of limited space, he'd jab his finger at a page of advertisements for cheap TVs or low-cost flights and instruct me to 'dump this silly rubbish'. As his inhibitions faded along with his memory, he would work himself up into explosive fury about the fate that would soon befall the planet, all because people spent too much time fucking! It was bizarre and uncomfortable to hear such an obscenity from my father, a previously fastidious and impeccably mannered man who would have recoiled with horror from anyone swearing like that.

My sister and I would endure his outbursts as best we could and it was only after he died, in the autumn of 2003 at the age of eighty-seven, that I was able to see the truth of what he feared. Until some populations started reducing in size, the world was on a terrifying trajectory. In AD 1, when Christ was born, there were between 100 million and 300 million on the earth. By 1500 there were 500 million. By 1825, one billion. By 1927, two billion. By 1960, three billion, by 1975, four billion. By Millennium Eve – which my father spent with Charlie and me, Daisy, my sister and her family and cousin Ander, watching fireworks from the offices of the *Daily Express* overlooking the Thames at Blackfriars – the world's population had reached six billion. Unchecked, that rate of population expansion would have meant sixteen billion people on the earth by the middle of this century, a completely unsustainable number. But, in fact, due to falling birth rates across the world, population experts now estimate that the world's numbers will level off between nine and eleven billion by 2050.

Charlie's family is a good example of falling birth rates. His maternal grandmother gave birth to twenty-two children, born between 1893 and 1916. There were two sets of triplets who all died, three sets of twins, one of whom survived, and seven others who grew to adulthood, his mother, Naida, being the youngest. His grandmother was called Rose Guest and when she'd come to the end of her years of breeding she set about planning her exit from her marriage. As the Depression deepened in the twenties, her husband Henry, a West Country cattle drover, transferred a sizeable amount of his company assets into his wife's name, in order to safeguard himself in the possible event of bankruptcy. Rose took the money and moved into the Clarence Hotel in Weston-super-Mare, from where she oversaw the building of a four-bedroom Regency villa, equipped with two bathrooms and all mod cons. Charlie has only eight cousins, a case of dwindling returns on Rose and Henry's original investment in procreation.

My father would not have been persuaded by their example. Nine billion people are still far too many for our planet to sustain comfortably. Most of the money I have invested in the farm came from the legacy I inherited from my father and I like to think that he would have been pleased with what we are doing, delighted by the pigs and the plants and our small attempt to put something back into the natural order of the world.

8

The Swallows Return

The last Saturday in March, a week before the official first day of spring on 1 April, turns into one of the worst days we've yet had on the farm. It isn't just because of what actually happens, although things do happen; it is also because the things that do happen bring me face to face with a whole slew of problems which I've been shoving under the carpet and refusing to acknowledge.

Mildred doesn't survive her fall into the duck pond: she shivers through one night and the following day she dies in the hen house. George is now a lonesome turkey and all that remains of poor little Mildred is a collection of five eggs which are awaiting their turn in the incubator. The new pigs have all settled in: Earl and the Empress are living in the caravan wood with Boris and his three brothers. This week the vet said there is every likelihood that Boris's fertility has been affected by his illness and by the antibiotics he's had to take, so we're going to have to bite the bullet and send Boris up the hill when he's fat enough. One of his brothers will be kept as the Gloucester boar. I want to call him Napoleon, as he's attained his status through another's demise, but the boars need short names which they can remember and Nappy seems very undistinguished for a breeding pig.

Poor Boris, getting the chop after all the misery of those injections, the tea-tree oil and iodine baths, the endless scabby skin and itchiness. Still, maybe he'll taste good, I think, as I go into Mr Bonner's expecting to see our name up on his blackboard, advertising our pork. Nothing. And no sign of Mr B. I find his dad, Mr B senior, in the back of the shop, standing beside the long chopping boards, expertly wielding a knife through a huge joint of beef.

'How's our pork?' I ask.

He frowns. 'Well, not very good, actually.'

'What do you mean?'

'Your pigs are too thin, there's not enough fat, and Clinton cut off a chop to cook and it was tough. And they're boars and they're not as good. We only sell gilts . . .'

He takes down a piece of meat that is hanging off a metal hook above his head. 'Clinton kept this for you to see.' He bends the piece of meat in his fingers: it's part lean flesh, part skin with a small layer of fat. It rolls together and, to my ignorant eyes, looks like a nice, though not large, chunk of pork. 'See how small it is,' Mr B senior continues. 'And look at this one.' He goes out to the main shop and returns carrying a huge rolled loin of pork in one hand and a smaller loin in the other. The first one has a thick layer of chunky white fat running right round it; the smaller one is almost wholly lean, the skin attaching directly to the meat. This is ours. 'We can't sell this kind of meat in a shop like ours.' He says this in a whisper, so that the people in the queue in the main shop won't hear. I could be in the clap clinic waiting for a test result. 'You could sell it in a supermarket, or somewhere that wasn't so particular, but it would bring us into disrepute. We've made the rest of the pigs into sausages.'

I feel sick: it is like having an article rejected or getting the sack. Does this mean Bonners won't sell our pork any more? I don't want to ask. Mr B senior is saying that we need to get some advice on how to rear our pigs and that we should ask David's uncle, Mr Sainsbury, who knows all about how to fatten pigs. He suggests that I call his son when he gets back from a short holiday in three days' time.

After apologising profusely for our substandard pork, I leave the shop and bump into Charlie, who is walking along Silver Street towards the butcher's. I tell him what has happened and we go off to get coffee in the Meeting House at the other end of the town. Apart from Mr Bonner, a pig is also going to Rowley Leigh, chef of Kensington Place restaurant in London, and heaven knows what he will think of it. Clearly, we aren't going to get much money for the pigs and, even though the walled garden is now full of seeds, at least another two or three months are going to pass when we'll still be far below the break-even mark. For the last five months our polytunnels, which could have been producing salads, have stood largely empty, and ground where winter vegetables such as leeks and Brussels sprouts and sorrel could have been growing has been fallow. The pork disaster acts like a catalyst to open the floodgates of doubt. Is this all completely crazy? If David had been borrowing the money from a real bank, rather than from a couple of ignorant townies, would he have done things differently? If Charlie and I were borrowing the money from the bank and we'd promised the manager an injection of cash once the pigs were sold, we'd be sweating with anxiety. It is only six days ago that we sat down in the kitchen with David, assessing our financial prospects for the coming weeks. It looked promising: Dillington House owed us £1,100, Rowley owed us £180, and the pigs would bring in at least £500. That would mean almost £1,800 into the account by the end of March, and on 1 April it's the farmers' market at Montacute where we'll be running the herb stall. They expect a thousand people and, by my back-of-the-envelope calculations, if they spent 40p each we'd be doing just fine. Now, I'm revising my estimate: to make up for the pig loss we'll need to come home with £600. I have absolutely no idea whether this is realistic or a complete pipedream. More importantly, is our eagerness to have a farm, and to watch the pigs and chickens breed and grow, to have the sort of romantic country idyll you see in picture books, actually preventing us from building a sustainable business?

As we set off to the bird market in Taunton, to see if we can find a female Kagyua duck and a replacement for Mildred, I am fearing just that.

'I'm out of my depth,' Charlie says, as we drive out of Ilminster and the rain starts pattering down on the windscreen. 'I know what makes a good vegetable, but I don't have a clue about what makes a good pig.'

The bird auction is being held in the Taunton cattle market. Trucks and trailers containing sheep, lambs, cows, sows and boars are loading and unloading their cargo. The air is thick with the sounds of the animals, the squealing of brakes and the shouts of the buyers and sellers. The rain is falling steadily by now, and the ground is running with the muddy yellow stains of animal muck. The rare-breed birds are being sold in one half of the pig barns: inside it is heaving with farmers, breeders and families with young kids out to buy a couple of fancy chickens to keep in their back gardens. Steam from wet clothes drifts into the air. It is smelly. The auctioneers, two young guys wearing green overalls, keep up a running mumble of inaudible words as they parade along the top of the pig pens, above the crates containing the individual chickens.

David and Josh are already there. There is no mate for our splendid blue-black Kagyua duck, only another drake, who is being sold as 'great breeding material'. There are no turkeys at all, male or female. Standing squashed up against a cage containing two blue buff Orpingtons, I find myself next to Darren Riggs and his two children. I ask him how much his dead pigs had weighed. He looks pleased. 'Eighty-four and eighty-seven kilos dead weight.' Ours had weighed fifty-six, fifty-eight, sixty and sixty-four. 'It's all been sold to friends in the village and our deep freeze is bulging with the rest of it.'

'What did you feed them on?'

'Grass, organic pig nuts and old vegetable scraps from the kitchen.' No substantial difference there, but Darren's fat porkers must have had a lot more of something than ours. I wonder if his were older, but in fact his two had gone to Snells at seven months, slightly younger than our four. There had been a good, inch-thick layer of fat on both his pigs.

'What sex were they?' I ask.

'One of each,' he replies, raising his hand to bid for a pair of Brahmas, which a second later go for £5 more than he is willing to pay.

'Don't boars taste different?'

'That's just an old-fashioned myth. If you eat them before they're sexually active, there's no difference. I don't know why people still believe that.'

God, how depressing. How come Darren can rear two good pigs in his small field, and we can't? I am angry that David hasn't seemed very perturbed about the Bonners' verdict on our meat. Charlie is angry that our polytunnels are only now being fully planted. We are both cross that our ignorance has been exposed. It had been humiliating standing in the butcher's shop, with old Mr B whispering so that the other customers wouldn't overhear. We walk back through the rain to where we've parked our car, in one of the car parks of Taunton Cricket Ground, to find the gate is locked and there's no one around. It takes us almost an hour to rescue the car and set off home.

Later that evening, I discover that we've run out of eggs. The rissoles I am making from a leftover piece of beef will fall to pieces without an egg to bind them, so I set off with the dogs and a torch to collect some from the hen house. The farm gate is closed and padlocked, so I climb over, leaving the dogs whining on the far side. The gate to the chicken run is padlocked also. I stand there cursing as the light dies in the sky, the walls of the garden black above me, the geese standing out in the darkness like large snowballs, their shapes indeterminate in the gloom. All the rescue hens and the rare breeds have gone inside their houses; only the geese and a handful of hens are still outside, displaying a complete disregard for the foxes and perhaps too much reliance on the powers of the electric fence. I can see the dogs silhouetted against the gate, and, as I walk back towards them, two of the new baby saddlebacks venture out of their house to see what is going on. I turn the torchlight on their curious little faces, their wrinkly noses twitching with interest and life. I make a silent vow that when it is their time to go up the hill, they will be as fat as barrels. I wish we'd just killed one pig and then fed the other three till they were fit to burst. Killing them when they weren't as good as they could be makes their death feel wasteful.

When I get home, I dig out an old copy of *Charlotte's Web*, the wonderful American children's story that I'd loved reading as a child. The porcine hero, Wilbur, was a ferocious eater, never more so than after he became a star, thanks to the cunning of Charlotte the spider, who saves Wilbur from the knife by writing words in her webs which Wilbur's owners believe have originated from the pig. Wilbur's meals are brought to him in a pail and then poured into his trough. 'The slops ran creamily down around the pig's eyes and ears. Wilbur grunted. He gulped and sucked and gulped, making swishing and swooshing noises, anxious to get everything at once. It was a delicious meal – skim milk, wheat middlings, leftover pancakes, half a doughnut, the rind of a summer squash, two pieces of stale toast, a third of a gingersnap, a fish tail, one orange peel, several noodles from a noodle soup, the scum off a cup of cocoa, an ancient jelly roll, a strip of paper from the lining of the garbage pail and a spoonful of raspberry jello.' I'm cheered, as always, by the story and decide to christen the new saddleback herd the Wilburys.

Over the weekend David talks to his uncle, who tells him that we need to double the amount the pigs are being fed. Those over three to four months will now be getting four pounds of nuts a day and the smaller ones, two pounds. Each pig will eat about £40 to £45 of pig nuts in its life. Then you need to add the £20 cost of 'going up the hill' and about £10 for straw and worming tablets. So if we rear the pigs ourselves, each one will cost £70 to get to market. We can reduce that cost, and improve the quality of the meat, by feeding them rejected vegetables and leaves, by turning them out to grass and by growing fodder beet for the winter. Fodder beets are out of fashion now: they're too much trouble to grow in bulk, so most pigs are fed on nuts all their lives. At my cousins' farm in Great Tew, I remember how delighted I'd been to carve Halloween lantern faces out of the oddly shaped mangel-wurzels that Giogia and Ben grew to feed their animals. In the days before smooth-skinned pumpkins were easily available, they were all we had.

Rowley Leigh's pig doesn't reach London till Saturday. It has a complicated journey: Dennis drives the carcass from Snells to Rowley's West Country fish supplier, who commutes up to London daily, delivering fish for the restaurant and the adjoining fish shop. The pig is loaded up with the cod, salmon, tuna, hake, turbot, crabs and prawns and delivered to Kensington. I ring Rowley after we get back from the bird market, worried that he is going to say we have sold him an inedible pig, but all he says is that he's heard that the pig is huge (which, of course, it isn't, at least not in the way that a pig can be huge). But there's still no word on the taste.

Charlie and I write a list of all the things that we feel aren't going right at the nursery, and just after nine on Monday morning I pull on my wellingtons and head across the field for a meeting with David. It is drizzling steadily and there are muddy patches in the park which suck at my boots. I can see David in the distance, feeding the geese and lonesome George. In the dull wet weather this work is no picnic, and my grumpiness starts to fade. As I go through the gate, I am confronted by the twelve little faces of the Wilburys waiting anxiously for their breakfast. I fetch their nuts and they squeal with hunger and expectation, jumping in and out of the trough, on top of each other, pushing and shoving, until finally they each have a place and there's a neat row of piglets, heads down, tails whirling, lined up along the feed trough. Earl and the Empress come charging out of their caravan: the Empress, looking fat, almost knocking us over in her eagerness to get at her breakfast. Bramble's stomach is heavy and hanging low: clearly a pregnant pig, due to give birth on 5 June. Robinson has been bonking Guinness and Cordelia with gusto: hopefully two more pregnant pigs. We will get it right next time.

I make coffee and David and I settle down in the office. There are pleasing, discordant sounds: the chirping of the small, newly hatched chickens in the storeroom, Radio 1 in the potting shed, the cackle of the rooks in the rookery up in the trees between the nursery and Dillington House, the soft hum of the incubator standing on a bench beside the desk, full of eggs, all due to hatch in the next few days. Any shreds of remaining grumpiness evaporate.

We go through the planting schedule for the year. To date we have planted:

> 26 kilos of onions which will, by the end of July, have grown to fill fifty bags of 25 kilos each. They'll be stored in the new, long store house by the south wall and sold when needed throughout the winter.

19 rows of carrots which will be ready to eat by early June, weather permitting. More carrots will be grown every month through to midsummer, resulting in enough to store to supply Dillington through the winter.

4 long rows of early potatoes which will be ready to eat in June. Chris Wilson, Dillington's estate manager, is uneasy about us growing spuds out in the new field. As we're organic we won't be spraying for blight, and if our potatoes get it his crop will too. So it probably isn't worth our while to grow anything other than an early crop.

6 rows of parsnips which will be ready to eat and over-winter in the autumn.

3 rows of Swiss chard in the tunnel which will be ready by the end of April. 4 more rows have been planted outside, to be eaten at the end of May. We'll keep planting new rows every month as Swiss chard is popular with Dilling-ton's chef, Mark.

4 long rows of broad beans, a total of 2,000 seeds, ready for June/July.

Courgettes have been planted in the tunnels and will be ready in May. More will be planted outside as the weather improves and we should have courgettes for sale from May till October. Aubergines, broccoli, celery have been planted and are doing well. Indoor climbing beans have been planted in the tunnels, as have tomatoes, cucumbers, peppers and chillis. They will all be up by the end of June and should keep producing till the autumn. We'll try some tomatoes outside as I'm keen to see if that changes the flavour.

We then make a list of what we'll plant in the last week of March and the early days of April: peas, spring onions, Swedes, cannellini beans, runner beans, French beans, more purple sprouting, kale, pumpkins, butternut squash, radishes and turnips. There'll be a huge, one-off planting of leeks out in the new field: Dillington wants between five and ten kilos a week throughout the winter, which means planting up almost an acre. The indoor climbing beans – a cross between a runner and a French bean – that we grew last winter were popular with the kitchen staff. They grow to almost a foot long and, unlike standard runners, don't need their tough outside edges removed. We make a note to grow as many as possible for as long as possible in the year. We're short of rhubarb: the house gets through five kilos a week and we won't manage that this year. Possibly we can take some from our garden: just yesterday Charlie decided to force our new growth and upended a large flowerpot over the pink stems which were pushing through the manure. In a few weeks, we'll have far more than we can eat. Six different types of lettuce and salad leaves are being grown. I don't think there's enough, but David says that we're growing enough for the house and there's no point growing more until we're sure of our outlets.

I sign cheques for chicken feed, pig nuts, two new tyres for the van, insurance for the Transit which we're going to need to transport the herbs to Montacute on Saturday, wages, a vet's bill and diesel fuel. As I tot up the amount of money that's going out, I wonder just how anxious we ought to be. Clearly, we've built something much bigger than we originally planned. Equally clearly, not everything has gone right. We have a pressing anxiety about herbs. Many of the seeds that we planted in January in the hope that they'd have grown into plants big enough to sell at the farmers' market in Montacute are still too small. Only the chives, parsley, salad burnet, mint and chervil are OK. We have a few rosemary plants which look healthy and even fewer sorrels which we transplanted from plants in our own vegetable garden and potted up. But the sage, basil and oregano are still tiny and we need more rosemary and more sorrel. To supplement our stock, David bought in some plugs from a nursery near Honiton and they're now stacked in rows in the greenhouse, growing bigger by the minute in the warmth, and, we have to admit, looking fantastic. Charlie and I aren't happy about the plugs, even though they haven't been sprayed or treated in any way. We never planned to go into a business whereby we bought up plugs, grew them on and sold them for 'a turn'. But David is gung-ho: the herbs are only costing 20p a plug, which, he says, actually works out cheaper when you take the labour costs into account. Charlie and I can see the sense and agree that it's a good plan to get us through a tight spot. But we are not letting up on our own herb-growing programme.

The swallows come back in the last week of March, over two weeks earlier than the last date recorded on the old potting shed door: 12 April 1852. They come in on the high south winds, straight from the Sahara to their old nesting grounds in nearby barns. I see them first on the 27th, swooping and dipping across the pond at the village end of the park, their blue feathers reflecting off the slanting evening light, the red patches on their heads appearing and disappearing as they turn and tumble in the air currents. They look effortlessly graceful above the water, diving here and there to catch an insect, soaring back up again to float aloft as if being carried by unseen hands. Suddenly, it seems, it is spring. There is the faintest green flush in the hedgerows above the yellow bursts of primroses; the countryside feels full of magic and life, the chains of winter giving way to the unstoppable miracle of rebirth and new life. The rains have cleared and the winds have pushed back the clouds, revealing pale blue skies. The air is soft and warm, full of the sounds of birds through which the swallows' twittering song is clearly audible. Costly it may be, but I don't regret this venture one bit.

The following day, back in London, I go to see Rowley at Kensington Place. 'It's a bit thin,' he says, as I follow him through the back of the kitchens, across the road leading into the parking lot and into the restaurant's storage department and deep freezes. He hauls the pig out of the fridge and lays it on a shiny metal table, then collects another, larger pig to put beside it. No doubt, ours looks skinny and slightly floppy. 'I'll carve it into a loin, roll up this end, and use the middle for a stew, maybe turn a bit into sausages, they'll be nice and lean.' I breathe a sigh of relief. It isn't a reject. A week later, Rowley tells me that his meat chef, Antonio, reported that the pig was a lot better than anyone had thought. It might have been a bit on the skinny side, but it tasted great and was very tender.

In the first week of March, Hygrade Meats, the meat-packing company in Chard that David used to work for in his early twenties, suddenly announces that it is closing down with the loss of all 305 jobs. Unemployment in Chard currently stands at just over one hundred, so the prospect of that number quadrupling when the factory doors slam shut for the last time at the end of June throws the town into turmoil. Hygrade's owners, the Tulip Corporation, say the closure is a sign of success: they are relocating to their head office in King's Lynn, where they plan to centralise all their operations to maximise profitability. The redundancy terms offered to the workers are the bare minimum and, the company announces, they'll be on offer only to workers who stay with the company till after 1 June. In a letter to the *Chard and Illy* in the days immediately after the closure is announced, Hygrade worker Steve Martin writes: 'The future for job opportunities in Chard is looking bleak. I have no means of transport to travel to surrounding towns. Like others, I relied on this job to support my family. After ten years plus, it has put me in a dilemma. Do I leave early and forfeit the redundancy pay I am due for those ten years' hard work, or search for a job afterwards when 300-plus people are also looking for work? We all put in a lot of hard work over Christmas, especially to keep up with Tesco's demand. As other factories weren't coping with the workload, they sent extra work to us. We were praised for our hard work and team effort, but now it feels like our dedication has been to no avail.'

Colin Rolfe, a friend of Tony Dowling, Hygrade's unofficial union rep as well as the Labour candidate at the last general election, is seething when I meet him in the Portuguese café in Chard a few days after the closure. He'd just been down to the unemployment office with his wife Zoe, who works at Oscar Mayer, and their two-year-old son Jack, who is recovering from a bout of pneumonia. 'There were no jobs that would be any good for someone like me,' he says, 'I'll get the job seekers' allowance of just £56.' Colin knows that the closure of their firm, where he's worked for the last two years, is directly connected to the ever-expanding power of the supermarkets. Many workers feel the supermarkets' continual drive for increased profits has been a major factor in the decision to close. Hygrade isn't closing because it has gone bust, it is closing because they can make more profits by relocating two hundred miles across the country. Tony Dowling told me later that 'many producers for Tesco are driven into the ground in order to keep prices down and profits up. There is nothing realistic about buy one get one free. It may be free to the customer and low-priced to Tesco, but somewhere, you know a producer is being squeezed – and then squeezed again.'

Keith Milton, the GMB branch president for Somerset, sums it up in another letter to the *Chard and Illy*: 'How many more factories must close, jobs be lost and lives changed for ever before big business realises they have a moral responsibility to their workforce which is not just motivated by more and more profit?'

There is another sinister thread running through this story. In 2003, when Oscar Mayer first started employing Portuguese labourers to work in their factories, filling the jobs with the dismal wages they were offering in their expanding empire, the town was targeted by the BNP. They renewed their campaign in February 2005.

Who, if anyone, gave Oscar Mayer Ltd the right to change the face of Chard? . . . Oscar Mayer Ltd acting, presumably, in the pursuit of profit, has over the last few years brought in hundreds of foreign workers and their dependants to work at their Furnham Road plant. . . . it is widely understood that Oscar Mayer has done so without seeking the views or opinions of local residents and with apparent scant regard for the impact their employment policies are having on Chard's social fabric, services infrastructure or local employment opportunities. Oscar Mayer's excuse for importing foreign labour, we are told, is that they cannot find enough suitable labour locally. Could we suggest to them they try increasing their pay rates to a level acceptable to Chard folk and in so doing contribute a little more to the British economy rather than to the Portuguese one?

When the leaflets first went out, the BNP were exploiting a spate of attacks that had been made on the Portuguese community. Two local cafés, Café Moca and Costa Brava, where the TV sets are tuned to pick up Portuguese TV and egg custard tarts and chorizo are sold alongside cheese and pickle sandwiches, had had their windows smashed. But the incidents were isolated and short-lived and the BNP's leaflets, heartily condemned by the mayor and other town dignatories, were largely rebuffed. Up until the closure of Hygrade there was almost full employment in Chard, and while there were complaints about immigrants pushing up rental prices, new affordable houses were being built. In the days following the closure of Hygrade it became clear from the sacks of letters received by Alex Cameron, editor of the *Chard and Illy*, that many young couples who had just taken out mortgages and started their kids in the local schools, confident that Chard would be their home for life or at least for a good long time, were very worried. Their contentment has been blown away.

Oscar Mayer, the town's largest single employer, currently has just over nine hundred workers on its books. Three hundred of those are foreign: the same number that are losing their jobs at Hygrade.

In the week after the closure, the first voice of protest is heard in the letters pages of the paper on 15 March. Mrs Coombs writes to say, 'Maybe it is time that local businesses reviewed their policy on agency workers. Many of them are foreign. I know they are all EU citizens, that they pay tax and national insurance like the rest of us, so they are entitled to work in this country. However, they are, after all, agency workers and migrant workers. In times like this jobs should go to local people with mortgages who have spent all their lives in the Chard area, brought up families, etc.'

In an instant, Chard becomes a first-rate recruiting ground for the far right: their messages offer the kind of protectionism that all the workers, faced with the loss of their jobs, want to hear.

On the last day of March, I'm back in Chard to join Colin and Tony on a march to protest about the redundancy conditions. Tony is adamant that Hygrade's new owners, Tulip, a subsidiary of the huge Danish Crown meat conglomerate, bought the company to get their hands on its valuable Tesco contract. Hygrade had been making £250,000 profit a month at the Chard factory alone at the time of its closure, but the government minimum redundancy payment being offered to the workforce is more in line with a company that has gone down drowning in debt rather than one which has posted a consistently healthy bottom line. Each worker is being offered £290 for every year that they've worked for the company. A pittance and, for someone like Colin, who started work only two years ago, a financial disaster.

The workers gather outside the Hygrade factory at 6.30 p.m., to time their departure to air on the BBC's Points West news programme. Red banners emblazoned with the slogan 'Workers of the World Unite' are carried aloft. Two young boys wave a placard saying 'You are as cold as one of your fridges'. Another billboard asks 'Tulip – how does it feel to ruin so many lives?' The local Methodist minister Marilyn Tricker commences the proceedings by offering up a prayer for the workforce.

'We are concerned for the impact this will have on the town of Chard. I believe in a God of justice and compassion and I would ask that God to act now.' The rain holds off and we march up Furnham Road, turning right at the traffic lights into Fore Street, where the mayor and mayoress are waiting to greet the marchers outside the Guildhall. Inside, MEP Glyn Ford kicks off the rally by explaining the impact that will ripple through Chard when the factory moves out. 'It is not just three hundred jobs that will be lost, it's six hundred. People who run sandwich businesses, cleaning businesses, small shops, they'll go too. I've been here before. Under European law there should be a ninety-day consultation period before terms are agreed on. Tulip made their decision without consultation and we will fight to overturn it.'

From round the hall there are shouts of support, but confidence is short-lived. Everyone looks angry, but mostly I think everyone looks worried. Wives, some of whom worked in Hygrade too, and kids who have picked up on the anxiety, mutter and shake their heads. The mayor, John Malcolm, pledges his support. The economy of Chard is in crisis: the closure of Hygrade will take £6 million out of the local cash flow overnight and this is an issue the whole community will have to face. No one will be left unaffected. Tony stands up to speak about what the union hopes to do to improve Hygrade's offer. Then I stand up and speak about the power of the supermarkets and how it is always the workers who suffer in the constant pursuit of greater profits.

There is a shout from the back of the room. 'Where is our MP? He's never here when we need him. If Paddy Ashdown still represented us, he'd have been marching with us.' This angry cry gets taken up around the hall and isn't pacified by Tony Dowling and Colin trying to explain that David Laws has an engagement he can't break and that he will be meeting with them on Monday. Cathy Morrison, the deputy mayor, picks up the microphone. In her hand she carries a bundle of brochures.

'I used to work in Oscar Mayer,' she tells the crowd, 'now I work at the employment centre in Chard. I want to reassure everyone that you will be able to claim the job seekers' allowance, even if your partners get other jobs. But I know that there aren't enough jobs for you all in Chard and I know that many of you don't drive and that you'll have to go to Yeovil, Taunton, even to Exeter to get work. So I've brought bus timetables with me. Not enough to go round, but after the end of April you can get more copies from the tourist information office next door.'

There was silence when Cathy finished speaking. After the feisty rhetoric from the unions about corporate greed and standing together, she has voiced the grim reality. There are almost no jobs in Chard and the lives that the workers had built up, revolving around the schools, the community, the known and the familiar, are being hurled into oblivion. A job in Exeter will involve spending three hours a day on a bus. How will the kids get to school without Mum or Dad to take them? Who will be there when they get back? And, even with a season ticket, the transport cost is going to make a big hole in the weekly pay packet, a hole roughly the size of the annual holiday budget. I look round the hall. Couples were holding hands and clasping their children to them. Now there is real fear on their faces. What on earth has this country come to?

Hygrade might not have been the nicest place to work, and no one really thinks that packaged, processed pork products add much to the sum of human health or happiness, but it was their place of work, where jobs had been a source of pride, belonging and security. Now, in the desire to 'rationalise' and maximise profits, they are being thrown on the garbage heap like yesterday's fish and chips. It seems to me that if this is what we call progress, then we have a very warped idea of how to run a successful world.

When Cathy has finished, the meeting is over and a long-haired folk-singer called Red Dirt takes to the stage. 'I'll be with you when the roses bloom again,' he sings in a gravelly voice that sounds as if it owes a lot to late nights and cigarettes. In small groups, everyone leaves the hall, gathering on the pavement to share a smoke before setting off for home. I find myself standing next to a white-haired, elderly man with a moustache who reminds me of my father. He has a nice grin and looks like he has once been in the army. He tells me his name is Andrew Fuller and that, for the last seven years, he's been in charge of hygiene at Hygrade. With his wife, he used to run the Langport Arms, but his wife became ill and they had to retire. After she died, Andrew had looked around for what to do and his path had taken him to Hygrade in Chard. 'Tesco were like terrorists for hygiene,' he tells me, 'they appear, unannounced, and check everything. Never sent the same person twice so that you had no chance of striking up any sort of relationship which might mean things got overlooked. Their sole object would be to find fault.' He pauses and adds with pride. 'We were the only firm in the country who ever got 100 per cent on the test.'

Over Christmas 2005, the firm had worked round the clock with almost all the staff putting in overtime to fulfil Tesco's last-minute Christmas order books. Hams and all kinds of pork products rolled off the production line: Hygrade was so efficient that orders that couldn't be completed in other

factories were often sent to the Chard outlet with demands
that they be filled in record time. 'It was a very successful
place,' Andrew says sadly. 'What a message to give out as to
how you want people to behave. "Work hard, do really well,
and we'll kick you in the teeth."'

The birds and the sunshine wake me up early the next morning
but we need to be up, as we have to load the Transit and get
the herb stall set up at Montacute by ten o'clock. It is a
beautiful morning, the light outlining every detail of every
branch, the daffodil heads turning towards the early morning
light. The garden, which has survived the long vicissitudes of
winter, is undoubtedly waking up and there is evidence of life
everywhere I look and in every sound around me. In the
garden pond there is a newt hanging in the water, a strange
small dragon with long fingers suspended in the stillness. Long
strings of toad spawn have appeared in the last few days, the
little black eggs held in the tapioca-like goo, hundreds and
hundreds of them, lying draped across the pond weeds like the
carelessly discarded necklaces of a forest fairy queen. In the
wood pond the wind has blown football-sized clumps of frog
spawn into one corner. A female can lay up to three thousand
eggs at a go, and there must be literally thousands of eggs in
the greenish white jelly.

Bob, David and I set off to Montacute with almost a
thousand herbs crammed into the Transit. David has rigged
up a makeshift two-tier system with a couple of tables, but on
the way a tray of mint falls off, scattering earth and plants all
over the other herbs. Montacute has been described as the
'most beautiful Elizabethan house in England', built in the last
years of the 1500s for the Phelips family. They used the local
honey-coloured stone from nearby Ham Hill, and in the early
morning light the mellow bricks look warm and welcoming.

Phelips had been chancellor to the young Henry VIII and his family lived there till 1911, when they hit hard times and moved to London, renting out Montacute to high-paying tenants. Lord Curzon snapped it up just after the First World War. It was grand enough for one of the more arrogant political figures of the time. In 1923 he was waiting there to be called by the king to form the new government, but the call never came.

The market is taking place in the old stable yard and we park close to the archway and cart the trays of herbs to our corner pitch. There is a jolly camaraderie among the stall-holders and, although we are clearly the newcomers, we feel welcomed. David isn't staying for the day as his football club is playing in the semi-finals of the local league. Earlier in the week Bob had phoned to ask me if he needed to wear a tie to the market. I reassured him that ties were absolutely not needed, but he looks touchingly smart in a neatly ironed shirt and jacket, by far the best dressed of the three of us.

Roughly 75 per cent of the food being unloaded from vans, containers and polystyrene freezer boxes has been grown or reared on the Somerset Levels, the mysterious region that occupies the centre of the county, running inland from the north coast. It is low-lying, with some parts below sea level, and the seemingly endless flat fields are dissected by small drainage canals or rhymes, as they are known locally. Flat land is always weirder and stranger than mountains: the mists swirl and it is easy to lose your way. Before the lands were drained the vast tracts of reeds and rushes concealed dank, dangerous marshes, where, legend has it, huge dragons hid, the smoke and flame from their breath mingling with the mists that rose from the bogs. Glastonbury Tor rises from the Levels like a lighthouse in a sea of green, the focus of the area, itself a place of so many myths and legends.

There are records of people living on the Levels for almost six thousand years, and in 1970 a peat digger called Ray Sweet discovered a pathway in the bog: here, between the autumn of

3807 and the spring of 3806 BC, the dwellers on the Levels first
figured out how to make a flat surface. They needed to
construct bridges and pathways to connect areas of dry land.
First they cut stakes which they would push into the earth in
an X shape, driving the bottom tips deep into the peat to give
the structure stability. They then laid branches between the
two arms of the X. But that winter they did something that, as
far as archaeologists know, had never been done before. They
used axes to makes splits in the ends of oak logs and, with
wooden mallets and oak wedges, forced the splits open till
they had planks, some of them up to fifteen feet long and three
feet wide. It was these traces that Sweet discovered a little over
thirty years ago, preserved by the peat over the centuries and
able to be dated so accurately through the growth rings still
visible in the wood.

By nine-thirty I am starving. At a stall selling pies, cakes and
jams I buy a couple of sausage rolls, the flaky pastry meltingly
delicious, the meat well-flavoured and juicy. Sue Warrington
used to be a full-time rep for a medical supplies firm as well as
a mother of three. She'd learned to cook as a child and had
always made her own jams, chutneys, jellies, pies and juices.
But three years ago, her fifteen years in the medical business
suddenly seemed like absolutely long enough and she chucked
it in to become a full-time producer of home-cooked food.

'It was amazing, it just took off,' she says, as she unloads yet
another box containing pies made of chicken and leek, spinach
and ricotta, lamb and apricots. 'Four months after I stopped
working, Keith gave up being a metal broker to join me. Then
we thought we'd have another baby and went and had twins.'
She laughs. 'That wasn't in the plan. With four boys and a girl
under ten, I'm often cooking in the middle of the night and the
twins always start yelling just when the jam is hitting boiling
point. My seven-year-old has become a dab hand at labelling
the pies.'

In their garden they grow their own vegetables as well as

green tomatoes for chutney. They have apple, pear and plum trees which, with storing or freezing, fill their pies throughout the year. Sue is at Montacute on her own, as Keith is manning their stall at another farmers' market at Axbridge. In addition to her own products, which include cakes as well as the pies and the jams, she's also selling a friend's cheeses. It's going to be a non-stop day, without a minute to sit down. She reckons that she now works far longer hours and knows that their bank statements never look as healthy as they used to. 'But I wouldn't change it for the world. The kids eat better. The community in our village of Chedzoy is lovely. I like being outside. I like being in charge of what we do. I like coming to the markets, you get to know people, they all value food and knowing where it has come from. Traceability, that sort of thing.'

At ten o'clock the punters start arriving. Many are elderly, careful with their money, eager to snap up something delicious to eat for the weekend and clearly enjoying the chance to turn the mundane Saturday morning food shop into an interesting outing. When I first met Colin Rolfe he had told me that most of his mates at Hygrade went to buy their meat from the Barley Mow, the farm shop just out of Chard on the road to Honiton. Colin initially went there because, after seeing what happened on the production lines, he couldn't face eating processed meat. But he was totally taken aback to discover that, gram for gram, it was no more expensive to buy meat there than it was to buy it at the supermarket. And, he said, he likes shopping there: it makes him feel good to know that he is feeding his kids proper meat, and, in the process, supporting the local economy.

Looking round the bustling stable courtyard, it is hard to imagine anything more different from the world I was in at last night's meeting. Both are part of the modern food industry, but where Hygrade stands for cheaper food, Montacute represents the other extreme: food that has been lovingly made and sold with pride. Charlie is much more down to earth than I am about the supermarkets, seeing them as a necessary part of our modern life, but I find myself becoming increasingly angry as I learn more about their practices and the effect they have on our health and our communities. I know that what's going on in the courtyard, while charming and wholesome, will never be the way we feed nations. But there are towns in America where the only shop is a Wal-Mart and the prospect of that being replicated by Tesco in parts of Britain is so depressing that I resolve to carry on with the markets, even if they make us only a small amount of money.

We make our first sale at about ten minutes past ten: two pots of mint and one of salad burnet. Charlie turns out to be a born salesman, offering advice about how to plant the herbs and how to cook with them. 'Make sure you don't put the basil out yet; there might be another frost and that will finish it off entirely,' I hear him say to a hesitant customer who goes on to buy two plants. 'Sorrel makes a delicious sauce to eat with fish,' he tells another. Business is OK, but it cannot be described as brisk. Brisk is what is happening at the stalls that sell food and offer free tasters – bits of sausage, cheese, chocolate, burgers, bread or sauces which can be scooped out of jars with plastic spoons and spread on broken bits of water biscuits. There are jostling queues at the Orchard Old Spots table, where Sue Tutton is selling variously flavoured sausages and burgers as well as joints of pork all from the offspring of her five Gloucester Old Spot sows, Brenda, Dorie, Sue, Joan and Molly. Sue and her husband Mark live near Kingsbury Episcopi, and in 2004 they bought the orchard next to their home after hearing that the picturesque plot was going to be sold to developers. It cost £27,000 and they had to find a way to pay back the loan. The first year they earned a meagre £260 from the apples, so in 2005 they bought five female piglets and a large white boar and went into business. Mark still works for Vodaphone, but, if they can get a grant to convert a shed into a 'clean house' where they can make their own sausages, burgers and salamis, he plans to chuck in his job and get into pigs full-time.

I'm still smarting from our own pig debacle, so I examine the fat content on Sue's pork. Maybe a half-inch, not enormous, but more than on ours. 'Why do you cross the breeds?' 'So they don't get too fat,' she replies. God, there's a lot to learn. On the table beside the saucers full of sausage slices, which I'm tucking into while we talk, are two small jars. The bottom of one is just covered by a layer of set, white fat. The other is almost full of a gunky yellow liquid, viscous enough to cling to the sides of the jar. On the first is a label saying: 'The fat collected after grilling eight of our sausages and three of our burgers.' On the other it says, 'The fat collected after grilling eight Tesco sausages.'

We didn't have any real idea of what we could expect to sell and by one o'clock, when the crowds started tapering off, it is clear that we have brought far too many herbs with us. It is also clear that what attracts punters to the stalls in the first place are the free snacks. Next time, we decide, we have to bake herb biscuits and offer bits of them on saucers to anyone who comes by. Our friend Yseult Hughes has written a recipe booklet for us explaining how to grow and cook with a dozen different herbs. Yseult and her husband Mark Ogilvy are brilliant cooks and the recipes are original and good. Full of optimism that this £1 masterpiece would fly off the table, I'd brought 150 copies along. We sell eleven. The market ends at two o'clock and it takes us almost as long to load up as it had to unload in the morning. We have made £183.50. Sue Warrington has sold every single pie, all her cakes, two-thirds of her jars of jams and jellies and a sizeable quantity of cheese. She tells me that their record taking at a market was £1,005. Still, £183.50 is roughly equivalent to 1,500 eggs, or one medium-sized pig sold to Mr Bonner. There are five more markets this year at Montacute and we've signed up for all of them. Perhaps we need more marketing: if we'd said 'buy five and get the sixth one free', and clearly displayed a laminated sign listing the prices (they were all £1, except for rosemary and sage, which sold at £1.25) and offered free biscuits, then I reckon we might have sold about £220 worth of plants. On our feeble income stream, this is pretty good money.

9

Bluebell Gives Birth

On 5 April, a dead swan is discovered in Cellardyke, a small coastal village nine miles from St Andrews. The swan is infected with the highly pathogenic H5 avian flu. The Scottish authorities quarantine the area, setting up a protection zone of three miles around the village. All bird-keepers inside the area are instructed to bring their domestic flocks indoors to protect them from wild birds. Measures to restrict the movement of poultry and eggs are put into immediate effect.

The dead bird was taken away for tests to discover if the strain of flu that had killed it was H5N1, which can infect humans; by lunchtime on the 6th that had been confirmed. Thank heavens, I thought selfishly, the swan came ashore six hundred miles away in Scotland. Since January the government has investigated forty cases of bird flu in the UK, but while a teal shot in eastern England was found to have a low pathogenic strain, it wasn't H5N1. The other cases weren't even carrying H5. Charlie, David and I had all started believing that bird flu was going to miss Britain. It's been fourteen weeks since it was first found on the borders of Europe, where it had swept in from South-East Asia, leaving 104 people dead in its wake. The first European victim was a fourteen-year-old Turkish boy called Mehmet Ali Kocyigit, who died on New Year's Day. His sister Fatima died three days afterwards and a week later a third sibling died too. By the middle of January the virus claimed two more local teenagers. Mehmet and his family had had very close contact with their chickens, picking them up frequently and breathing the same close air. Zeki, the children's father, told a local news agency that the whole family had eaten sick birds, but that only the children had become ill.

By mid-February H5N1 had spread to France, Germany and Italy. By the end of the month cases had been detected in Greece, Austria, Hungary, Slovenia and Slovakia. Two dead ducks heralded the virus's arrival in Sweden on the last day of the month. And although David King, the government's chief scientific adviser, warned that bird flu would arrive on our shores, the long gap since those two ducks were discovered in Sweden had led me to believe we were going to be OK.

David has laid an old piece of red carpet across the entrance to the farm, soaking it in disinfectant and covering it with straw. We keep the gate shut and there are buckets of disinfectant at the entrance to both of the chicken runs to dip your wellingtons in before going through the gates. Three years ago, when Britain had been gripped by a brief panic about the possible spread of the SARS virus, 45,000 gas masks had been bought in Scotland within days of the first reports of a possible pandemic. Then, as now, there was talk of huge numbers of people dying and of how the government was going to dig mass graves to bury the infected corpses. I was editing the *Express* during the most serious health panic, BSE. It was a fear that ran throughout the 1990s and the science suggesting that the disease could be passed to humans was indisputable; indeed, new variant CJD has killed 155 people in Britain, though the peak for these deaths was in 2000 when twenty-eight people died. So far this year there have been two deaths.

Tragic, but far less tragic than some of the stories I remember publishing, which warned that there might be up to 130,000 people with the fatal brain infection.

In 2005, 3.1 million people died of AIDS worldwide and 1.2 million died in traffic accidents, almost three thousand of them in Britain. But pandemics, like bird flu, accelerate us into panic. One reason is that we know we have no control over viruses and that they don't respond to antibiotics. BSE and bird flu also play into another fear, a general worry that modern farming is fiddling with nature in dangerous ways. Is disease our reward for cheap supermarket food? The disgusting use of mashed-up bovine remains as cattle feed, a form of unnatural cannibalism which resulted in BSE, did indeed turn out to have deadly consequences. In vast battery cages, where our cheap chickens lead their miserable little lives, the flu virus can spread like wildfire and infect humans. The government has been at pains to tell the public that it is quite safe to keep on eating chicken and eggs, but in Italy, after the discovery of a few dead birds, chicken consumption fell by 70 per cent. However, when I ask Mr Bonner how his chicken sales fared during the weekend scare he reports business as usual.

On the farm we have a surprise: Bluebell has suddenly given birth. No one had thought she was pregnant since she remained quite slender throughout, and although David had suggested that I should pop along to the chemist and buy a pregnancy testing kit as he was too embarrassed to go himself, we didn't get round to it, assuming that her mating hadn't caught. But it had, and at 8.30 p.m. on a Friday in April she produces six perfect, evenly sized little piglets. We get to the Dairy House very late: at roughly the time that Bluebell went into labour I was sitting in the make-up room at the BBC, getting ready for that week's *Late Review*. Charlie picks me up just before midnight and we drive through the night, comparing notes on our respective weeks. He has been in the House of Lords, pleading a case concerning illegal immigrants and their status under UK law, especially where it relates to divorce. Family law is now his main speciality and I know he finds it a welcome relief after almost twenty years working primarily on cases of child abuse. I like these times in the car: sometimes we hardly see each other during the week and the two and a half hour journey is the time we catch up. It is one o'clock before we pass Stonehenge, the mysterious stones clearly outlined in the moonlight, standing like guards marking the real beginning of the West Country. An hour later and we're turning off the main road and into the park. In the headlights the eyes of the sheep glow like fireflies in the darkness.

The next morning we find David, Adrian and Bob clucking around Bluebell like a group of proud dads at the maternity unit. She's been moved into the biggest hut, which will be hers for the next two months until the piglets are weaned. She is lying on her side, the six small pigs searching frantically for her teats, sucking, gasping, squealing, clambering over each other to gain a good purchase. They are about six inches long and four inches high with stubby wrinkled noses; their pink skin is covered with the finest white hair and they have flattened little wrinkly ears. Their black spots are clearly marked, so precise they could have been drawn on their bodies with a kohl pencil. Bluebell is quite unconcerned by the attention as we all stand round her, cooing our admiration. I sit down on the straw and rub her behind the ears and on the snout. She grunts contentedly and looks at me through her long-lashed eyes. Pigs' eyes are very human. Unlike dogs and horses, whose eyes seem more like pools of liquid darkness, pigs' eyes have pupils and irises and they study you in an unblinking and measured manner. Bluebell, who has always struck me as a wayward creature, seems resigned to motherhood. She might not have wished for it, but now that it has arrived, she is going to do her best for her piglets. There is something touching about Bluebell and her piglets, a sort of innocence; animals always manage to teach us that we are not superior to them in any way, and it is humbling to sit beside her and watch how perfectly she deals with her babies.

Later in the morning, I go to Mr Rendell's greengrocer's to buy her a treat: a bunch of carrots, a sweet potato and a huge parsnip. It's Grand National Day so I go to make my annual bet. Since I always base my selection purely on names I like, I look for a name which relates to the pigs. Nothing. But since she has had six piglets, I back one called NumberSix Valverde.

During the afternoon Charlie and I are in our small vegetable garden, planting seeds and preparing the ground for the summer vegetable harvest: from over the field I can see a series of cars arriving at the farm, disgorging excited children to visit the piglets. But after the race, which Bluebell's horse amazingly wins, I go back to see her. It is quiet now and I sit down on the straw beside her to give her the carrots, the parsnip and the sweet potato, which she guzzles enthusiastically, making Wilbur-like sounds of slurping, chewing and chomping. It is warm in the shed and it smells of a mixture of clean straw, dried grass, milk and something indefinable which I can only think of as the smell of sweetness. I curl up beside the pig, my head on her shoulder, the little piglets making small squeaks and barks beside me, and think how astonishing it is to feel so comfortable beside such a huge, strange beast.

Things had been happening to friends of mine this week which weren't good. On Monday an old chum of sixty-three suffered a colossal heart attack and was lying in a west London hospital in a coma; no one knew whether he would survive. Another friend has been trying to get pregnant through IVF and the attempt ended in a miserable miscarriage. Another was undergoing radio therapy for cancer of the throat. A very dear girlfriend has dislocated both shoulders and broken her arm in seven places in a skiing accident. Just two days ago I met with another friend, who has been having a tough time coping with her drink problem: she was on her way to residential care and I wonder how she's doing, remembering my own first few days in the treatment centre and how frightening it had seemed. Another's father has died after a long and depressing period of dementia. And Chris, the estate manager here at Dillington, has had to go suddenly to Newcastle as his brother's child died yesterday after a long illness.

Two years ago, I had little faith in my own ability even to survive, let alone to thrive, and if anyone had told me that one day I'd be lying in a pigsty next to a nursing sow and her babies, I'd have told them they were hallucinating. Life feels incredibly fragile and terribly precious. Bluebell seems to have fallen asleep, her slow breathing interrupted by deep grunts and snores. I shut my eyes, aware that the sunlight is dancing on my eyelids, and suddenly I am back on the bench in the treatment centre, under the heavy boughs of the copper beech, thinking that the tree breathes out what I breathe in and I breathe out what the tree breathes in. I don't believe in a god as he is manifested in the ordered religions of the West, but I most certainly believe that something has a hand in ordering this world and that there is a time and a place for everything, and if you let go and let the river of life guide you, you will find yourself precisely where you are meant to be.

Bryan Ferris and Mike Fry-Foley have fixed up a meeting with Norman Campbell, the mayor of Ilminster, in a last-ditch attempt to try to reverse the planning decision which would create the proposed one-way system in the town. I ask to tag along. Heading off to meet Bryan at his shop, I bump into Mr Bonner on his way to work. It is the first time I've seen him since the pig fiasco, and he immediately tells me to come and see him to collect the money he owes us and in the next breath asks when the next pigs will be ready. I tell him we've had our first piglets, but such is small-town life that he already knows, as he also already knows that I am on my way to the meeting with the mayor. He's just walked down to the far end of Shuddrick Lane to see for himself how far away the new car park is from the butcher's. 'It is bad news,' he says, 'our shop is as far away as possible – at least two-thirds of a mile. No one is going to pop up and buy their sausages from us if they've parked all the way down there.' Mr B and I are standing outside Isle Books, owned and managed by Chris Chapman. Chris is in his eighties and most days the store shuts down while he takes a long lunch. There's a press cutting from the *Daily Mail* stuck to the window with Blu-Tack. Underneath the headline 'Now Blunkett Is Set to Make Millions from a Tell-All Memoir' a story reveals that the ex-Home Secretary is planning to tell the world the secrets of his affair with Kimberly Quinn. Next to the cutting, Chris has added a handwritten note, also Blu-Tacked to the glass: 'In the unlikely event of any of my customers requiring a copy of this book, I would prefer them to get it elsewhere.'

The meeting is being held in the council chamber, a stuffy ground-floor room in the council HQ on North Street, a few metres north of the town square. It smells, Bryan says later, like the old clothes department in a charity shop. Mike is already there with a display board and photocopied briefing reports of his presentation. The mayor arrives with the town clerk, Stephen Fisher, and the meeting gets under way. Norman Campbell looks like a farmer and his hands are tough and workmanlike, but Brian tells me that he was in oil in Africa, a fact that the Chamber of Commerce seem to hold against him as he's never been involved in the business of shops and trading. Mike sets out the arguments, which the two men listen to impassively. The traffic, he says, is hardly a serious problem: the middle of Ilminster isn't the centre of London. Even the most pessimistic (or optimistic, depending on your point of view) projections only estimate that another twenty-five cars an hour will want to drive through the middle of town in peak time once the supermarket is open.

'We don't need this huge detour to control the traffic, a detour in which all roads lead to the supermarket but only two of them to Silver Street.' I can see that Mike is getting annoyed by their apparent lack of interest and he issues a challenge, saying that, as yet, the townspeople aren't walking down Silver Street carrying placards and protesting. Norman wakes up. 'We don't want any of that,' he says quickly.

'We understand,' Mike goes on, 'that the traffic department looks only at traffic, not at the situation of the town as a whole.' This also rattles the mayor. Up on the wall, a wooden plaque lists the names of the mayors of Ilminster over the last twenty years. Each had held the position for only two years, scant time to oversee the arrival of a supermarket. Of the fourteen members of the council, only five are elected: the rest are co-opted by the existing members as there are not enough people willing to stand for the posts. Many of the crucial decisions were taken before Norman's time in office, but they are the decisions that the council seems determined to stand by and I don't feel optimistic that anyone, or anything, is going to change their mind.

'This plan is going to split the town in two,' Mike says.

'We don't see that,' Norman replies. 'We believe that the supermarket will bring increased numbers of people to the town and that they will come into the old town after visiting the store. It will help the town, not detract from it.'

Tesco currently takes 30 per cent of the country's grocery spend and its sales have gone up by 23 per cent in the past two years. There is no evidence in any study I have seen that a single supermarket has actually boosted the local economy.

Bryan turns to me and asks if I will tell the mayor some of the statistics that the New Economics Foundation has published in the last few years about the impact of supermarkets on market towns. I rattle off the main findings: £10 spent in a local shop puts £25 back in the economy, £10 spent in a supermarket puts back only £14. Profits go to head office and are never ploughed back into the town. All sorts of other businesses, such as key-cutters, small printers and local accountants, pay the price along with the shopkeepers. Supermarkets can afford to drop prices for as long as it takes to hound out competition. I add that their financial clout is so huge that anything that can be done to help level the odds needs to be done and, on that basis alone, the road scheme must be reconsidered.

'We listened and it is right that we listened,' Norman says, after Mike and I have finished. 'But the whole scheme was the subject of full discussion. As far as everyone is concerned we have the best answer to our main concern – keeping the town alive – and that needs to be appreciated. Out of courtesy we have listened to your objections and we will give your proposals some thought. But can we go back on planning? How can we take this idea forward?'

Bryan points out that, for him, the number of people actually visiting his shop is critical. Only one out of every five people who goes into Lane's actually buys something, and that can be a £1.50 greeting card or a £400 garden bench. 'What will hurt the town is the slow chipping-away, and it doesn't take much. People are anxious. What would happen if one of the banks decided to close down? The others would too,' he says.

Norman brings the meeting to an end by saying he has an appointment to meet his wife for a cup of coffee before going to Lane's to buy a birthday present. 'I'm telling you after the meeting, Bryan,' he adds, 'so you didn't think I was trying to bribe you.'

I go to visit Colin Rolfe in Chard. He lives in a modern development on the edge of town, in a red-brick corner house. There's a barbecue outside the front door. Inside, Zoe and her mum are watching *Narnia* on a video she describes as 'dodgy'. On the kitchen table Colin has laid out papers, labels and packets of Tesco's ham. He talks me through the process. Hygrade buys pigs at 'best price', and if they're not available at the best price in the UK then they are bought from other EU countries. They're butchered at Beechings in Chard and then, if there's an oversupply, or if Tesco have suddenly decided they don't need so much ham that month, the pork is sent to Taunton, where it's stored and frozen at Novacold. It is sent back to Chard either when there is a shortage of meat or when it's over ten months old. Under law, the pork from the dead pigs has to reach your shopping basket within a year of the animal's demise. It is generally the case that what we buy in the supermarkets labelled as 'fresh meat' can be anything from thirty-five days to eleven months old.

Colin explains to me what happens in the factory. Once there, the hams are dunked in vast vats which inflate the meat with water, at the same time adding salt, dextrose, stabilisers such as diphosphates, triphosphates, and polyphosphates, and the antioxidants sodium ascorbate and the preservative sodium nitrate. The hams are tumbled around in these vats of chemical solution for one hour continuously, then for ten minutes on, fifty minutes off, for another twenty-four hours. The minimum time the meat spends in the stainless steel tumblers is thirty-six hours, the maximum is five days. The resulting hams are cooked to a temperature of 70.5°C for two minutes, then cooled to less than 5 degrees. Then they're bagged up and can be stored for another twenty-eight days. After that, the hams are taken out of their bags and roasted at 250°C for a minimum of thirty minutes, cooled again, and refrigerated for up to two days. Colin gives me a copy of the internal flow diagram for pre-sliced ham and I notice that at this point on the list of what-to-do-and-when, the ham ceases to be described as 'meat' or 'legs' and becomes simply 'product'. The product is then transferred from the fridge to a spiral slicing machine. The hock bone is removed and a cutter whizzes round in endless circles, slicing off pieces of what will be sold as 'fresh ham'. The product is then vacuum packed and each pack is inflated with preservative gases. The check-list notes that 'each pack is inspected for seal integrity'.

'That bit's important,' Colin tells me. 'Once you break the seal, you may have only a couple of days left. When you buy ham, you think you're buying something fresh; in fact, you're buying something that is right at the very end of its usable life.'

Our talk turns to Hygrade, where the union attempts to increase redundancy payouts have, so far, come to nothing. A £500 relocation payment has been offered to any workers who need to move house to find new employment, an offer that Colin says would be a joke, were it not so serious. So far, twenty-two of the workforce of 305 have found new jobs, even though taking the jobs means they don't qualify for the redundancy of £290 per year of work.

'We're all taking any jobs we can find,' Colin says. 'The food industry is menial and specialised. What can someone who has worked in Hygrade since they were a teenager, shoving bits of pork into stainless steel drums, actually do? Not much.' Colin's been offered a job with the union: it won't pay well but he knows he is lucky. He shows me a document that he's got hold of – 'Don't ask me how!' – which outlines plans for the relocation of the company. It sets out the dates and the stages when works are to be completed and demonstrates clearly that Tulip's primary concern is not to miss a single day's production. There are two corporate logos at the top of the page: Tulip on the left-hand corner, Tesco on the right.

Zoe has been out shopping with her mum and her youngest son, Jack. They arrive back with twenty carrier bags which they dump on the kitchen floor. Astonishingly, they've been to Tesco. Jack has a small plastic bag containing a colouring book and set of cheap, waxy crayons: Tesco's Easter offering

to kids. After the announcement in March that there would
be a competition inquiry into supermarket chains, Anatole
Kaletsky, writing in *The Times*, noted that 'anyone who has
tried to find anything worth eating in the garish monoculture
of a Tesco "convenience store" will surely pray that some *deus
ex machina* will save what is left of the small greengrocers,
butchers and delicatessens that Tesco, in particular, seems
determined to eradicate from Britain's high streets'. But, he
goes on to say, 'hopes of reining in the big four through
regulation are almost certainly forlorn. Tesco's depredations
will not – and from a legal standpoint cannot – be stopped by
the Competition Commission or the Office of Fair Trading.
Controlling planning, liberalising parking, banning deliveries
by articulated lorries or enforcing rent controls to support
small shops artificially are all measures that might nibble away
at the growth of the megastores. But,' Kaletsky concludes,
'none will work. Only consumer choice has a real hope of
cracking the supermarket monoculture. If people genuinely
value local shops they must be prepared to pay higher prices
for the goods they sell. They must be prepared to resist the
blandishments of the cut-price retail chains and distinguish
between those that offer quality and socially responsible
behaviour, as opposed to merely competing on price.'

When I was editing the *Daily Express* my boss, the Labour
peer Clive Hollick, invited Terry Leahy, CEO of Tesco, to
lunch. In the retailing world Leahy is a god, and I could tell
that Clive was hoping that his magic might rub off on the
Daily Express. At the time we met, in 2000, the *Express* was
struggling with its sales, constantly being beaten into second
place in the mid-market by the might of the *Daily Mail*. Like
the *Mail*, Tesco was just getting bigger, seemingly by the hour.
Leahy had taken the helm from his predecessor, the flamboy-
ant Lord McLaurin, who went on to become the chair of the
MCC. He told us that when McLaurin took over, Tesco was
playing second fiddle to Sainsbury's. Thinking about Sains-

bury's dominated the thinking of the Tesco executives: if they produced a new product, be it a single variety of yoghurt or a whole product range, Tesco did so too. If they dropped their prices, Tesco followed suit. McLaurin's first command was to 'forget Sainsbury's'. He said he didn't want to see the Sainsbury's name on any documents, or hear about the company in any meetings. From now on, Tesco was going to do its own thing. It worked. When McLaurin retired Leahy took over a company that was already winning. Leahy's masterstroke was the introduction of the loyalty card: until then, only Green Shield Stamps had rewarded customers for continued business. Other companies now started copying Tesco.

I remember Leahy as a middling sort of man: middling height, middling looks, unflashy clothing and a quiet turn of phrase. He was likeable and self-contained. No, he wouldn't do an interview with his brother (who ran a corner store in their home town of Liverpool); indeed, he wouldn't do an interview at all. His personal life was just that; his politics were private. Tesco always supported the government of the day, regardless. He'd driven in from his office in Cheshunt, north London, a journey that takes well over an hour on a good day. Not for Leahy a flash West End office. He works where he lives, where his customers shop. Every year, he spends two weeks working in one of his stores; he is so anonymous that even his own staff fail to recognise him. I wondered what he did with all the money he reputedly earns: his home is modest, his kids have been to state schools, his wife is a GP in the NHS, he drives himself to work in the morning. The first job of his life was as a shelf-stacker for Tesco and he's never left. My friend Chris Blackhurst, who was then the deputy editor of the *Express* and also a guest at the lunch, later told me that Leahy regards Tesco as his religion. By 2006 it's become a religion that is taking over the world: they're the fourth largest company in Thailand, the ninth in Hungary. They're in Japan and looking at China. Leahy told us he was confident that he gave his customers what they wanted, and in

2004 he told Chris that he thought it 'right to fight the farming and corner-shop lobbies'. Some farmers can't match the quality he demands and corner shops go out of business anyway. Tesco is the biggest customer of British farming and the creator of over 100,000 jobs.

Over lunch in the *Express* boardroom, high up on the sixth floor of our Blackfriars office, overlooking the bustling life of the River Thames, I asked him what advice he would give the *Express* in its war for the middle ground of Britain. Our situation was comparable to the Tesco/Sainsbury's stand-off that Leahy and McLaurin inherited a few years earlier. He didn't hesitate: 'Stop thinking about the *Daily Mail*. Be your own masters. Don't mention the *Mail*, don't even read the *Mail*. You're doomed every time you make a comparison.' It made incredibly good sense, but it was insufficient to save us; five years later, as I sit in Colin's kitchen watching Zoe unpack the contents of the bulging Tesco carrier bags into the cupboards, I look around to see if I can see a newspaper. Sure enough, there is a *Daily Mail* lurking under a pile of papers on a chair in the corner.

That same evening, Bryan goes to a meeting of the council to try to repair the bad feeling that exists between the town council and the Chamber of Commerce over the Ilminster in Bloom campaign: both sides feel the other should have done more to support the annual initiative. The meeting doesn't go as he hoped. Norman Campbell, the mayor, after gratefully acknowledging that the chamber will be throwing its weight behind the floral bonanza, announces that he thinks that the issue of the one-way street should be looked at again. 'There is a strong feeling we have not got the ideal solution for the town. I feel that out of courtesy we should explore whether the mechanisms for re-opening this debate are in place.'

Bryan is surprised and delighted but Norman's open-

minded approach is instantly rejected. 'It sets a precedent to go
back too soon,' says Councillor Richard Jacobs. Mike Henley,
another councillor, adds that 'it would undermine the credibility of the council . . . We will be going down a very slippery
slope because we will take all credibility from decisions made
by this council in the future.'

Only one councillor, Margaret Excell, speaks up for Bryan.
'Some councillors become entrenched once they have made a
decision. I can't see any harm revisiting it. When you actually
talk to the people of Ilminster they think this is a travesty.'

Bryan feels marginalised and humiliated. 'The whole situation stinks,' he tells me. We're sitting by the desk at the back of
Lane's Garden Shop; a new shipment of terracotta pots from
the Far East is cluttering up the floor. Shoppers are few and far
between. 'There is no reason why they could not have given
the issue another hearing. Those councillors are guilty of doing
their best to wreck the commercial viability of the town for the
independent shopkeepers.' He and Mike Fry-Foley have
decided to call an open meeting of the town directly after
Easter to try to force the council to re-open the debate.

When they're five days old, Bluebell's piglets venture outside
for the first time. They walk with delicate little steps, picking
up their hooves and putting them down warily, still uncer-
tain of the ground beneath their feet. Bluebell has become
much more protective and when the piglets are outside, she
walks backwards and forwards in front of them, keeping us
away. She also checks us out more assiduously, subjecting
any visitor to a thorough sniff of hands, boots and trousers.
On the far side of the fence the other sows watch the piglets
keenly. Babe, Guinness, Collette, Cordelia and the incredibly
fat Bramble follow their every move, standing in a line like a
group of young mums in the playground, clucking over the

antics of their kids on the swings. Once Bluebell had given birth, Robinson, the saddleback boar, had to be moved out of the main pen and into the rescue chickens' run, along with Lonesome George. It is a temporary residence while new fencing is erected, but with four more pigs already pregnant we don't need another, and Robinson will have to live alone for a few weeks. He spends his days lying on the ground, belly towards the sun, only bothering to stir to escape the shifting shadows as the hours pass. Two days after Robinson joins the chickens, Bob goes into the hen house to collect any eggs that had been laid outside the nesting boxes. He finds the lengths of wood which the chickens use to perch on at night thrown every which way across the floor. All the straw which he scattered over the floor the night before has been pushed into a pile in one corner. Bob puts the perches back up, but when it happens again the next night it becomes clear that, despite his bulk, Robinson is managing to get through the small, chicken-sized doorway in the side of the hen house. Once inside, he's been shovelling the straw into one corner and using it for his own bed, leaving the chickens to spend the night on the floor. Definitely a budding Napoleon of the farmyard.

'Six pigs: minimum £600. Max: £1,200.' I write this down in my notebook under the heading, 'Now we are pig breeders.' In 1862, the American government passed the Homestead Act, which entitled migrating families to 160 acres of land in the Midwest. The land would be theirs for good provided they spent the first five years farming. Within a decade, millions of immigrants from Germany, Scandinavia, Scotland and Ireland occupied 300,000 square miles of middle America. To make ends meet and to pay off the starter loans they needed crops that made quick money. The answer was to grow corn and keep pigs, and by 1880 there were 50 million hogs in the Midwest.

The economics went like this: a good sow could be bought for $5. With proper care, she could produce five or six breeding gilts a year who would farrow in their turn the next season. In the third year, the sows could be sold at market for $30 and the farmer still had his original pig, who was still breeding. It was a farmer's best, most reliable investment and pigs soon had the nickname of 'mortgage-lifters'. All too often, 'hog-money' was all that stood between the farmer and the demands of the local bank. If he had pigs, he could afford a few cattle. The pigs would be turned out on to the standing corn in the autumn: they'd feed themselves on the stalks, root up all that was left, fertilise and plough up the land and leave it ready for planting in the spring. This labour-saving device was known as 'hogging down'.

Today the value of pigs in the USA is over $5 billion, contributing to the worldwide need for 75 million tonnes of pork and 2 billion pounds of lard every year.

Four days after the discovery of the dead swan in Cellardyke, the bird flu scare is over. Scientists discovered that the bird had most likely contracted the disease in Europe and died as it attempted to migrate across the North Sea. Andre Farrar, a spokesman for the Royal Society for the Protection of Birds, says it 'looked like this was a whooper swan that spent the winter in Europe, set off on its migration, got halfway across the North Sea, felt like crap, and landed and died before washing up in Cellardyke. It can put the spring back into people's step because it makes it much less likely that other positives will be found.'

Mr Bonner pays us £159 for the two pigs. Not much profit. They cost us thirty quid to buy, plus £20 for Snells, and heaven knows how much on food. But, assuming that we get Bluebell's six piglets up to size and that she has twelve to fourteen in her next litter and we sell them at seventy-five kilos dead weight, rather than forty-five, then we're looking at our own 'mortgage-lifters'. I gave Mr B a tray of twenty white goose eggs; the local deli sells them for 99p, so I sell them to Mr B for 40p each, as I'm keen he should make some profit from us to make up for the pork fiasco. He's selling ten-pound bags of beef bones for £1 a bag to raise money for the Christmas lights so I take one home for the dogs. Fat-Boy hugely over-eats and smells like a raw chop for two days. Mr B sells twelve goose eggs in a couple of hours.

On Easter Sunday, Charlie and I go to church in Wells Cathedral. In our age of regulation and automation it is extraordinary that the dates of Easter, in the northern hemisphere at least, are still determined by the cycles of the moon. Easter falls on the Sunday after the first full moon after the spring equinox, which means that it occurs any time from 23 March to 24 April. It seems to me that whatever you believe in, it can be no coincidence that the great Christian festival of Christ's rebirth happens at the same time that the earth undergoes its own annual renewal. Nothing lasts, nothing stays the same. All life is about renewal, about picking yourself up if you've failed, about trying again.

We find two seats about six rows from the front. To the left of the altar, a six-foot-high cross has been painstakingly covered with spring flowers: daffodils, tulips, primroses, camellias, hyacinths, primulas and scillas, its fragile beauty bursting with colour. For over a thousand years Wells Cathedral has been a great centre of Christianity, but its importance has always been overshadowed by Glastonbury. No mythical king ever strode through its doorways and it lacks the legends that have sustained and taken Glastonbury into the realm of the spiritual, divorced from its Christian beginnings. Yet Wells is without doubt one of the finest cathedrals in England. It is small and set at the far end of a green which is surrounded by pretty houses. On a clear blue day, its eastern façade stands against the sky, the gargoyles and sculpted scenes as elaborate as anything you would find in an Italian city where tour buses would deposit their cargo all summer long. But Wells, sitting on the edge of its small market town, with only a few hundred yards separating the great front door and the open fields and the start of the footpath to Glastonbury, just seven miles away across the Levels, is spared the crowds. Charlie and I once spent a night here in winter and after dinner we walked around the cathedral green in the moonlight, the only people there to appreciate its powerful beauty.

I think I am like many people, perplexed by belief but disturbed that so many dismiss faith with secular cynicism: the towering edifice of Wells has been for centuries the recipient of the prayers, hopes, sadnesses and joy of countless people, and it is hard to feel wholly cynical in the presence of such permanence. Now faith is being abused by fanatics of all persuasions who argue that their faith is guiding them towards war, punishment and repression. Sitting in the magnificent knave, the curved arches reaching above me, I find myself remembering a man I met in the early 1990s called Steve. Steve was in his sixties, with two gold teeth which twinkled in his wrinkly, smiling face. It was shortly after Mandela's release from prison and Steve had defected to the ANC from the South African police force. He had been in charge of a little-known unit and his job was to eliminate ANC dissidents and trouble-makers who the authorities wanted out of the way. His team of three, himself and two black special constables, would kidnap and murder on demand, driving their victims into the hinterlands to the north of Johannesburg and burning their bodies to destroy the evidence. He told me that they had special songs which they sang as they watched the bodies burn, drinking themselves into a stupor as the flames went to work. I felt transfixed with horror that this man should be sitting at my dining-room table. Steve touched my hand: 'I did this because I believed this was right. That God had told me so. No one ever went to war believing they were on the side of evil.' I know my father went to war and killed German soldiers, confident of his belief, but when belief is used to justify cruelty, it is no wonder that we become so cynical of religions' deepest goals.

It is easy to dismiss the church and say that it no longer matters, but I believe that it does. In Wells this morning, on the long pew beside us, is a family with young children, the youngsters turning the pages of picture books. Behind us and in front of us are old people, middle-aged people, teenagers in jeans. The message is simple. It is for peace, for love of one's neighbour, for a moment of calm within the relentless stream of modern life. There is nothing here for anyone to quarrel with. Like it or not, the Christian story is the one that I and so many have grown up with. Christmas and Easter might nowadays represent nothing much more than a few days off work and a chance to shop even more extravagantly than usual, but the Christian year is embedded in all our lives. It is estimated that this year we spent £10.5 billion over the four-day Easter break, a record burst of consumerism, but I know that I certainly have a hankering for something over and above spending and acquiring, and that I am increasingly drawn towards the mysterious and the unknown, towards something that will forge a reconnection with a narrative that links my life into the great human quest for social justice, fairness and equality. If we reduce the world to just the bare bones of stuff, of rationality and of materialism, we deny that part of ourselves that is capable of rising a little higher, of yearning to be at one with something that money can't buy, and if we forget that, or say that it doesn't matter, then any chance of forging a better world is gone. We do not need to believe in God to care about the human condition or to believe that there is some- thing in this world which transcends materialism or to believe that our lives are a journey in which we can strive to make moral progress. I do not know if we evolved a need for religion, or if there is a religious gene, as some scientists attest, but faith is stubborn and our need for it so primeval that no amount of shopping malls will ever replace it.

The service opens with the hymn 'Jesus Lives', followed by a sung psalm and then the first reading from the Old Testament, from the book of Genesis, which tells the biblical version of creation. Creationists tell us that this, indeed, is how the world was formed and they are rubbished in turn by devotees of Darwinism, who say that we all evolved in a random fashion, with the fittest being the long-term survivors. Clearly the world was not made in seven days, as the creationists believe, but I have never understood why a belief in some kind of god, a god of one's own understanding, is incompatible with evolution. Creationists like to challenge evolutionists about missing links, attesting that as we do not fully know how worms evolved to be human beings, this therefore implies the presence of a creator. I'm with the scientists here: in time and with diligence, we will discover all those missing links and our progress from single-celled life to fully evolved human being will be understood in all its minutiae. But what evolution doesn't answer is what started it all off in the first place, what kicked off the big bang which led to life on earth. Evolution doesn't, and I think cannot, explain that, and neither can it explain our need for beauty, for love, for human emotions. The fact that God can't be explained in any way that makes satisfactory scientific sense doesn't mean he doesn't exist.

But religion has a lot to answer for, not least in an environ- mental respect. The reading from Genesis tells us that God said, 'Let us make man in our image, in our likeness and let them rule over the fish of the sea and the birds of the air, over the livestock, over all the earth and over all the creatures that move along the ground.' In Christian theology, humans were given *carte blanche* to rule the planet; indeed, it was stated that it was God's will that we should bring nature under control. But as our population has increased and our technological skills have advanced we have become a rogue species, dominating all others, convinced by our own righteousness. Until recently, humanity had evolved happily within living communities, all profoundly interdependent on one another. The natural world was our kin; maybe this is why we find it so restorative today. We need to rediscover this interdependence, and this involves learning to live lightly. The founders of Alcoholics Anonymous stressed the importance of this. Anyone struggling to recover from addiction knows that one of the secrets of recovery is learning to take life seriously, but not so seriously that we lose our sense of humour, wonder and fun. Living lightly means living with respect for others around you, it means losing the crippling self-absorption that is the trademark of an addict's life and it means becoming aware. As a species, we need to rediscover how to live lightly once again.

On Easter Monday, the piglets discover that they are small enough to squeeze under the gate, Peter Rabbit-style, which leads out of their pen and on to the path along the side of the walled garden, where we're growing rhubarb and cut flowers. They trot along, noses in the air, looking this way and that, full of curiosity and then, for no reason that I can ever detect, they stop, stiffen, their ears prick up and they squeak loudly, turn round and dash back to the safety of their mother as fast as they can, their little pink legs moving in sequence as they race along the grass. They seem to behave exactly like Piglet, who was always in a state of alarm and agitation at real and imagined fears. When Winnie the Pooh decided that he was going to track a Woozle, he enlisted Piglet's help. The two animals paced round and round in circles, unaware that the tracks they kept encountering were their own. 'Suddenly Winnie the Pooh stopped, and pointed excitedly in front of him. "Look!"

' "What?" said Piglet, with a jump. And then, to show he hadn't been frightened, he jumped up and down once or twice more in an exercising sort of a way.'

Out in the big field, pheasants have eaten all the small new leaves of the cabbages and the broccoli. We had planted fifty metres of each and now the plants look like shredded lace made by a bunch of drunken elves. They've left the red cabbages, possibly considering them too bitter. There aren't many solutions to the pheasant problem: we have tried bird-control devices which fire off blanks every few minutes but the birds seem to know instinctively that this is just a ruse. CDs or bits of silver paper strung on lengths of string are similarly useless. Charlie's father used to have a Labrador that was so well trained that he would sit by the growing vegetables for hours on end, provided his dad left his shooting jacket on the ground beside him. As an anti-pheasant tactic, it is not much use for us: Fat-Boy can't sit still for a minute, let alone be entrusted to keep watch over the cabbages. So I write a cheque for two 250 × 8-metre lengths of gauze which will cover the new plants until they're big enough to withstand the onslaught of the pheasants. Another £334.96 to add to the bottom line, but, as David points out, we can use it over and over again.

'This is our town and we love it. Mark my words, it is going to change.' On the Tuesday after Easter, Bryan Ferris is standing in front of a crowd of almost one hundred in the Ilminster

Parish Hall, making his last-ditch attempt to garner enough support to force the council to reconsider the planned one-way system. He, Mike Fry-Foley and Mr B have set up stands around the room which show in detail what the proposed routing will do to the town, in particular to the shopkeepers of Silver Street. 'If we don't have a commercial heart to the town, we have nothing,' he says. Mandi and Graham Bulgin, owners and proprietors of 'Allo 'Allo taxis, look gloomily at the maps. 'From May 1st the Somerset County Council is making it compulsory for all taxis to have meters,' Graham says. 'This route change is going to add £3.50 to a fare for someone coming from the south who wants to get to the north or east side of Ilminster. There won't be any point in us having a taxi rank in the square, so we'll just be available by phone.'

The Parish Hall stands at the top of North Street: it's a large stone building with scuffed wooden floors and a stage at its southern end. It's the biggest meeting place in Ilminster. Three town councillors are present and, once everyone has studied the road plans, Bryan asks them if they want to speak. 'We'll keep our powder dry and listen,' says Mike Henley, who had been so dismissive of Bryan at the meeting the week before. Bryan and Mike then invite the townsfolk to come up to the microphone and share their views of the one-way system.

'I'm a member of the Ilminster First Response Unit,' says Steve Mayor, owner of the Dolls' House shop in East Street, 'and we pick up 999 calls and go to help. We often arrive well before the ambulance. But the local ambulance is usually parked in Chard and the one-way system will add eight minutes to the journey. That could be a matter of life and death.'

Deirdre Cargen, proprietor of Bishop's Funeral Services in Chard, says that she hopes to open an office in Ilminster and she wants to warn the town about the effect Tesco might have. 'I've watched Chard go downhill: it's a beaten place now. Even though Tesco agreed not to sell various things, they do. Take pot plants. When they won the contract to open in Chard, they agreed never to sell them. But on the day before Mother's Day the store was full of pot plants. The same happens at Christmas. They take them away before anyone has a chance to complain. Ilminister is a lovely little town. I don't want it to go the same way.'

The councillors are getting annoyed. 'This was meant to be a meeting about the road system,' shouts Mike Henley. I am sitting next to Steve Mitchell from the picture framer's and we agree that he sounds like an arrogant windbag. 'Now you're all talking about the supermarket. There's no debate about that. Tesco *is* coming.'

His words are greeted with loud jeers, but the next group of speakers stick to the question of the road system, raising issues to do with parking, whether Tesco, who own the car park, will charge people who just want to use it but not shop at the store, how the signposts will work, where the buses will stop, what will happen while the store is being built on the site of the existing car park. It soon becomes clear that the issues have not been thought through at all.

'The one-way system didn't just happen. There's been full consultation,' interjects Mike Henley, to more raucous boos and jeers.

'I'd like to contradict that.' The calm-voiced speaker is at the back of the hall. 'It was a split vote at the original meeting last year and it was only pushed to a vote because the councillors wanted to get off to dinner. It was never fully discussed. It wasn't democratic. I was there.' I look round to see if Mr Henley plans to answer, but he's gone, slipping away through the crowd to the side exit. The atmosphere is now highly charged and excited. There is a goal towards which everyone is working and, it seems to me, there is now a villain in the person of Councillor Henley. I get a lift home with my neighbour, Henry Best, who used to be the regional representative for the Campaign to Protect Rural England. Henry is

six-foot-six tall and he folds himself into the driving seat of his
small Ford Mondeo like a collapsible walking stick. 'It's not
going to work, they're not going to listen.' I don't want to
believe him, but Henry is a wily old bird who has, over the
years, worked tirelessly to support the rural communities
around the town. He's seen the closure of countless village
shops, and watched what happens in towns when supermarkets move in and, one by one the shops close down, or move
away. While I concede that the supermarket battle is lost,
winning the fight over the one-way system still seems not only
possible but an important victory to strive for. It will make a
difference to the shopkeepers, but it will also be a unifier for
the town, making us all aware of what we stand to lose.

The week after Easter we set up an honesty table in the front
porch of Dillington House. Several hundred people go in and
out every week, taking courses, attending conferences or local
council training days. Dennis has built a table to fit precisely
into one side of the porch without disturbing the passing
traffic: six feet long and eighteen inches wide. In *Freakonomics*, Steven Levitt and Stephen Dubner's unconventional
take on what makes life tick, there's a story about the
economics of honesty boxes. In Washington in the 1960s, a
man named Paul Feldman was employed to analyse weapons
expenditure for the US Navy. He was a good boss and every
Friday he brought in bagels and cream cheese for his staff.
Employees from other departments heard about the bagels
and wanted some too. In time, he was bringing in fifteen dozen
a week and to recoup his costs he put out a cash box and a sign
with the suggested price. His collection rate was 95 per cent:
he attributed the underpayment to oversight, not fraud.

In 1984, his research institute was taken over. His kids had
finished college and his mortgage was paid off so he quit and

decided to sell bagels. The plan was simple. In the early morning he would drive round all the companies who had signed up to his scheme and deliver bagels and a cash tin: at lunch he'd pick up the money and the leftovers. Within a few years he was delivering 8,400 bagels a week to 140 companies and he was making as much money as he ever made working for the Navy. He was also, quite unwittingly, carrying out the field research for an economic experiment into white-collar crime.

He expected to continue receiving the same 95 per cent payment rate. What he didn't bargain for was that his presence in the research unit deterred cheating and that in the real world, he had to settle for less. A company that paid above 90 per cent he considered 'honest'. Anything between 80 and 90 per cent was 'annoying but tolerable' and less than 80 per cent would elicit a snappy note of complaint ending with 'I don't imagine that you would teach your children to cheat, so why do it yourself?' He noticed several curious trends. Cheating went down immediately after 9/11. It is more pronounced in big offices than small ones. Warm weather makes people more honest, while unseasonably cold days make people cheat prolifically. The week before Christmas is shocking, as is Valentine's day and Thanksgiving. However, around the Fourth of July, Labor Day and Columbus Day, people are more likely to pay up. The reason? The high-cheating holidays are fraught with miscellaneous anxieties and the high expectations of loved ones. Feldman also concluded that people who were happy in their work were less likely to cheat.

Wayne is optimistic: he's had experience of honesty boxes and tells me confidently that we will probably end up getting more, not less, money. 'People always round up – not down,' he says. 'Otherwise they think they're being dishonest.' I bought a new notebook to keep a list of what is on sale: eggs, soap, herb recipe books, herbs, hostas, irises, daisies, grasses, flowering currants and larger pots stuffed with four or five different herbs.

On the first day of the experiment, Dillington House is hosting a West Country education conference for 146 people. Over the weekend, there are courses taking place in digital photography, 'Women in Ancient Egypt' and 'Plant Hunters', as well as a course on the importance of hand evaluation in bridge; some 150 people are expected to attend. By teatime on the first day we have made £58, on the second £46 and on the third £38 – as much as we made in Montacute after deducting the rental price of the stall. Suddenly, the farm's financial future looks quite different. If we can sell £200 of produce on the honesty table every week, we'll earn £10,000 a year and that, in our parlous financial set-up, is a fortune.

Charlie is chuffed: throughout that first weekend he goes to check the table every few hours, making sure that anything that has been sold is replaced and that the pots are tidy and earth isn't being spilt on the flagstone floor of the hallway. Unlike Members of Parliament, visitors to Dillington are clearly an honest lot. The honesty box in the Strangers' Canteen in the Commons, which had been introduced to allow MPs and staff to pay for cups of tea without having to queue for the checkout, has just this week been removed after too many 'forgot' to pay. I get out the old cash flow charts and revise them with this new, unexpected addition. It looks good. The chickens are now laying two hundred eggs a day, we have six more pigs, and we are shortly going to be able to sell the first of our home-bred rare-breed chickens.

Eggs – 1,400 a week: £160 a week
Pigs – by the autumn selling six a month: £900 a month
Vegetables – by midsummer selling to DH: £1,600 a month
Honesty table: £800 a month
Plants to the South Petherton Flower Shop: as yet unknown
Herb markets: £200 each time, five more markets to go

That adds up to £4,140 a month, not counting the flower shop, the sale of rare-breed chickens and the proceeds from any other markets at which we can rent a stall. It also doesn't count selling vegetables to other outlets with which we may strike up deals over the summer when the produce is full grown and ready to eat. Are we finally turning a corner? David has pinned up a plastic notice on the door between the office and the potting shed. Illustrated by drawings of cartoon pigs with stubby little wings, it reads:

Another Month Ends –
All targets met
All systems working
All customers satisfied
All staff eager and enthusiastic
All Pigs Fed and Ready To Fly.

10

A Market Stall at Langport

The strings of toad spawn hatch into tadpoles just before the end of April, when the weather warms up and spring arrives like a tidal wave, unstoppable, changing every day, the trees seeming to explode into a million shades of green. There are hundreds and hundreds of tadpoles clustering round the edges of the garden pond, clinging to the muddy black lining, next to the water snails which the warm weather has lured out from under the weed in great quantities. Early one morning I watch a group of tadpoles eating the pale grey innards of a snail which hangs limply out of its shell. The first time I look I can still see the eyes on the tips of its two front tentacles, but quite soon afterwards the eyes have been gnawed away and by the following day the whole nibbled body has parted company with the shell. Like a shoal of piranhas, the tadpoles are feasting on the stringy flesh which floats slowly through the water like a life raft.

Bluebell's piglets need tagging, and when they are three weeks old David and I decide to brave their indignant screams. Using a device that looks like a stapler, we clip their ears with a metal tag which has been engraved with our licence number.

No pig can be moved around the country and thus to slaughter without such identification, and it is easier and less painful to do it to the piglets when they're tiny and their ears are still soft and pliant. We bribe Bluebell to leave the run with pig nuts and half a dozen parsnips, then, with the gate firmly shut between us, David grabs the first piglet and passes it to me. For something so small, piglets make an incredible amount of noise. They squeal, bark, kick, wriggle, whistle, grunt and honk, keeping up the same level of outrage right through the process, without any change of emphasis or volume at the moment David punches the metal tag through one ear. But once back on the ground, all noises instantly cease and they trot off to join the rest of their siblings, wholly unaffected by the experience. Any maternal instinct that Bluebell might still be harbouring is clearly insufficiently strong to displace her interest in the parsnips: she chomps and chews throughout her offspring's ordeal without even bothering to look up. All the same, David and I are glad of the gate: sows are unpredictable and Bluebell now weighs about 200 lbs.

As I watch the punching machine pierce the piglets' ears, I remember having my own ears pierced. It was 1974. I was twenty-three and living in a first-floor hotel room in a dusty little street in the Kathmandu bazaar, known locally as Freak Street. It was so called because it was where the countless hippies and exiles from the sixties congregated to explore Hinduism and Buddhism and, above everything, to take drugs. With my boyfriend, John Steinbeck, I'd arrived in Kathmandu on a green Royal Enfield 350 cc motorbike, a machine developed by the British Army and the workhorse of the Indian police. We'd come to India three months earlier, accompanying an old friend of John's to Bangalore to visit the guru Sai Baba. Steve had cancer and Sai Baba had a reputation for performing miracles. As we discovered when we arrived, most of these miracles involved producing quantities of holy ash from his fingertips and the occasional Rolex watch, which

would emerge from the folds of his long saffron robes. Despite
liberal applications of holy ash, or *vibutti*, after two months,
Steve died. We cremated his body, flew north to Delhi and
bought the Enfield. From the bazaars we acquired mattresses,
sheets, a mosquito net, cooking pots and pans, a gas-canister
cooker and plastic containers for food. We loaded it all on the
back of the bike and set off north, travelling up the Ganges to
Rishikesh and then east to enter Nepal.

Within minutes of checking into the hotel, there was a
knock on the door and a young Nepalese, carrying a square
leather briefcase, was offering us the contents of his mobile
pharmacy. John had been a soldier in Vietnam and after his
tour of duty he'd returned to the country as a journalist.
He'd broken a lot of stories, lived as a monk on an island in
the Mekong and become briefly addicted to heroin. He'd
made the experience sound exciting and I wanted a part of it.
Inside the bag there were slabs of rich brown hashish, lots of
multicoloured pills and little white vials of clear liquid with
the words 'Welcome Drug Company, Bombay' etched on the
glass. I persuaded John to buy the morphine, plus a couple of
syringes. Then I lay back and let him inject the liquid into the
vein in the crook of my left elbow and floated away on a tide
of opium dreams. A few days later, he bought me a pair of
circular gold earrings, forgetting that I didn't have pierced
ears. Undeterred, we sterilised a needle in a candle flame and
he pushed the point through my ear lobe and into a cork.
The holes that resulted were out of balance and messy: one is
lower down than the other, which makes many styles of
earring look ridiculous. They bled on and off for days. But I
put the earrings on and carried on drifting through the
opium haze.

In the days that followed, we would spend hours lying on
our twin beds, the windows open, the noises of bells and
drums and chanting drifting up from the street outside, and
reading aloud to each other, working our way through as

many of his father's books as we could buy from the local bookstore: *East of Eden*, *The Log from the Sea of Cortez*, *Cannery Row*, *The Grapes of Wrath*, *The Red Pony*, *Of Mice and Men* and, one of John's favourites, 'St Katy the Virgin', a short story about a wicked pig who undergoes a religious conversion after chasing two monks up a tree. Fearing for their lives, the monks try to exorcise the evil out of Katy. They lower a crucifix suspended on a girdle down to the sow's eye level.

'The face of Katy was a tiger's face. Just as she reached the cross, the sharp shadow of it fell on her face, and the cross itself was reflected in her yellow eyes. Katy stopped – paralysed. The air, the tree, the earth shuddered in an expectant silence, while goodness fought with sin. Then slowly, two great tears squeezed out of the eyes of Katy, and before you could think, she was stretched prostrate on the ground, making the sign of the cross with her right hoof.'

John Steinbeck's motto had been 'To the stars on the wings of a pig,' a sentiment he felt was both 'earth bound but aspiring'. Steinbeck had always liked escutcheons; he liked the way that people with a profession had symbols of their trade: cobblers had shoes, pawn merchants had their three gold balls, aristocrats had seals which told of their armies and castles and worldly possessions. He claimed to be proud of his common stock and thought that a flying pig aptly represented the aspirations of a hard-working, ambitious though lowly man. The image, which he called Pigasus, was turned into a gold and steel seal by a craftsman in Florence, with the words 'Ad astra per alia porci' stamped around the flying pig. He took delight in punching the seal into hot red wax to close his letters.

The idea of flying pigs dates back to a 1586 Scottish proverb which curiously states that 'pigs fly in the air with their tails forward', but Steinbeck, according to his eldest son, Thom, pinched the idea from Lewis Carroll, a writer he much admired. It appears in the poem 'The Walrus and the Carpenter', which Tweedledum recites to Alice shortly after she has met him and his brother, Tweedledee, in a wood.

'The time has come,' the Walrus said,
'To talk of many things;
Of shoes – and ships – and sealing wax –
Of cabbages – and kings –
And why the sea is boiling hot –
And whether pigs have wings.'

Steinbeck taught his sons to memorise 'The Walrus and the Carpenter' when they were old enough to read, along with all seven verses of 'The Jabberwocky', which they would have to recite before their father would consider granting a favour, like staying up late or going fishing on a weekday. He never owned a pig himself because, he told his sons, a pig wouldn't take to life in New York City, but when his famous black poodle Charley died, shortly after their marathon trip together round America which formed for the basis for *Travels with Charley*, he bought a white bull terrier, which he named Angel, after a pig that had been owned by his best friend at junior school in the Salinas Valley. One Halloween, he cut out a pair of wings and taped them to Angel's sloping shoulders and walked her round Sag Harbour, his two sons following behind, doubled over with laughter.

By mid-May, every inch of the walled garden is planted and the seeds are growing well. Outside the walls in the five-acre field, 1,000 cabbages and 1,000 cauliflowers are safely sheltered under a long length of white fleece, which looks as though someone has chucked a giant blanket across the earth. Another length of the white material covers early carrots, and

1,000 sprouts, 2,500 parsnips, 1,000 French beans, 1,000 spring onions, 500 Swiss chard and 3,000 leek seeds are beginning their magical underground journey, which will, in a few short weeks, transform the small dry seeds into lush, energy-rich plants, full of taste, nutrition and vitamins. If Alice in Wonderland had been asked to choose which of the following two scenarios was most likely to happen, that pigs would learn how to fly or that a tiny seed could become an eight-foot-high leafy plant, producing well over one hundred red flowers and well over one hundred pounds of green beans, which taste delicious and which, moreover, if you eat them yourself will make you grow tall and strong – and it will do all this in about eight weeks – I think she would have plumped for flying pigs as being by far the most plausible.

I am beginning to understand how lucky we are to have the walled garden. Correctly positioned and designed, the temperature inside the walls is estimated to be 7°C higher than outside, which means that inside the garden we're effectively in Bordeaux. Melons, pineapples, peaches and grapes were all grown here in the eighteenth century, when Dillington House, under the ownership of Lord North, had a reputation for its excellent kitchen. Thomas Beedall, a parson from Langport, recorded in his diary in 1769 that he had occasion to call upon his Lordship.

'Read the newspapers until his Lordship came back when I was hard into his Lordship's room and he talks with me and gave me five guineas . . . at five o'clock I went for dinner with the head servants and had for Dinner a Dish of fish, a sirloin of Beef roasted, a Loyn of Veal with colly flowers, carrots etc. for the first course, and for the second a Roast Turkey, a Hare, Pidgeon pye, fried Oysters, Chicken Tarts, Lavor etc. Drank water at dinner, after Dinner drank 4 glasses of Port Wine.'

A huge variety of vegetables were cultivated and, though there are no records of exactly which were grown in Dillington, records from the nearby Selborne estate in 1749 show that the head gardener was planting forty different varieties, including endive, mustard and cress, white broccoli, skirret and scorzonera, marrowfat peas, leeks, squashes, cucumbers, three types of artichoke, asparagus, all manner of lettuces and onions for pickling. His hot bed for growing melons was forty-five-feet long and used thirty cart-loads of dung a year. Our range of vegetables is modest in comparison.

Walled gardens are of ancient and almost universal origin. There is detailed evidence of Egyptian gardens dating from the fourteenth century BC with huge walls, towering gateways and oblong outlines, echoed by a garden within, which would always be laid out in the same, symmetrical lines. Instinctively, when we first looked at the garden in early winter of 2004, we wanted to carve it up into straight lines, pathways, perfect circles, above all into symmetrical shapes which would complement and perhaps soften its innate austerity. The Egyptian love of gardening was echoed and enhanced by the Persians, who had several ideal forms of garden: small ones, built close to the house, protected by mud walls and containing pools, watercourses, trees and flowers, and much larger, free-flowing parks. In Sardis, Cyrus the Younger created a famous palace garden when he walled in an area of park land and referred to it as a *pairidaeza*, from *pairi* (around) and *daeza* (wall). The original meaning of the word 'paradise' thus describes an enclosed garden in the Persian style.

Traditional Persian gardens were designed in great right-angled crosses which symbolised the four corners of the universe. Running water would divide each section, which would be planted with scented flowers, fruit and shade trees and embellished with architectural details. The Old Testament descriptions of the trees in the Garden of Eden follow this pattern. Now I can see that, with the exception of flowing streams, we've created something that more or less accords to the old designs. The apple trees on their wires create areas, or gardens within the garden. The walls cradle the peaches, apricots and plums. The herb bed is a semicircle against the west wall. The whole area has gradually filled up, until there is not a wasted square inch, but somehow it is in proportion and it looks right.

The walled garden had lain fallow for forty-three years before we took it over. The last occupant was called Leslie Barker. He'd acquired the tenancy in 1951, the year I was born, and like us he'd supplied the college with carrots and cabbages and onions. After nine years of trying he went broke and moved to Sussex, where he found a job as head gardener to Lady Astor. I learn all this from an elderly lady in the village, Ellen Doble, who, as a young mother, had started working for Leslie Barker in 1954. In 1947, Ellen had married her childhood sweetheart, Maurice, a thatcher. For four years they lived in a tied cottage near Honiton on the estate of Lord Sidmouth. After his death in the early fifties, his heirs sold up and Ellen and Maurice moved to Whitelackington, where Maurice became the Dillington estate thatcher. Initially they lived in the mews of the main house, but when the house was converted into a lecture theatre they decamped to the village, to the house where Ellen now lives alone after Maurice went into care.

'If Mr Barker had had his own shop, it would have been different.' Ellen and I are walking along the path between the rows of flowering plants and the vegetable beds. Ellen uses a walking-stick; since my accident I'm no speed freak, and I find we naturally keep pace with each other. 'Mr Barker used to sell his vegetables in town and he never made very much money. He also grew flowers in the glass houses – chrysanthemums and irises and really lovely dahlias – which we'd pack into brown cardboard boxes and send to the markets in Bristol. He was very fussy: all the flowers were individually checked: we had to pick off any loose petals. We packed the flowers in rows, alternating the direction of the heads so that the box was very full and the flowers didn't move around and get damaged.' Ellen worked five days a week in the garden, from nine till one o'clock, and she was paid two shillings and sixpence an hour.

On the inside of the south wall there are two rectangular patches of flaky white paint which were once, respectively, the back walls of a shed and a small house where, Ellen says, the gardeners used to live in the days when Dillington House was a home, not a college, and the gardeners worked exclusively for the family, supplying all their fruit, flowers and vegetables. 'There was a black kitchen range and that's where little Maureen, who was two when I started work here, used to play when it was cold.'

She shivers, although the day is warm and she's wearing a thick grey coat over a blue wool jumper. Ellen's eyes are bright blue and I can see that she is really pleased to be walking around the old garden again, pleased to see that it is coming back to life. 'It was often very cold. I remember digging the celery, throwing it backwards into a pile, then cutting the outside leaves and grading it. Our hands would be blue. We would freeze. And it always seemed to be raining when we had to bring in the parsnips and the carrots.' Ellen's first job had been picking and grading the strawberries, so I showed her our strawberries, growing in boxes, standing on top of two rows of bales of straw, out of reach of the slugs. 'How did *you* stop the slugs?' I asked. She thought for a minute.

'We never had any problems with slugs, or snails, or pheasants, or rabbits, at least not inside the walls. Outside it was much more problematic. There were rabbits everywhere: we ate a lot of rabbits in the war. Then the myxomatosis came and Maurice wouldn't go anywhere without a gun. He would put them out of their misery, poor little things.'

I offer to take Ellen into the pig pen to get a close look at the piglets, but she prefers to keep a wary distance. When Ellen was a young girl, her family had kept a couple of pigs in the back garden. Her mother fed them every day, pouring the food from a bucket into a long trough. One day, desperate to get at her breakfast, one of their sows had lunged forward to grab the edge of the bucket with her mouth. Unfortunately, her mother's thumb had been in the way. Ellen remembers her mother running back to the house, her thumb hanging by sinews, blood pouring from the wound. 'If it had happened today, they could probably have sewn it back on,' she says, leaning on the gate, watching Bluebell and the piglets ferreting around in the dust, searching for stray pig nuts that might have eluded them. 'We didn't get rid of them,' she continues, 'and in the war, it was good to have your own pigs. Along with the rabbits, we were able to eat well.'

Ellen's father used to say that you could use every bit of a pig except for its squeal: bacon and sausage from the body, brawn from the head, faggots, savouries, lard and pâté from the innards; rind and gristle were turned into jelly stock or minced up for faggots, and trotters and tails were pickled and kept in jars. In the war, pigs were prized although the Ministry of Agriculture didn't regard them as 'priority' animals. Cows, since they provided milk, had first rights, after humans, to meagre rations. The numbers of pigs on farms were reduced by half and imports fell by 70 per cent after Germany occupied Holland, Belgium and northern France.

But two factors helped ensure that pigs played their part in the war effort. In 1940, the Minister of Agriculture, Lord Woolton, passed a law which stated that owners of usable rubbish could be – and occasionally were – prosecuted if they didn't recycle it for animal use. The other was the establishment of the Small Pig Keepers' Council (SPKC), which persuaded local councils to turn a blind eye to health laws and allow people to keep pigs in their back gardens. The SPKC also pioneered pig clubs; these had been popular in the First World War and some had survived the intervening years. If you were a club member you qualified for cut-price feed, help with collection of food scraps, and for 2/6 you could get insurance for your pig. Pig co-operatives flourished in urban areas. In Hyde Park, the police started their own piggery. A correspondent of *Farmer's Weekly* visited the park in 1941 and reported: 'The sty that houses these important pigs was built by policemen, and built like a gaol. Evidently, the police were afraid that the pigs might escape.' After the lions, elephants and giraffes were moved out of Regent's Park Zoo to the safer environs of Whipsnade, pigs, also belonging to the London constabulary, were moved into the cages. As part of the pigs-at-war drive, canteens were encouraged to recycle their scraps. In Tottenham, sixty-eight garbage collectors bought one hundred pigs; they bolstered their diet from scraps which they collected in special buckets carried on the refuse lorries. Under ministry regulations, any waste that was intended for pig consumption had to be boiled for an hour to destroy organisms that might pass on foot and mouth or swine fever. The Tottenham refuse collectors developed a steaming system which could process huge amounts of waste under pressure, resulting in a concentrated swill which became known as 'Tottenham Pudding'. Any leftover pudding was sold to other pig-keepers.

Local councils saw the benefits of the pig clubs and helped by placing 'pig bins' on street corners. Labels reminded people not to put in certain types of waste – tea leaves and rhubarb leaves, which make pigs very sick. But stories from the time recall strange objects finding their way into the bins: in Bath, a young man called Gordon Tucker found a pair of false teeth and an ebony and silver pepper-grinder which is still in his family today. By 1942, there were over four thousand pig clubs. Despite all the domestic scraps, pigs were eating too much imported food, so their numbers were restricted. Co-op clubs were allowed two per member per year and domestic owners were limited to the same number.

Ellen's father kept pigs, as well as cows, which he rented. And when Ellen and Maurice were newly married, they kept pigs in their back garden. 'A pair of saddlebacks who ran wild all over the orchard,' she recalls. 'We would buy them as weaners and then sell the pork. I used to feed them on scraps from the big house: in those days you were allowed to give pigs leftover cooked food. I think it's a pity that you can't do this today. Such a waste.'

On the evening of 3 May, there are two separate but linked meetings in Ilminster. In the community school, three hundred people join Bryan Ferris, Mike Fry-Foley and Clinton Bonner to protest against the one-way system. I would have been there too, if I hadn't already agreed to take part in a debate on climate change which has been organised by the South Somerset Climate Group and is scheduled to take place at exactly the same time, five hundred yards away, in the town theatre. Both venues are packed, with people sitting on chairs on the stage and standing up at the back. The one-way meeting is clearly the noisiest. At the outset, the councillors are challenged by town resident Malcolm Young, who says, 'There is a great tide of public opinion that thinks you are no longer working for the people of this town but for a £2.26 billion supermarket.' There are representations from emergency services, the taxi companies and the bus companies. None of them feels they have been adequately consulted. The councillors are told that the overwhelming view of the town is against the new one-way system. 'We don't live a particularly grand lifestyle and many shops operate on a shoestring. Tesco has got it all sewn up,' claimed Bryan Ferris, to hearty cheers. At the end of the evening, they take a vote. All hands are raised in favour of asking for a rethink of the decision, except one. Councillor Adam Kennedy draws a sarcastic round of applause when he becomes the only person to vote against.

Kennedy owns a small engineering company, and claims to do much of his family shopping in the town. A few days after the meeting, I reach him on the phone to ask why he is such a strong supporter of both the one-way system and the arrival of Tesco. 'It gives us more choice,' he replies, 'but I won't talk about the supermarket.'

'Do you think there are any downsides to this road system? What about the fact that the emergency services say the new road system will add eight minutes to the journey if you live in the northern end of Ilminster?'

'Not true,' he replies. 'You can drive round a different way and come along the main road.' I point out that this would add several miles to the journey, but he tells me that an ambulance 'with its lights flashing' will be able to speed along the A road and cover the distance in the same time.

But his main reason for voting against re-opening the one-way decision, it transpires, was that it had been agreed at a meeting which he had chaired. 'So it would be disloyal of me as I was in the chair,' he says crossly.

'You mean you would lose face?'

'Much worse than losing face, I would be disloyal.'

Kennedy was co-opted on to the council six years ago. As such, he has never been voted into the job. I ask how much he cares about the town. 'I live here, my children go to school here, I shop here, I'm on the town council . . . I put myself out every week for this town . . . I can't be accused of not caring . . . it makes me very annoyed that people ask this question.'

'So I take it that you are convinced that the arrival of Tesco and the new one-way system are the very best possible things that could happen to Ilminster in 2006.'

There was a pause. 'I won't answer that question.'

I have the phone pinned between my shoulder and my ear as I type his answers directly into my computer. 'So you'd like me to say that in answer to the question, Mr Kennedy said he wouldn't answer.'

'Yes. But you need to ask the question of who is most loyal

to the town . . . those friends of yours in the Chamber of Commerce or me. Just ask them where they send their children to school. It's not the local school.'

At the Ilminster theatre I've been teamed up with the writer Mayer Hillman, author of *How We Can Save the Planet*, to talk about the morality of climate change. Mayer's talk is gloomy in the extreme and his solution is based on his belief that the government is shortly going to introduce individual carbon rationing and, in effect, take the moral dilemma about whether or not to drive a more energy-efficient car, change your household heating system or buy yet another cheap flight to Europe, out of our hands. I don't agree with him. Politicians play the green card as a crucial part of their PR and they pretend that we can lower our carbon emissions without having to radically change our lifestyles. Gordon Brown, who says he sees the environment as the biggest crisis we face, maintains that it will provide enormous economic opportunities. But one of his first acts as Chancellor was to cut VAT payable on gas and electricity. In 2006 he taxed owners of fuel-guzzling 4 × 4s just £45 extra, less than the price of a tank of petrol. At the 2006 Tory Party conference, a leaflet had been issued to delegates urging people to make a contribution to preserving the planet by not overfilling their kettles and by picking up a piece of litter every day.

In mid-February 2006, the *Guardian* obtained a leaked copy of a draft treaty between the European Union and the United States which would prevent the British government taking any action to reduce the environmental impact of airlines without the approval of the US government. It is not the first such agreement, but it may turn out to be the most wide-ranging. The 1944 Chicago Convention, now supported by no fewer than four thousand bilateral treaties, rules that individual governments may not levy tax on aviation fuel. The airlines have, in effect, been spoon-fed all their lives. The only area of air travel where we can, as a country, make a decision in isolation from the rest of the world is in airport development.

Our government could contain, or even reverse, the growth of flights by simply restricting airport capacity. But the opposite is happening. Heathrow is soon to get a new runway, and Stansted, Edinburgh, Birmingham and Glasgow are expanding. Twelve other airports have announced plans to increase capacity. According to the Commons Environment Committee, the growth in air travel the government forecast will require 'the equivalent of another Heathrow every five years.'

One-fifth of all international passengers fly to or from an airport in the UK. That number has risen five times in the last thirty years and is expected to double to 476 million passengers a year by 2030. Aviation represents the world's fastest growing source of carbon dioxide emissions; unchecked, aircraft emissions will exceed the country's entire output of greenhouse gases in 2050 by 134 per cent. Unlike Mayer, I don't feel hopeful that governments are going to be introducing any sort of serious rationing in the foreseeable future. I argue instead that the change will have to come from all of us and that, until we make it a vote-winning condition, no politician will risk his re-election by announcing an intention to impose any sort of restriction, let alone actual carbon-rationing. Centuries of believing that we live on a planet which has a limitless capacity to support us and feed us, ad infinitum, regardless of what we do, have been proved wrong; our world has limits.

Maybe this crisis will give us the chance to be part of a generation with a mission. While I never envied my parents having to live through the miseries of the war, I did envy the way they often spoke about it. For them and for their generation, those years of terror bound them into a higher purpose, one towards which everyone in the country was striving. Circumstances had forced them to put aside the bickering and petty squabbles and jealousies of everyday life; they were all in the same stream, heading towards the same goal, united by a wish for peace, both for them and for their children. In my lifetime of prosperity, I've known a few such moments when I think I have had the opportunity to rise above the scratchiness and competitiveness of everyday life and I have treasured them. Working with a team to accomplish a goal brings a happiness which self-centred pursuits never can. Solving the climate problem won't be accomplished unless we can change the way we think and start genuinely working together towards a goal which is bigger than all of us.

The following week, in early May, there is a letter in the *Chard and Illy*, under the heading 'Climate and Store are Linked'. 'Supermarkets and climate change are connected,' wrote Peter Langton. 'Car journeys to or from the south of Ilminster will soon be two miles longer and the new supermarket will bring us food which has been flown and trucked halfway round the world. We desperately need to cut down our transportation and it would be in all our interests to support local shops which sell local produce.'

That same week, Tesco announces a £100 million environmental initiative. It is unclear what they plan to do. To date, the company's environment record has been less than brilliant. It failed to achieve its target of cutting carbon dioxide emissions by 4.2 per cent in 2004 – because, the company says, of unexpectedly high sales growth. It would take more than thirty corner shops and greengrocers to match the CO_2 emissions from one average-sized superstore. Grocery packaging still makes up roughly a quarter of household waste and the UK's biggest supermarkets distribute some 15 billion plastic bags a year, which end up in landfill. Peter Langton's connection between the supermarkets and climate change illustrates only a tiny part of the argument. A 2004 study entitled 'How Green Is Your Supermarket?' said that the UK food industry accounts for more than one-fifth of total greenhouse gas emissions. In 1980, the UK imported 6.3 million tonnes of food, feed and drinks; by 2000 this had risen to 17 million tonnes. If the environmental predictions are correct, that figure is wholly unsustainable and we will have to return to growing our food much, much closer to where we live.

Our first cut flowers are ready for sale in the middle of May – just chrysanthemums to start with, but soon there will be sweet peas, and sweet williams, day lilies, pinks and small carnations in mixed, bright colours. When we first proposed selling them to Dillington House, along with the eggs and the vegetables, Wayne asked Lorraine, his highly competent manager, where she bought the flowers for the dining-room tables. Lorraine said she went to Asda in Taunton, where she could buy a bunch for as little as £1.99. By cutting off the stems and dividing the mix of carnations and greenery, one bunch could stretch to fill six or seven small vases and they lasted for at least two weeks. We'll never equal let alone beat that price, but Wayne is enthusiastic about having Dillington flowers on the Dillington tables so, early on in the planning of what to grow in the nursery, we decided to grow cut flowers. Now that we have the honesty table, I wish we were growing more, as they'd be a good addition to the eggs, plants and bags of vegetables.

To coincide with Mother's Day, I've made a short film for the BBC's Sunday morning programme *The Heaven and Earth Show* about the ethics of the flower trade, which I learned about in the first place from the town greengrocer John Rendell. John's flowers arrive twice a week via a refrigerated truck which trundles down Silver Street dropping off its cargo. The driver is Dutch. Every Monday he loads up three containers from the flower markets of Holland and crosses the Channel. In Bristol, two of the containers are detached and coupled up to local trucks. Two go south into Devon and Cornwall and one follows a regular route around Somerset, dropping off cut blooms at local florists. The flowers have been grown abroad: our own flower-growing industry now accounts for just 20 per cent of the flowers sold in the UK. Even the once prized daffodils of the Scilly Isles are now little more than a cottage industry. Supermarkets sell 75 per cent of all the cut flowers we buy: their huge buying power is reflected in the fact that a bunch of five red Cassini tulips retail for the same amount today, about £1.50, as they did twenty years ago.

John sometimes finds that he gets an attack of asthma shortly after the flowers have been unloaded into the back room of the shop. He reckons it is caused by the chemicals on the flowers. I often find him in the early morning, seated at a small table, creating someone's name, or a cat, out of flower heads for a funeral later in the day. Births, weddings and deaths form a large part of his income. We're not yet ready to entrust our floral tributes for our dear departed to the hands of the supermarkets and the hatches, matches and dispatches business is what is keeping many a small-town florist alive. When John was fifteen, he used to bike to Taunton, then catch a lift with a trader who went daily to Exeter, where he studied flower arranging at Constance Spry's West Country school. John was the only boy in the class. Now he's in his seventies and, with his younger wife Mary, he works every day in the shop, selling vegetables, eggs, fruit, honey, local biscuits, bird food, cheese, butter, bird food containers, cane baskets, artificial flowers, ribbons, plants and buckets of cut flowers.

The supermarkets such as Asda, where Lorraine has been buying flowers, achieve their rock-bottom price by flying the blooms in directly from South America or Africa. Over nine

million red roses are sold in the UK every year and 85 per cent
of the flowers we buy are imported, not just from the flower
markets of Europe but from Kenya, Colombia, Ecuador and
Zimbabwe, where the environmental standards are low and
bosses don't spend much time considering the welfare of workers. The majority of Asda's mixed bunches come from Ecuador
or Colombia, where flowers are grown under glass, miles and
miles of it. Pipelines carrying water laced with pesticides and
fertilisers criss-cross the farms. Trucks loaded with flowers
shuttle between the farms and the airport, ensuring that the
newly picked blooms are airborne as fast as possible. In order
for it to travel so far in a box without any water, a complex
cocktail of chemicals is added to the plant, on top of chemicals
to speed growth, enhance shelf-life and kill bugs. A survey of
8,000 Colombian flower workers revealed that individuals had
been exposed to 127 different pesticides, 20 per cent of them
banned in the USA because of their known toxic effects, many
of which are carcinogenic. Working in glasshouses enhances the
effects of the chemicals, and workers – the majority of whom
are women – suffer skin trouble, breathing difficulties and
miscarriages. In Kenya the story is repeated, with extra environmental consequences. In a region already short of water, a
large flower farm can use upwards of 80,000 litres of water a
day, leaving local supplies struggling. Lake Naivasha, famous
for its extraordinary flocks of flamingos and a crucial water
source for much of Kenya's wildlife, is drying up due to the
greed of the flower farms and its waters are being contaminated
by the pesticides that leach back into the lake.

When John was a teenager and first learned to arrange
flowers under the watchful eye of Constance Spry, the flowers
he had to work with came from Cornwall, the Channel Islands
and the glasshouses where his father used to grow carnations.
Until the 1950s, Ilminster had its own railway station, and if
he wanted something special he could phone Covent Garden
at six in the morning and the flowers would arrive, in

returnable wooden boxes, by three o'clock in the afternoon. The station master, attired in a black suit, waistcoat and fob watch, would deliver them directly to the shop. To make a complex funeral wreath, John first had to make a frame out of wire, then stuff it with wet moss or straw, to support the flowers and keep them fresh. It could take ages. The most elaborate funeral display he ever made was a three-foot-high steam engine, crafted out of wire, moss, carnations and roses. The deceased was the young son of the owners of a travelling fair that toured the West Country in the summer months, transporting the merry-go-rounds and coconut shies on the back of huge steam engines, which lumbered slowly along the country lanes. Just outside Ilminster the boy had slipped off the coupling between two wagons and been crushed to death by the relentless steel wheels.

I like watching while John's nimble, clever hands create arrangements saying 'Beloved Dad' or 'You will be missed' out of carnations and roses and 'mums. Fashions, he says, have changed, and now that most people opt for the crematorium fewer flowers are wanted. It has been ages since he has had to make a vacant chair, or a replica of the gates of heaven. Even the once popular symbol of praying hands is hardly ever asked for. Animals are still popular and John finds it easy to create a floral cat, or dog, but a request for a tortoise made him think. How to make the neck? He solved the problem with a chunk of courgette, finishing it off with plasticine eyes.

Flowers have extraordinary designs. The numbers of petals in a single flower are almost always part of a series known as the Fibonacci numbers; 3, 5, 8, 13, 21, 34, 55, 89. While it is well known that number sequences occur throughout the natural world – for instance, years have 365 days and the moon's cycle is twenty-eight days – the curious pattern that occurs in the world of flowers is something that I have always found wholly awe-inspiring. Lilies have three petals, butter-cups have five, many delphiniums have eight, marigolds have thirteen, most field daisies have thirty-four, fifty-five or eighty-nine. These are all in the Fibonnaci sequence, and while there are exceptions to this rule they are rare.

This number series is obtained by adding together the two previous numbers. $1 + 1 = 2$, $2 + 1 = 3$, and so on into infinity. If you dissect the head of a sunflower the same numbers crop up in the spiral patterns of the seeds. I first learned about the phenomenon of nature's numbers from the scientist Ian Stewart. He was talking about his book *Nature's Numbers* and I took Daisy along to listen. As she was only ten I expected that she might be bored, but I was very keen to go and so she had no option but to tag along. Ian showed slides of the sunflower heads, pointing out that, in addition to the numbers of seeds, there was another even more amazing natural pattern in the shape. The seeds, or florets, are arranged on the head of the sunflower in two intersecting groups of spirals, one moving clockwise, the other anti-clockwise. In some species the number of clockwise spirals is thirty-four, and the number of anti-clockwise ones fifty-five. In other species you find fifty-five one way, eighty-nine another, or even eighty-nine one way, with 144 going the other. Pineapples have eight rows of scales sloping left, thirteen sloping right. Daisy was spellbound and so was I.

The number system inherent in plants and flowers was first understood by Leonardo Fibonacci, who was born in the 1170s in Pisa. His lifelong fascination was with numbers and numerology's impact on the natural world. But as Ian Stewart asked some eight hundred years later, 'If genetics can choose to give a flower any number of petals it likes, why do we observe such a preponderance of Fibonacci numbers?'

Ian explained that the number sequences show up in DNA codes and then went on to talk about how, as the cells of the plant differentiate themselves into leaf cells, this precise pattern occurs. Plants grow from their tips. The tips are conical and leaves near the top are nearer the centre than those which are farther down the stem. If we could draw a line connecting the points from which the leaves grow, we'd find we have a spiral. The important number in this spiral is the angle between the lines connecting the stem's centre with each leaf. In 1837 a crystallographer called Auguste Bravais and his botanist brother, Louis, discovered that this angle is usually close to 137.5 degrees. This number is important because, if you take any two consecutive numbers of the Fibonacci series, turn them into a fraction, and multiply them by 360 degrees you get 222.5 degrees. But since this is greater than 180 degrees it needs to be measured in the opposite direction, so has to be subtracted from 360 degrees, resulting in 137.5. As an example, if you take 34 and 55 and multiply the fraction by 360 degrees you have 222.5. As their size increases, the ratio of the Fibonacci numbers gets closer and closer to 1.618034, or phi, the Golden Number, a number which crops up in the shapes and designs of the natural world with extraordinary regularity. When you look on the head of a sunflower, it is easy to see the clockwise and counter-clockwise pattern. The florets grow in a way that makes the most efficient use of the space. But if the angle was slightly different, for instance if florets were positioned at 120 degrees apart, (which is exactly a third of 360 degrees) then there would be gaps in between. But nature, using the proportions of the Golden Number, ensures that the space is completely and efficiently filled.

The Golden Number, or ratio, or phi, is a never-ending, ever-repeating number: 1.6180339887 . . . When it was first realised that there exist numbers like this, which go on for ever, it caused a philosophical crisis among mathematicians in the fifth century BC. Numbers were meant to be manageable things: now suddenly, there were numbers which had no end, which stretched into infinity. The Golden Number is present in flowers and the numbers and position of their petals, in the growth pattern of spiral sea shells, in the structures of galaxies, in branches of mathematics, and in the arts, where, in the search for 'perfect proportions' in design and architecture, the golden ratio has been found to be the most pleasing. Maybe we like it because it reflects shapes and dimensions which we understand as natural, but it is so pervasive that it is impossible not to share Albert Einstein's sense of wonder. 'The fairest thing we can experience is the mysterious. It is the fundamental emotion which stands at the cradle of true art and science. He who knows it not and can no longer wonder, no longer feel amazement, is as good as dead, a snuffed out candle.'

By the middle of May, Bramble has grown so fat that she is finding it difficult to walk. It has been hot and she looks quite defeated, her belly hanging huge and heavy, her teats long and pendulous. If Bluebell had six piglets, Bramble's stomach would indicate that she must be having twice that number. She's been moved into the maternity ward on her own and when I go to bring her a carrot she follows me around the run like a lost dog, eager for strokes and, it seems, for conversation. One of the rescue chickens has moved out of her pen and into the pig pen with Bramble: every time David or Bob catches her and puts her back she flies out again and back in with the pig. The hen had started escaping when Bluebell and her piglets were still occupying that run: the little pigs would watch the bird with fascination, lying in their piggy heaps, eyes focused on her as she pecked the ground for grubs. We could trim her wings, but David thinks the hen might be a diversion for Bramble as she waits out the last days of her pregnancy.

Bramble's re-housing means several other moves for the pig community. It's now Babe's turn to become a mother, so she is bivouacked with Robinson, a move she doesn't appreciate at all. Her method of vengeance has been to kick the food trough over and then to keep kicking it as the pig nuts spill on to the ground, making a great racket with her hooves smashing against the tin. Even when it's empty, she becomes periodically overwhelmed with fury and rushes at the trough, shoving and kicking, turning it over and over, making banging and crashing noises which disturb the otherwise peaceful sounds of the farm.

Robinson is having problems of his own: he's been sunburnt on the white skin under his 'saddle' and his skin is peeling and flaking off through his wiry hairs. Pigs roll in mud to provide a sunscreen, but Robinson had been too lazy to walk down the hill to his wallow to muddy up his back and the sun has been beating down on his tender white stripe. Even though he's almost a foot taller than Babe, it's clear she has the upper hand. I watch her vent her fury on the empty trough and then turn on Robinson, who is snoozing in the shade by his water trough. He's splashed water on to the ground, creating a huge muddy puddle and he is lying in this to keep cool, balancing his head on the edge of his watering trough. With her snout, she pushes him hard in the side. When he pays no attention, she redoubles her efforts, until he is forced to get up, where-upon she immediately leaves him alone and goes back to beating up the trough. The moment she comes into season, all this behaviour will cease and she will become Robinson's willing and eager sex slave.

In the adjacent run, the other pigs watch their antics, clustered together like a group of aunts having a jolly holiday in a nudist colony. Babe is the only virgin left among them and they seem to be enjoying her evident discomfiture. But they've all been through a pig's version of the first-night jitters, none with more anxiety and annoyance than Bramble, so I guess they know how she feels. When the vet comes to check on Boris's persistent health problems, he points out that the Empress has grown so fat that she won't get pregnant, so she has been moved in with the grown-up sows, where she is having to fight a bit harder for her rations. It's true, she is very fat. She looks as though she is wearing huge slabs of bacon as a topcoat. She still sticks her tongue out when she's thinking

about things and I notice that she even sticks it out when she's
having a drink. Guinness and Collette and Cordelia, the two
saddleback sows, haven't been very welcoming to their new
companion and are constantly barging into her and butting
her in the softness of her underbelly. David says she is losing
weight after just a few days, but it seems tough to be a pig on a
diet, sort of against nature and instinct.

Bluebell and her piglets are now living next to Hyacinth,
Blossom and Lobelia and alongside the fence around the
rare-breed chickens. The piglets are venturing further and
further with every passing day, wriggling under the gate or
through the square holes in the pig wire which they can still,
just, force their bodies through. They explore in small
groups, wriggling their way first into Hyacinth's run and
from there, through another wire fence and out into the field.
They stand next to dandelions which are about their height,
staring in amazed delight at the big yellow flowers, then they
scamper off through the tall grass, pausing to root up a divot
of grass, pushing their noses into the soft, damp, muddy
earth, their tails wagging furiously as they uncover a tasty
stash of grubs. Then suddenly they'll all stand stock still,
look this way and that and, as though summoned by a
distant whistle, they'll race for home and the safety of
Bluebell's belly. I watch one piglet fail to get through the
fence first time and start to panic. He screams and jumps up
in the air, then darts back and forth along the fence, looking
for a suitable gap, but going so quickly that he clearly won't
be able to see anything. Finally, he flings himself at the fence
snout first and, pushing his head through the square hole,
scrabbles with his front trotters for purchase in the earth on
the other side. He finds it and wriggles his bottom, popping
through the fence like a cork leaving a lively champagne
bottle. Back on his feet, he shakes himself thoroughly and
looks around, as though to check that no one has witnessed
his moment of cowardice. Satisfied that all the other pigs are

gainfully occupied, he trots back to his mother and latches his gums on to a teat, curling his tail upwards into a contented coil.

Our second outing as stallholders is to a market at Langport, on the banks of the River Parrett. Langport is deep inside the Levels and, as its name implies, the town was once an actual port, servicing the boats which chugged up the Parrett into the heart of the swampy lands. Charlie went to school there between the ages of four and ten, commuting alone by train from Charlton Mackrell every morning and then home again in the afternoon. In the days before Beeching ripped out so many of the rural lines, Somerset was criss-crossed by small trains, which enabled a small boy to safely travel eight miles twice a day on his own.

The night before, Charlie was at a dinner for his head of chambers and I was on *Late Review*, discussing the disappointing and rubbishy film version of *The Da Vinci Code* among other new arts events of the week, and we didn't leave west London till well after midnight.

Shortly after 9.30 a.m., still half asleep, I climb into the old white Transit with Bob. David has built a precarious arrangement of shelves to enable us to transport hundreds of plants and herbs, but as we bump over a small bridge on the drive across the Levels the table lurches to one side, sending a tray of lavender plants flying. Half a dozen of them come loose from their pots and earth scatters over the other plants and the bottom of the van. The marquee is almost empty when we arrive, a clear advantage as we set up shop in a prime location by the entrance. After shaking off the soil, I arrange fifteen different herbs, petunias, hostas, rosemary plants, lavender, marigolds, geraniums, sedums, grasses, lupins, busy Lizzies, and royal blue irises on a rickety wooden table. I make a pile of copies of the herb book which has turned into a steady seller, earning us 50p on each sale. We've also got three boxes of different lettuces – Webb's wonder, lollo rosso and unico – on sale for 60p each.

Next to us, Angela Davage from nearby Curry Rivel is putting out her stocks of homemade pasties, sausage rolls, bacon and tomato rolls, cakes, scones, cheese scones, all neatly wrapped in cellophane and labelled by hand. She is yawning too, after cooking till ten the night before and then getting up at five to finish the packing and sorting. Angela's husband had to stop work at Westland Helicopters due to ill health. Now he is unemployed. Her baking hobby is the mainstay of the family finances and she cooks for farm shops and works the local markets. Her mother helps out, and while Angela is manning the stall in Langport her mum is doing the same thing at the nearby Drayton market.

Bob and I lug the trays of herbs and plants from the back of the Transit into the tent. I realise that we've brought no bags, no signs and no tin to put any money in, but luckily Charlie hasn't left home yet and I am able to reach him on the mobile and divert him towards the office for brown paper carrier bags and flat-pack cardboard boxes. By ten-thirty we are set up and ready so I go to look round. Langport town extends into the village of Huish Episcopi, home of one of Somerset's most remarkable churches. In 1972, when Britain converted to decimal currency, the first decimal stamps featured great English church towers. Huish took pride of place, appearing on the 9p version, the most expensive of the issue. The tower is celebrating its 550th year, although the church dates back to the 1200s. Huish was reputedly the model for Plumstead Episcopi in Trollope's *The Warden*, and in an adjoining tent an exhibition of paintings, photos and collages of the tower are being auctioned in aid of its upkeep. Outside on the rough grass beside the river, nine members of the Wessex Highlanders, splendid in tartan kilts, hats and bum-freezer black jackets, are warming up their bagpipes. A little later in the day, one of them comes by the stall and tells me that he learned to play the bagpipes in a piggery, where the noise was sufficiently loud to drown out the shrieks and wails that he made while trying to master his instrument. He thought the pigs quite liked it, as they'd cluster round him as he went through his scales.

There's no formal opening of the market, but by 11.30 we've already sold two herb books, twelve different herbs, two irises and all the lupins we bought – sadly only three: we could have sold many more. David had packed the Transit the night before and Charlie is annoyed to find that there is no coriander in with the herbs, as we've grown loads of it and it is already going to seed. But Bob is enjoying himself. On the drive over he told me that he was particularly chuffed that Bramble had finally started to treat him as a friend. The day before, he'd been spreading extra straw in the maternity ward and the fat sow had shown a keen interest, helping push the straw this way and that, creating a big luxurious bed in which she will soon give birth. Apparently, she'd nudged him several times on the leg, not her usual pushy shoves, more a gesture of thanks. She had bestowed a little gift of grace on Bob and it was touching to see how much it delighted him.

'Make eye contact and smile,' Charlie says. It's late in the morning and, exactly as happened at the Montacute market, the stalls selling food are doing a roaring business while trade on our plant stall is lurching along in fits and starts. Mark and Sue Tutton of Orchard Old Spots are nearby. Since opening time, Mark has been frying pork burgers, bacon and sausages on a portable gas grill and one of his daughters has been stuffing the meat into buns, adding fried onions or generous dollops of Sue's home-made apple sauce. By twelve-thirty there's a queue and the smell is mouth-watering.

I go back to the car park to fetch some more parsley plants from the van and when I come back Charlie is talking to a couple about the value of sorrel: great as soup, brilliant in omelettes, grows all through the winter; he's got his sales patter down to a fine art. The woman is in her forties, pretty and vivacious, and she is laughing at something Charlie has said, her husband leaning forward across the table to join in the conversation. I look at her and I shudder. She is in a wheelchair and it is a serious wheelchair: not the kind I used to have, which was a one-size-fits-all model, the sort you have if you are unable to walk only on a temporary basis. This chair has been customised and fitted with a motor and gadgets to steer by.

As the days approach the third anniversary of my accident, the second anniversary of when I finally put down the booze, I find myself thinking a great deal about the car accident and about how I very nearly became permanently disabled. I have no idea how I would have coped. I make myself busy at the far end of the stall, moving pots that don't need moving, keeping my hands occupied, acutely aware that I am standing upright, able to fetch parsley plants from the van. If you are given a diagnosis for any condition that is going to last a lifetime, you have to grieve for the future you will never have. I nearly had to face a future of never walking freely again, of never being able to carry a cup of coffee across a room or board a train without help or just walk down a street, blending in unnoticed with the crowds. People used to tell me that I was brave and I am sure that people tell the woman in the chair, who is counting out some money to hand to Charlie in return for a couple of basil plants, the same thing, over and over again. It is not about bravery though, because you literally have no choice but to keep pushing forward and making the best of things. Bravery is about doing something over which you exercise a choice, being the first one, so to speak, to charge over the barricades, or risk your employment in order to tell the truth, or standing up to the bullies in the school play-ground who are making another child's life a living hell. That's being brave.

I now think that I was given an extraordinarily precious gift, that almost losing my leg, almost dying, has put beauty back in the heart of everyday life. To see my child grow up and blossom, to be able, in my fifties, to start a whole new life with a partner I love, is priceless. When I was a young woman in my twenties, inspired by the rallying cry of the 1960s that everything, in order to be anything, must be far out, extreme, on the edge, I rebelled against any notion of settling down and leading a life that was ordered, that had routine. Routine smacked of boredom and compromise. Knowing what time you would go to bed at night meant your life was dull and proscribed. I never for one moment dreamt that what I thought of as stultifyingly boring would, in years to come, become so extremely rich and satisfying. The woman in the wheelchair and Charlie are still laughing, turning a brief encounter into a moment of uncomplicated pleasure. I wonder what trials she has been through, how she has come to terms with her life of immobility. What is so clear from her merry deep laugh is that it is a life rich in things that matter: in human connection, relationships and nature.

On my travels through recovery I met a young rabbi called Shalom. On the day before I was due to get the final verdict from my surgeon as to whether my leg would survive intact or face the chop, he sat with me in the garden at the clinic and said, 'Don't ever forget that the adventures of the mind are always far, far more rewarding than the adventures of the feet.' My experience was nothing compared with families facing a terminal sentence on one of their own, but my brief glimpse into the abyss of disability has made me truly thankful for so much we all take for granted. In my case, sometimes just the act of getting out of bed in the morning, unaided, unimpeded and, above all, without a hangover is enough to carry me happily through the day.

Outside the tent, two men are performing the Chinese Lion dance inside a brightly coloured paper lion. They've come from the Lee Palace Chinese restaurant in Dorchester as part of a cultural initiative. Our neighbour in the tent, Angela, has been along to a cooking demonstration held in a local village hall earlier in the week. For £7.50 they were shown how to cook a range of Chinese dishes, which were then laid out as a multi-course banquet fit for a king. Only eight people showed up and they all got stuffed. The Hong Kong-born owner of the restaurant used to work in London's Chinatown. He moved to Dorchester six years ago and doing the Lion dance is now a regular, if bizarre, feature of West Country life. The lion shimmies its way between the rows of flags stretching from the flag-pole, between the kids and their hula-hoops, the black-suited members of the Langport Brass Band and the bagpipe players who have struck up a chorus of *Auld Lang Syne*. It should, I think, be utterly incongruous, but somehow it's not. The wind whips up the sides of the marquee tent, sending our hanging baskets, which aren't selling at all, banging against the canvas walls. The surface of the river breaks up into flurries and the yellow rape that grows in profusion on the far bank weaves and bends against the sudden gusts. A springer spaniel hauls itself out of the water, dripping wet and wagging its tail. It rushes, barking, into the middle of the pipers, scattering water on nine pairs of thick white socks. Overhead, the clouds gather and part, threatening a downpour which never quite materialises. As we pack up to go, Charlie and I count up our takings: £164.50, of which probably less than £50 is pure profit. As an hourly rate it leaves much to be desired: three of us have been on the stall for over four hours, which means we've each earned roughly £4.20 an hour. But as a way to spend a day, it's been priceless.

On 10 May there is an acrimonious meeting of the town council. Fifty protesters storm out shouting 'resign the lot of you' after the councillors block a discussion on whether to re-examine the one-way decision. Four of the thirteen councillors backed a motion calling for the council's rule book – the standing orders – to be suspended, a necessary move in order to allow discussion of the same item twice in a six-month period. But Councillor Adam Kennedy led the decision to overrule the motion, suggesting that the council simply take note of the public's position. Norman Campbell, the mayor who was so sympathetic to Bryan, Mike and myself at our recent meeting, chooses this moment to tender his resignation as mayor, citing his unhappiness at the councillors' decision not to re-open the debate.

Now all efforts are being focused on the last-ditch attempt to make the council reconsider the planned one-way system at a meeting that will take place at Dillington House on 30 May. Relations between the town council and the Chamber of Commerce have reached such a low point that a new organisation has been formed called the Ilminster Democracy Action Group. The IDAG is led by Dave Bailey, an ex-shop steward at the local Glacier Metals company. In 1995, Dave and his wife Jennifer organised Ilminster's own special millennium celebrations, which recalled that in 995 the town had been ceded to the abbots at nearby Muchelny Abbey, by order of King Ethelred the Unready. At a meeting at Christchurch, Canterbury, three bishops, two dukes, five abbots, five thanes and the shepherd of Sherborne, one I. Wulfsige, signed a charter which gifted the town – and all its taxes – to the Muchelny abbots. The charter survives to this present day, stored in the records office in Taunton, the oldest such document in the British Isles. I have a copy of it beside me as I write. It begins, 'In the name of the gracious one who thunders and rules in perpetuity, who guides and governs the kingdom and the three fold mechanism of the entire universe, the lofty height of the heavens and the deepest depth of the flowing ocean, everything in the heights and depths, with the power of his majesty, now and for ever more.'

During the dissolution of the monasteries, Henry VIII gifted
Muchelny to his wife Jane Seymour. The document disappeared, but in the late nineteenth century it was discovered
at the now ruined abbey and was moved to Taunton, where, in
the early 1990s and with the help of the vicar's Latin primer,
Jennifer began the task of translating the Anglo-Carolingian
script into modern English. At the celebrations in 1995 the
document, which hadn't been seen for a thousand years, was
brought to Ilminster and displayed in the minster. Dressed as a
monk, Dave carried it up the aisle during Sunday morning
service while a libretto Jennifer had written about the Canterbury meeting was sung by the choir. They seem to me to be the
perfect couple to help spearhead this last protest.

On 19 May, Dave organises a meeting of the IDAG in the
Parish Hall. One hundred and fifty people pack the room to
capacity. In his opening speech he sets out the arguments: 'Bus
fares will have to increase, some taxi fares will more than
double. One of my concerns is the environment. Over the last
week I have been doing a survey of the traffic passing through
the north end of Ditton Street. Currently, I reckon a one-way
system would increase the mileages driven within Ilminster by at
least 6,800 miles per week. That's over a quarter of the way
around the world! Think of the pollution and global warming.'

Opinion is canvassed as to whether there should be a march
from the town centre to Dillington House for the next meeting.
The idea is quickly abandoned out of worry that older people,
who won't be at work at that time, might not manage to get up
over the hill, and that the march would end up being poorly
attended and thus fuel to members of the local council who
support the one-way scheme. Jennifer and Dave have printed
posters for the shop windows advertising the next meeting and
urging as many as possible to attend. Over a cup of tea in our
garden, she tells me that she fears the break-up of the community if Tesco is allowed to have everything its own way and
the shops in Silver Street start going broke. I ask her how she

defines community and she immediately says, 'There wouldn't be a Christmas shopping evening if we didn't have the small shops. And I wouldn't be able to go out to the shops, discover I'd left my purse at home and still be able to come home with food for supper.'

Politicians like to eulogise the importance of communities but do little to maintain them. The separation between those who make decisions and those who bear the impact of them is one of the most destructive aspects of corporate globalisation. The board members at Tesco head office don't give a fig about whether Bryan Ferris and Clinton Bonner go broke; their decisions are taken purely to maximise corporate profit, without any sense of who will be affected. Over in Chard, Colin Rolfe and his fellow workers at Hygrade are now only days away from their factory being shut. Again, the footprint of Tesco is stamped all over a decision that will have disastrous implications for a local community. There is something hugely reassuring and quite irreplaceable about doing business with your neighbours and with others who have a vested interest in the community. Communities aren't created by any one single thing and they can't be created overnight, as planners and politicians fondly imagine every time they sign off the plans for a new 'dormitory' town. Communities grow out of people stopping at the teashop or the pub for a beer, getting advice from the grocer about how long to cook the new potatoes, or ideas for a recipe from the butcher, from comparing opinions with other customers at the baker's and nodding hello to an acquaintance in the chemist's. They grow out of shared interests and concerns: how's your daughter doing, did your dad get his hip operation, how was the holiday? Individually each exchange is trivial, but added together they weave themselves into something unique. The sum of all those casual encounters creates a feeling of respect and trust, a resource in times of personal or neighbourhood need.

'Can you imagine,' I say to Jennifer, 'going into Tesco and

saying that you've left your bag at home, and can you have tonight's dinner on credit?' We laugh together, but it isn't a laughing matter. The global economic system under which we function shatters communities in its wake and, once shattered, it is almost impossible to glue things back together. Profit has become the sole pursuit of our society and it has overthrown morality as a way of deciding the validity of a decision. That makes it all right for three hundred men to be chucked out of work in Chard, because it will make more money for Tulip and Tesco, and all right for Tesco to move into Ilminster and change the traffic flow, because it will make more money for the head office. It is considered sissy to be concerned about the worries of little people, as though a politician would be seen as less powerful and macho if he said that there needs to be a limit on economic progress. But study after study has proved that once basic needs are met, money does not enhance the happiness quotient of humankind.

Still, there's no denying that there is a lively sense of involvement and anticipation in Ilminster. The shops are all displaying protest signs and leaflets with the times of the next town meeting. In preparation for the meeting a Battle Bus has been hired, which will leave the town square at one o'clock to take anyone without transport out to Dillington House in time for the meeting. Tickets are on sale for £5, but that sum will be refunded when you get on board. On the way to Mr Rendell's I bump into Mr B senior, a clutch of leaflets in his hand and an undeniable spring in his step. There is much talk about 'last-ditch efforts' and 'final stands' and 'now is the time to be counted'.

Sometime during her first night with Robinson, Babe digs a hole under the fence between his run and the sows' woodland home and escapes, virginity intact, back to the safety of life among the girls. 'Typical woman,' David says dryly. 'She's going to give in sooner or later.'

Just after lunch on 23 May, Bramble goes peacefully into labour, lying on her side on a thick bed of straw, breathing deeply and evenly until the moment when she gives a shudder and a loud grunt, flexes her hind leg upwards, and out slither the wet little piglets, sometimes nose first, sometimes feet first. With the umbilical cord firmly attached and a coating of mucus all over their bodies, the little pigs sneeze and cough to catch their first breaths. But within seconds they are up on their feet, struggling to find purchase on the straw, groping their way round Bramble's fat back legs towards her teats. Josh and I, who've never seen piglets being born before, crouch on the straw and rub Bramble behind the ears. By nightfall she's given birth to ten.

Even though they are Robinson's babies and he's a pure-breed saddleback, they all look like Gloucester Old Spots, pink and spotty and naked, with silky ears lying flat against their heads. While Bramble is deep in labour, David notices Guinness shoving her shoulders against the gate into Robinson's run, trying to get in where Babe has just broken out. Wondering if she is on heat, he opens the gate and Guinness shoots through. Robinson is instantly aboard. They stay locked together for a full twenty minutes, not moving, staring straight ahead, looking bored and disinterested, barely exchanging a grunt. When Robinson has finished he lies down under a tree and goes to sleep while, a few feet away, the first Mrs Robinson puffs and pants and brings his first ten children smoothly into the world.

11

The Midsummer Pig Roast

Six days before the Dillington meeting Bryan assembles the towns' traders to decide how best to structure the face-to-face encounter with the councillors. Thirty minutes will be allocated to the public and no one individual is allowed to speak for more than two minutes. Bryan suggests that those who wish to speak should have specific points to make, not general objections based on future fears. However well-founded these might turn out to be, he knows that this isn't going to cut the mustard with the councillors. To date, 4,344 people have signed the petition objecting to the one-way system and the names have been sent to the town council. Bryan also said that he's sent two letters to Terry Leahy, asking for Tesco's comments on the impact of the one-way, but so far the superstore's CEO hasn't bothered to reply.

Richard Westworth, owner of Sarah's Dairy, the cheese shop on the site where David's uncle once ran his butcher's shop, reports on the impact of a recently implemented one-way system in nearby Tiverton, where he has a branch of the dairy. Although a bigger town, Tiverton echoes Ilminster's current predicament because the one-way system was implemented to accommodate increased traffic following the opening of a Tesco superstore. His business is down 30 per cent, and a local wine merchant, The Jolly Vinter, has suffered 25 per cent losses. Richard thinks several shops might close before the end of the year. David Bailey reiterates his environmental concerns about the extra miles cars will be travelling. The question of the emergency services and the increased distances they would have to travel is also discussed.

Sitting behind me in the Minster Rooms beside the church, Councillor Adam Kennedy mutters his objections to every point. 'All these issues have been discussed when the planning was originally approved,' he announces. There are angry murmurs around the room.

Bryan ploughs on with the central point of the meeting. It is important, he says, that the issue of the road is kept separate from the issue of the supermarket. But, as it becomes apparent just what has happened, that is clearly impossible. Under the arcane methods by which planning works in this country, the decision to build a supermarket couldn't be granted until the traffic flow was changed. But at the time that the town considered the traffic flow, no one knew which supermarket was bidding to come to Ilminster, or how big it was going to be. Additionally, at the time of the road decision, everyone understood that the car park would remain where it was, and the store would be built further out of the town. Now the situation is radically different: the supermarket is going to be built in the car park, the car park is being pushed out into the fields, and the store that is coming is Tesco, the biggest and probably the most ruthless of the big four.

David has seen a cable TV programme about a couple with a farm in Devon: they've got pigs and sheep and cows but their real money comes from city folk who want to work on the farm and pay £200 a week for the privilege.

'That's quality, what a deal . . .' he keeps saying, as we're walking round the nursery working out when the different vegetables will be edible. 'We could buy a caravan and park it over here.' He points to the area under the corner of the walls, at the end of the rows of herbaceous plants. 'To think they'll pay *us* to work *here*.'

'Why don't we just stick them in with the chickens, in tents, or in the huts?' I ask. He beams. He thinks I'm serious. I imagine David trying to rent out what is left of the pigs' caravan in the wood and we both start laughing. But it isn't such a bad idea: David would be a great teacher to anyone who wanted to learn the ropes, but I know that it is just further confirmation to him that people in the cities lead grim and deprived lives. Ever since we began the project I've been trying to persuade him to come and visit us in London, to see for himself just how much money topiaried box balls, or privets shaped like clouds, or bay trees sculpted into descending spheres sell for in the posher London garden centres. I know he doesn't believe that they can fetch several hundred pounds apiece. Like paying to live in a caravan and working ten hours a day, breaking your back weeding carrots, it's just another sign of the insanity of city folk.

Just before the end of May, I spend the evening with Zoe and Colin Rolfe at their house in Chard. Hygrade is now in its last days. Of the workforce of 305, 282 are still without jobs and the factory gates will shut for the last time in less than five weeks. Colin and the union representatives have fought hard: Tulip is also closing another one of its meat packing plants in nearby Chippenham, making a total of 850 workers qualifying for redundancy. Another £850,000 has been wrested from the management, to be divided up according to length of service. For Colin, with only a little over two years' service to his record, it means another £400, but for some of the workforce it takes their final settlement to five, six, seven, even eight thousand pounds.

The few that have found jobs have found them in the food sector, but the wages are low and most jobs involve travelling. Colin's mate Lance, who held the rank of supervisor at Hygrade, earning around £18,000 a year with overtime, is taking a menial job at Ilchester Cheese which pays only £5.50 an hour and involves an hour's commute a day if he wants to carry on living in Chard.

Colin plans to go on working with Tony Dowling to try to change the law about redundancies: the minimum £290 per worker per year in work was originally intended to apply only when a company had gone bankrupt and the workforce faced being laid off with no money at all. 'That's what it was instituted for, but what's happening is that successful companies are using it as a guideline for how little they can pay. If the firm hasn't gone broke, we want to see redundancies being fixed according to the weekly pay each person has been receiving.' We are sitting in their neat, orderly kitchen. Outside, Jack is playing in the small garden. I'm annoyed with myself for forgetting to bring a bottle of wine or a gift of some sort. We're drinking tea, but it's now seven o'clock and I suspect that they'd like a drink.

'I've had an offer of working as a store man in a packing company,' Colin says, 'but none of us has any qualifications. They've set up a Skills Analysis Training to help people find jobs, but they're only interested in getting you a job, any old job, not in helping you find a job that might be different, or better, or require a bit of new training. It's all about keeping the unemployment figures down. I know that I've got this job for the simple reason that I have a licence to operate a forklift truck. And that's it. It's not because I've got A levels in English and maths, or because I once stood as the Labour candidate for this region.'

Colin is starting work on 5 June, and he doesn't plan to stay for long. He's hoping to work in one of the council-run homes for troubled young adolescents in Chard, a job he could do for three days a week, spending the rest of his time working with the union to try to ensure that others in his position don't get screwed by the vagaries of the redundancy laws.

'All this has made me pretty sure of one thing: I don't want to go on working till I drop, making profits for some bloke in Denmark, or some geezer sitting in Tesco's head office.'

'Colin would be great with young kids in trouble.' Zoe beams at him with pride. They're in this together, as a couple, and their affection is solid and durable. 'Because Colin is getting a job straight away, we won't have to live off the redundancy,' she continues. 'But lots of the guys, they haven't done anything about finding work. They just seem to think, hey, great, I'm going to be getting five or six thousand pounds, so much more money than I've ever had in my life, and I can live off that for months. What's the worry, what's the problem? There'll be another job.'

Lots of them, Colin says, have a staggering level of debt: £2,000 on one credit card, £1,500 on another, £1,800 to the bank, a mortgage, loans from stores to cover the cost of TVs and fridges and cars. One of their friends owes over £18,000 and Colin is worried that he's not planning on using his redundancy money to start clearing his debt.

'It just hasn't hit them yet what is going to happen,' he says. Zoe gets up to put the kettle on for another brew. There's a small telly in the corner and Jack's toys and books are spread out at one end of the table. 'It will, and soon. The first lot of us are leaving at the end of next week and I think that will really bring it home.'

I ask if people are frightened yet. He shakes his head. Not yet, but they will be.

Colin is also worried about the growth of racism in the town. Chard, he reckons, has coped well with the influx of Portuguese workers, who now make up almost half of the Oscar Mayer workforce of eight hundred. He grins. 'Everyone thought there'd be a barney when the European Cup was on in 2002 and our guys were playing the Portuguese in Portugal. But it went OK. But when the factory shuts and there's some two hundred guys on the dole and there's just no work around here, then they're going to be fair game . . . it wouldn't take much to stir it up.'

Chard is home for Colin: after he left school he went to London, where by twenty-two he was the manager of the Athena poster shop in Piccadilly's Trocadero Centre. He'd commute in from Stanmore every morning, hating the fact that no one talked to each other on the Tube and that, even after a couple of years, he knew so few people in the anonymity of the city. He's had several jobs in Chard, including running his own company, which was where he met Zoe, his second wife, but his world revolves around a town, not around a job, and that's how he wants it to stay.

Zoe gives me a lift back to Ilminster. On the way she tells me that she ended up in the West Country because her father and his sister were evacuated as children to Somerset: they were posted to Ashwell Farm House, one of the properties on the Dillington estate. If I stand in the field where we're now growing carrots and leeks and fighting the pheasants over rights to our newly sprouting cabbages, I can look to the west, and there is Ashwell Farm, a big, square stone building. Zoe wasn't sure exactly where I lived, so she hadn't mentioned it before. Now we drive round there together, to have a look at the house, standing like a black shadow in the dark of the night. We're both rather taken aback by the coincidence. 'My aunt, Brenda, she lives in Ilton and I know she'd like to tell you about it. If I remember rightly, her mum, my gran, got a job up at the big house as a cook. And I think my granddad worked in the gardens.'

We lose the war of the one-way system. After it is over, it becomes clear that it wasn't a contest at all, that minds were made up long before the meeting takes place at Dillington Park on that Tuesday afternoon. The Battle Bus set off from Ilminster town square shortly after one o'clock with seventy-eight people aboard. It rained heavily over the weekend, but by Tuesday the weather is turning again, and the sun feels hot when it breaks through the scudding clouds. Twenty years ago the council converted the old stable block into classrooms and one long hall, which can seat almost two hundred people. Wayne stages concerts there, and I've once given a talk about newspapers and on another occasion interviewed Fay Weldon in front of an enthusiastic local crowd. That day, the room is packed when Charlie and I walk in. Bryan has saved me a seat next to him in the second row. Charlie stands at the back. I look around; it seems that everyone I know in the town is there. There is Henry Best sitting next to Mr Bonner. Mr B is wearing smart mustard-coloured trousers, a yellowy tweed jacket, a blue shirt and a red tie. In front of them sit Dave Bailey and Jennifer. Aaron Driver is next to Elizabeth Ferris. Everyone nods and smiles, most are holding bits of paper on which they've written what they want to contribute to the meeting. In the front, on a small raised stage, sit the Somerset councillors in whose hands the decision rests. Two women and one man and, on one side, members of the transport group and, on the other, three men, including the clerk of the meeting, who are supposedly responsible for ensuring that all legalities are followed. Hazel Prior-Sankey, the senior councillor, occupies the middle chair.

She opens the proceedings: 'This meeting might get rowdy, please don't boo or cheer or clap and don't intimidate anyone, we want to be able to hear.' She says it with a smile but she's addressing the room in much the same way as a head teacher might scold a group of unruly ten-year-olds. Hazel is about my age and I think she looks friendly and open-minded. 'We cannot alter the planning – all we can do at this meeting is deal with the TRO' – short for traffic regulation order – 'We only have a small remit. We're elected to represent the public interest, but what is in the general public's interest may not be in the interest of a small group.' The small group means all of us, sitting upright on smart metal chairs covered in blue velvet. Bryan stirs beside me and mutters, 'Oh God . . . that means she's upholding the decision.' His pessimism seems premature, but I can see other faces droop. The councillor to Hazel's right, a blonde woman in her thirties called Cathy Bakewell, speaks up: 'Why has it all taken so long? When this was first agreed there weren't many protests, just twenty-seven people against the traffic scheme and of that fifteen were against Tesco.' She doesn't invite any answers and her words hang in the air like ominous clouds. 'I'm going to allow an hour for people to speak,' Hazel announces. 'Two minutes each, that's all.' She's increased the time allowed, but I have no idea if this is a good sign or not.

Henry Best goes first. He's written out his short speech in his spidery handwriting and he towers over the seated rows like a benevolent giraffe. 'I represent the Somerset branch of the Campaign to Protect Rural England, and our job is to protect the market towns of England. You may not have to consider the controversial decision of a superstore. The laying of that cuckoo's egg has already been settled. But you must deal with the consequences – more traffic, longer journeys, higher pollution, disruption of community services, turning an old, workable street system into one huge roundabout. The majority of people do not want this TRO. They said so in a petition: we have signatures representing 3,540 souls and Ilminster's 2001 population was under 4,000. Please heed the cry of those whom you have been empowered to represent. More would have been here but for having to earn their livings or care for their children.'

As Henry speaks, Dave Bailey waves a copy of the petition in the air. He is still waving it when Henry sits down. There is a burst of noisy applause. People stamp their feet on the floor. Hazel and the other councillors look annoyed and tap their pencils, points down, on the table in front of them. 'Can I ask you to refrain from applause as this will intimidate anyone with a different point of view,' she says in a school-mistressy tone. The stamping increases, accompanied by loud boos.

Looking upwards across the old stable courtyard, I can see a thin sliver of blue sky where puffy white clouds are moving eastwards, like giant tennis balls pumping out of a machine. Down in the courtyard, the flagstones surround a small pond, dense with irises and water lilies: it was once the main water trough for the horses, the place where Lord North's sweating animals must have come after bringing their famous master back home from Westminster when he was prime minister. Local legend has it that he once delayed so long at Dillington that he was too late to warn George III that he was about to lose the American colonies.

The meeting wears on. One by one the town's traders stand up to make their pitches. The room grows hot and someone opens up the big doors out into the courtyard. 'This will result in degeneration, not regeneration,' says Mike Fry-Foley. 'You do not need the wisdom of Solomon to realise that this will split the town in two,' says Clinton Bonner, whose shop, being the furthest from the car park and the supermarket, is likely to be hardest hit. There is a catch-22 element to the proceedings. The issue under debate is not the supermarket, but the super-market is the cause of the proposed one-way system. When planning was granted for the store, no one knew that it would be Tesco, or that by some sleight of hand the car park would be pushed out of the town and into the fields to accommodate the needs of the supermarket. The town seems to be fighting with one hand tied behind its back. Standing at the back of the room, looking over the shoulders of the two councillors who were for the one-way system, Mike Henley and Richard Jacobs, Charlie watches them writing notes to each other on a pad of paper. After I finish speaking, Mike Henley scribbles 'yet another supermarket ranter'.

We hear about the elderly, we hear from a driving instructor, we hear from someone in the first response unit for the emergency services. Next to me Bryan slumps lower in his chair. I am exhausted: I came that morning from the Hay-on-Wye book festival where the previous night I'd listened to Al Gore's impassioned speech about the environment. Dealing with climate change, he said, promised us a chance to create a better world where communities pulled together, united by common purpose. My ankle is hurting, my cheeks feel hot and, as we wait for Hazel to pronounce her verdict, I feel like crying.

'I want you to know that our decision has not been cooked up in advance,' she says, casting her vote in favour of the one-way system but noting that things could stay as they are until building work starts. Cathy Bakewell concurs, but says the one-way system should be implemented immediately, and the third councillor, who has sat silently throughout the proceedings, votes with Hazel. And that's it. We file out into the late afternoon sun, past the entrance to the main house and towards the park. I can hear the pigs grunting in the wood and the geese are making a racket from the other side of the trees. The Battle Bus is waiting in the car park, its engine already running, ready to take everyone back to town.

Charlie and I wave goodbye as the bus sets off down the single-lane track, scattering a large herd of sheep that are sleeping on the hot tarmac. We turn off the lane and down the path leading to the farm, where David is preparing the pigs' second meal of the day. The pigs start squealing, kicking at their metal feeders and pushing past each other in their anxiety to get to their food. Charlie gives my shoulders a rub as we watch the pigs guzzle up their dinner. 'Maybe it won't be as bad as everyone thinks,' he says, 'We've already got the Co-op and that hasn't caused any problems. Maybe it *will* stop some people going all the way to Taunton to go to Sainsbury's. We've got good shops in Ilminster. They'll be OK.' I'm grateful for his optimism, but at this moment it seems impossible to share.

At the Hay festival I interviewed James Lovelock, creator of the Gaia theory and one of the world's leading climatologists. Professor Lovelock will be eighty-seven on his next birthday but he looks much younger. He's small, trim and energetic, asking where he could go walking around Hay, saying six or seven miles along the river was just the ticket. He smiles a lot and it's impossible not to be charmed by his warmth. Even when we were on stage and he was delivering his apocalyptic message, the smile is still there, completely out of keeping with his words. If Professor Lovelock is right – and all the evidence suggests that he is – there is now no chance of reversing the climatic disaster that is engulfing the world. By the end of the century, the central latitudes will be uninhabitable, reduced to deserts where the wind howls and the dust blows. Nothing will be able to live there and the human population will be forced to flee north, where the climate will still sustain life. The British Isles and everything north will be habitable, so will New Zealand and the southern regions of South America. Lovelock was unfailingly bleak, delivering a message that no politician hoping to get elected or re-elected would dare to utter. He was telling us that all we can do is hunker down, start going back to the land, live more simply and set up small farms to provide food on a local basis.

I'd recently seen pictures of the deepest coal mine in the world, an open-cast mine in China where the coal had lain buried for fifty million years. Was this part of what Lovelock meant by Gaia's Revenge: that we were burrowing deep into the earth to extract waste that the earth had stored away so well, confident that it would never be brought to the light again? He nodded. I then asked him if, as we came to the end of the world's fossil fuel supplies, climate stability would be restored, that Gaia would somehow, in the nick of time, regain stability. He smiled and shook his head. 'It's too late for that.'

I told him about the farm and my plan, if we succeed in becoming economically stable, of trying to establish other small farms to feed other institutions, such as hospitals, large schools and prisons. As I push the gate open to allow David access to the pig feeder, holding it back against a small army of porcine strength and greed, I think about what he said. One day, in the not too distant, we're all going to be living off small farms like ours. I'd just read a news report from Japan, where the government is so worried about the potential collapse of the meat market that it is warning people that, within ten years, they may have to return to a largely vegetarian diet. It takes two kilos of grain to produce one kilo of chicken, but a huge seven kilos of grain to produce one kilo of beef and the world has only a limited supply of land on which to grow feed to fatten animals, rather than growing food which humans consume directly. About-to-retire Japanese baby boomers are being encouraged to start small farms in their retirement as they may be feeding their country in years to come.

I go back to the store house to fetch a plastic tray to collect the eggs, 129 of them requiring five trays and as many trips. Some of the chickens have become broody and, every morning, David sprays those that are sitting on their eggs with purple paint and then, if they're still there in the evening, turfs them off and out of the hen house. The eggs are warm, and so many different colours, some as dark as an autumn chestnut, through shades of toffee, cream and white. As I collect the eggs, I worry: will Daisy really grow old in a world where no one can live in Africa, or India, or the Middle East or the southern states of the USA?

In the office, next to the slogan about pigs being ready to fly, David's brother Julian has pinned up a picture of David holding a huge, ugly, ruddy coloured carp. The fish weighs thirty-four and a quarter pounds and it dwarfs David, who is kneeling down on one knee, holding the giant scaly beast towards the camera. David caught the monster on his week's fishing holiday to France. He'd gone there with Julian in 2005 and reckons he caught the same fish then also. 'A great way of making money,' he said. 'They cost about £500 but they get caught over and over.' It is the end of the second week of June and it's hot: 80°F and more by midday. The heavy rains of May seem like a distant memory. From the office where we're sitting, I can hear the thwack-thwack of the sprinkler systems as they pump water across the rows of carrots and beans. So far this morning, I've eaten a handful of small snap peas, a tender broad bean, its flavour sharp yet delicate, a couple of indoor flat climbing beans which are big enough to sell at £4.50 a kilo, a juicy spring onion and a still-too-thin though delicious carrot which is a week or so away from being ready to harvest. Fat-Boy has shown great interest in the proceedings, especially in the carrots: he loves all vegetables except for onions, garlic and cucumbers, and carrots are one of his favourites. I pull one for him and he chews it enthusiastically, thumping his shiny black tail on the baked earth before carefully dropping the spidery green leaves on to the ground. In a week, they'll be ready to sell, along with the beans and the peas, the turnips and beets. In the polytunnels, the tomatoes hang heavy and green, needing only days more sunshine to ripen them into delicious redness. Dark green cucumbers hang down under their big, ungainly leaves. Minute peppers are beginning to show beneath the foliage. The straggly leaves of the garlic plants have grown to two feet and the bulbs beneath the soil are swelling and ripening. Safe from slugs in boxes on top of straw bales, the strawberries are beginning to change from white to pink; soon, like the tomatoes, the sun will bring on the rich colour and the sweetness.

'It wasn't working out,' says David. He is drinking coffee out of a mug with a fat brown and white cow painted on the side and is wearing a grey T-shirt bearing the words 'Dowlish and Donyatt FC'. 'He just wasn't that interested in what happens here and when I told him that we couldn't go on employing him, he didn't say anything, didn't say that he liked working with the animals or growing stuff or anything. He just shrugged and said that he'd been thinking about retraining as an HGV driver.'

Charlie and I know that the question of Bob's employment at the nursery has been under question for the last couple of months. 'We don't have to work with him, David does,' Charlie had said to me recently. 'You and I can't interfere and we're not running a charity.' True, but I've been touched by Bob's willingness to give up his Saturdays to stand behind a market stall, dressing up in his best garb to flog herbs to the middle classes, clearly awkward that he isn't gifted with a snappy repartee which can turn the purchase of one herb into the purchase of three or four, but giving it a go, nonetheless. I feel bad that I don't know more about him, that he is going to pass through our lives, disappearing without leaving a trace. Once, when we were out together to fetch some chicken feed, he told me that his jobs never lasted long. As he said it, he shrugged, as though accepting that this would probably be his fate this time around as well.

'We can't afford him,' David says, knowing full well that this will be the clinching argument. He opens a drawer and rummages around for a pencil. 'Look,' he says, writing down numbers on a piece of paper. 'This week we've made £362 from the honesty table and from people wandering down here from Dillington House to buy plants. Plus we're owed money by Rowley for the eggs and we're owed money for the veg that we've sold to the House. We're going to break even this week, but we'd be in the red if we still had to pay his salary. And honestly, Rosie, he just didn't get it. He never got enthusiastic about anything. Me and Adrian, in just one morning this week, we got through more than Bob and I could get through in two days.'

'How are we going to cope at the village open day?' I ask. It is now just two weeks till 24 June, the day when we are opening our garden, selling cream teas, helping to organise a bookstall, a bric-a-brac stall, and a plant and produce stall. Ellen Doble's daughter, Sandra, has organised an art exhibition which is going to be held in the village hall. In the evening, we've offered to hold a village pig roast, with one of our pigs as the star attraction. So far, almost eighty of the hundred tickets have been sold. On top of that, the second Montacute market is taking place the same day and our plan has been that Bob and I will go to Montacute leaving Charlie and the Bellew family to deal with events back home.

'Dennis is going with you.' I shrug. I like Dennis and I know we'll have a good time, but it doesn't stop me feeling sad that Bob has gone.

The weekend before the open day I take the dogs swimming in the pond at the end of the park. There's a rickety pontoon attached to the shore by a couple of wobbly planks which stretch out into the still, green water. The dogs, especially Fat-Boy, love swimming and they swim alongside me, every so often swerving off to investigate the thick plant life on the banks. Wild mint grows near the shore, and yellow flag irises and cow parsley crowd towards the water's edge, their reflections leaving streaky yellow and white patterns on the softly ruffled surface. Swimming is the only physical activity that has been completely unaffected by my accident and I stay in the water for over an hour, watching the swallows swoop down to feed, the dark brilliant blue of their heads and backs standing out against the sky, the red feathers round their beaks flashing in the sunlight. They fly with an effortless grace, soaring out of the sky, breaking the surface of the lake and scattering droplets of water that break into rainbow colours beneath their wings, then gliding upwards to turn and tumble in the air, as though the entire space above the pond is a playground for their acrobatics.

Every year since we've been at the Dairy House, the swallows have nested in the garage, but this year the roof has been repaired and the old nests have been destroyed. I was worried that they wouldn't return, but they have, to the shed which adjoins the garage, into a newly built nest in the eaves. They are wonderfully cosmopolitan, creatures that connect two continents and two entirely different ways of life, weaving the world together, crossing warring nations and increasingly unstable climate zones. What will happen to them, I wonder. According to James Lovelock, their winter world in North Africa will soon become so hot that they'll have to change their millennia-old migratory patterns, wintering here and spending their summers high on the slipstreams above the Norwegian fjords, hunting for flies in the endlessly long light nights of the Arctic circle.

Fat-Boy and Bingo crash through the reeds on the banks, the tall cow parsley waving above them, as they follow the smells of the water voles and the occasional moorhen. Fat-Boy glances up constantly; it is as though he is checking that he can see me and every few minutes he's back in the water, swimming out to touch me with his nose. When he swims, only the top of his head above his nostrils is visible above the water and his silky ears float out beside him. Using his tail as a rudder, he creates barely a ripple as he crosses the pond; he reminds me of a crocodile. He's so perfectly adapted to swimming, unlike Bingo, who swims in a frantic, jerky style, her head, back and tail well above the water, a nervous look in her eyes. Before we had Fattie, Bingo never went in the water, preferring to stay on the bank and bark at passing ducks. But she's a plucky dog and, even though she looks terrified, she hurls herself into the water alongside Fat-Boy and expends huge energy trying to keep up. On the bank, Bingo has found a two-foot-long thick stick in the rushes and I watch Fat-Boy try to take it from her, holding on to one end with his teeth, locking his front paws into the mud to increase his tugging power. Bingo growls back through her clenched jaws: at any moment, Fat-Boy could whip the stick away from the smaller dog, but it's a game they like to play and he's a generous-hearted animal. I let my feet sink down into the pond, feeling the water grow colder with every inch. Even though the pond is large and very deep in the middle and my bad foot has a tendency to buckle up with cramp, I feel safe in the knowledge that Fat-Boy would tow me ashore within minutes of my asking.

Under the overhanging branches of an alder tree, there's a cloud of brilliant-blue damsel flies whirring like small helicopters. This last week, from 12 to 19 June, the nursery has, more or less, broken even for the first time. Earlier today David went through the invoice book: even though he's exhausted, he's clearly thrilled. This is what we sold:

Monday 12th: Dillington House bought 234 eggs,
   12 lettuces, 5 kilos of rhubarb, 7 kilos of broad beans,
   4.5 kilos of peas, 12 bunches of spring onions,
   6 cucumbers and 5.5 kilos of flat beans.
   Total: £107.30. We also sold them 8 lavender
   plants for their garden: £16.
Wednesday 14th: 300 eggs at £37.50.
Thursday 15th: 246 eggs at £30.75.
Thursday 16th: 12 lettuces, 8 spring onions, 6 cucumbers,
   7.5 kilos flat beans, 6 kilos of Swiss chard, 3 kilos of
   turnips and 6 bunches of parsley. Total: £83.05. David's
   mother, Anne, bought £19.50 worth of plants for her

garden. Mike Fry-Foley bought a tray of eggs, 1 kilo of courgettes, 1 kilo of baby carrots and 3 lettuces. Total: £7.35. Two village residents bought eggs, plants and herbs totalling £44.70. Dillington House ordered another 200 eggs late in the day: £24.99. Rowley Leigh at Kensington Place took 250 eggs: £30. The honesty box earned £108.

We add it up on the calculator: £509.14.

We have spent: David £250, Dennis and Anne £60 each, plus £140 for a new electric fence for the pigs as the little ones have been escaping under the existing fences and wandering off to the car park, acting like schoolboys playing truant. Total: £490.

The cost of animal feed takes us over our break-even figure by about £50, but nevertheless it's the best week we've ever had and there's comfort in knowing that, for the next two months at least, we'll have even more vegetables to sell. This week, plants are being delivered to the flower shop in the nearby village of South Petherton and David is optimistic that we'll earn a steady £50–£60 a week.

I watch two damsel flies mating, the male curving his body into an arc above the female, binding them together so they seem as one, a triangle of flashing blue above the water. They move like creatures from an animated cartoon, in one place, then another, without ever apparently travelling in between. They don't make a sound, but they ought to, a sort of snapping sound as their bodies twist, turn and jolt. Up above, the swallows are rolling and diving through the sky, their fast, chattering speech sounding strangely human, like stutterers on speed. The Chinese believed that if you administered a broth made of swallows it would cure a person's stutter, but then there was also a cure for epilepsy that involved one hundred swallows, white wine and an ounce of castor oil.

The coming of the first swallows is universally regarded as a sign that the spring has detonated, as they begin their journey north only when the currents that carry them towards our shores heat up to 48°F. There are always the first birds, the outriders, who forge ahead a couple of weeks earlier than the rest and who often suffer because they get caught by a late frost. It proves the old saying, 'One swallow doesn't make a summer': one week of more or less breaking even doesn't mean that we're out of the woods but, like the single swallows of early spring, it is a very good sign.

Ten days before the pig roast, David phones Snells to book in one of the pigs. Too late. Snells are overloaded with work and they can't fit in a single extra pig, however much of an emergency. Fliers have already gone out advertising the week-end: open garden, plant stall, bric-a-brac, cream teas, guess the weight of the pig, produce, the art show and in the evening the pig roast, where for £5 you get a hunk of pork, apple sauce, stuffing, salad, strawberries and cream. We were planning to eat Lobelia, and though I am relieved that she's had a stay of execution, this is a potentially embarrassing turn of events. By the time David tells me, he's already ordered a whole pig to be picked up from a farmer in Barrington, which will arrive boned, roasted and ready to eat. It will cost us £190.

Outside our gate, David has mowed a rectangular space where a marquee will be erected. Our own village marquee has been put up outside the village hall. The plan is that the pig roast will take place by the hall where the art exhibition is on display and that the rest of the events – cream teas and stalls – will happen in the field beyond our garden fence. Mary Rendell gave me the name of the keeper of the Barrington village tent and at two o'clock on the Friday afternoon six men, like characters from *Last of the Summer Wine*, disgorge themselves from two tiny cars and bang in poles and ropes and bright red strapping and the tent is up. Cars and vans bustle to and fro from the village, carrying trestle tables and grey plastic chairs, benches and tea urns, cups and saucers, plates, cutlery, extension leads, paper napkins and two large teapots. I haul boxes of old books out of their storage place in the garage and lay them out on tables. Old clothes are hung up on a portable clothes rail. David and Adrian drive to and from the nursery, delivering plants which we arrange on another table inside the marquee, sheltered from the hot sun. I position a small, sturdy, square wooden table by our gate and write out price-of-admission labels and arrange the raffle prizes – two bottles of Vladivar vodka, three bottles of wine, a plastic flagon of local cider, a box of Fonte Verde spa treatments which I was given after a visit to an Italian spa two years ago, a wooden picture frame, a large box of After Eights, a mechanical apple-slicer and corer, and a huge bowl of fruit wrapped in clear plastic and topped with a huge green and red ribbon which John Rendell has donated. I pin up a sign saying 'Garden Open – £1'. Manning this desk is to be Charlie's job for the day. Inside our house my old friend Sophie is at work in the kitchen, making the stuffing and the apple sauce and preparing food for the lunch party we've decided to hold on the Sunday.

Sophie lives in Norfolk and she's cooked for Charlie and me at every occasion in our married life when we have reckoned we can't cope. Our wedding, our birthday parties, our big parties which are just for the hell of it. The dogs are devoted to her and greet her when she arrives like a long-lost relative. My stepson-in-law, Charlie, husband of Miranda who is David Leitch's eldest child, has arrived to take photographs of the pigs and the garden and the preparations. Miranda and her two children, Fen and Jessie, are due to arrive tomorrow, when Daisy is also coming in on the morning train.

As the sun sets into a vivid red and pink work of art beyond the vegetable garden, I feel a rare sense of comfort and ease.

We've been at the Dairy House for just under four years and the coming weekend feels like a celebration of all that Charlie and I have made together here. I walk round the garden, conscious of its loveliness in the fading light, the scent of roses heavy in the hot night air. In the wood, a lone green woodpecker is still hammering away in a branch above my head. The old oak by the pond is silhouetted against the coming night, the five-foot bamboo wind-chimes that hang from one of its branches still and quiet. Somewhere an owl hoots and another answers back. I sit down on the bench by the oak, leaning back against its gnarled trunk, and watch the still water of the pond grow steadily blacker as the light leaches from the sky. In the undergrowth beside me I can hear the rustling of some small creatures of the night, and out in the fields a cow is lowing. I look out across the pond towards the park, where the oaks are slowly being swallowed up in the darkness, their shapes becoming increasingly indistinct until they are just a blacker part of the blackness. It would have looked the same to someone sitting under this oak tree for the last few hundred years, the continuity of nature which feeds and nourishes the soul. The owls start hooting again, several of them this time, calling and answering each other, their eerie cries carrying through the stillness. I imagine them swooping down through the darkness to find mice or frogs or other small creatures who haven't managed to get home in time. In East Anglia an old chimney stack was recently opened for the first time since it had been capped in 1913. Barn owl droppings revealed an exotic and varied diet: bats, water shrews, dormice and weasels, bits of frogs, swallows, yellowhammers and a great many different insects. Then the darkness is broken by the lights of Charlie's Land Rover travelling through the park and within minutes the dogs are racing noisily through the garden, barking wildly as they charge through the flower-beds.

Fat-Boy wakes us up at five o'clock, leaping on to our bed and lying down above the pillows, more or less on top of our heads. It's a position he favours, since, once *in situ*, he is impossible to ignore. I heave him off but he keeps padding around the bedroom, sticking his nose into my face, until I have to get up, kick him out of the bedroom and shut the door. The reason for his early morning energy is apparent as soon as we get up. The previous afternoon, Mr Bonner delivered eight chickens, two small truckles of Cheddar and a whole Somerset Brie for our lunch party. They have all been stored in the spare fridge outside in the shed, but dear Mr B also included a whole Cheddar, 56 lbs of it, a magnificent circular wedge covered in cheesecloth, yellowed and stained from the fat which seeps from the cheese. He sent it along as a loan which he thinks we might like to display on the table. The unexpected gift has been placed on the floor of the back kitchen, well sealed in a brown cardboard box. It was too heavy to move on to a shelf, so I left it there when I went to bed. But I forgot about Fat-Boy. Overnight, he's bitten his way into the box, ripped a hole through the tough cheesecloth and eaten a large circular chunk out of the cheese. Charlie is less than amused and he sets off to town to tell Mr B of the disaster that has befallen his cheese, which, we reckon, would have cost over £400. Fat-Boy goes too, sitting in the back, looking terribly pleased with life. I set off to Montacute with Dennis, the back of the van full to the roof with herbs and flowering plants, brown bags of beans, peas and beetroot, bunches of freshly picked carrots with long green feathery stalks, herb biscuits in small clear bags, and recipe leaflets jammed in wherever there is a spare inch.

The incident with the cheese has made us late, and by the time we arrive at the market it is already full of stallholders setting up their wares under green-and-white-striped umbrellas. The sun is beating down on the old stable yard as Dennis, who's recently had a hip replacement, and I, with my limp, start carting trays of herbs and plants across the cobbles towards our stand. Our second disaster of the morning: we've

forgotten to load the trestle and have to borrow a small table
from the National Trust. We can't fit much on it, just half a
dozen herbs, four boxes of eggs, a small pile of recipe booklets,
a selection of sweet herb biscuits and a dish of herb dip with
some cracked biscuits. We arrange the trays of flowering white
daisies and purple osteospermums, chives, parsley, rosemary,
basil, sage, oregano, thyme, coriander and chervil on the
ground around us. When we've finished, I walk back to the
archway to inspect our efforts. The stall looks good and
inviting, a leafy contrast to the tables bearing rows of jams
and honey, cheeses, pies and tarts and cakes, or the mobile ice-
trays full of pork or lamb or water buffalo, or the table
groaning with handmade chocolates which is next to the
one selling fish from Bridport. The edible samples smell
delicious: scallop shells full of prawns, slivers of squid in
oil and smoked trout pâté, chunks of black, bitter chocolate,
little wedges of ewes' milk cheese, squares of stoneground
brown bread spread with local organic butter, slices of hot
sausage flavoured with apple, leek and herbs, crispy bacon
which you can skewer on a toothpick, broken water biscuits to
dip in jars of strawberry and raspberry jams.

As we wait for the market to open I walk round the stalls,
saying hello to the stallholders I've come to know over the
summer: Sue and Keith Warrington, Andrew Moore and his
wife Lavinia, and Tanya with her wonderful display of fresh
bread and croissants, as well as the organiser, Elaine Spencer-
White. At the water buffalo stand, the whiskered butcher tells
me that they expect to take over £1,000 by lunchtime. Then it
is ten o'clock and a sudden rush of people surge through the
archway into the stable yard, falling on the food stalls with the
sort of voracity normally reserved for the first day of the post-
Christmas sales. Supermarkets might dominate our retail
world, but for the first hour of that Saturday morning I reckon
any retailer would have been pleased to be there, as money
briskly changes hands and food is eagerly stashed away in

shopping bags. By providing people with trolleys, supermarkets ensure that people usually buy more than they actually
need and I reckon that if there'd been trolleys at Montacute the
stalls would have sold out of food within the hour.

Business on our stall is intermittent. Despite my certainty
that snacks would boost our income, our piles of biscuits are
only rarely sampled and hardly ever seem to translate into a
purchase. Dennis and I shelter from the heat and bright light
under our stripy umbrella and drink tepid water out of plastic
bottles. I ask him if he and Anne are worried that David is
overworking and he laughs and shakes his head. 'He's tired,
but he's always wanted to do something like this.' David is
their eldest child, born in 1968, eighteen years after Dennis
and Anne married. They met as teenagers, when Anne lived in
Dinnington and Dennis in the nearby village of Kington.
Anne and her sisters would bicycle to Dinnington to catch the
bus to Taunton on a Saturday afternoon to go shopping.
Dennis and his mates would whistle at the three long-legged
blondes as they cycled by. Their first date was a walk around
the village. They married when she was nineteen and Dennis
was twenty. Dennis's job as a cowman, and Anne's looking
after the calves, meant six-and-a-half days' work a week,
including weekends, bank holidays, Christmas Day and
Boxing Day. His first job in the early 1960s paid £12 per
week; his second, towards the end of the decade, paid £22.
The days would start with bringing seventy cows in from the
field, milking them, turning them out again, trimming feet,
performing artificial insemination, cleaning and washing the
milking parlour, hauling the churns out on to the roadside
stand for the delivery lorries. They lived on the farms where
they worked so they'd go home for breakfast and home again
for lunch. Then in the afternoon the process would be
repeated. 'You worked until the work was done,' he says
ruefully. By eleven-thirty, I'm feeling exhausted. Dennis, by
contrast, is chipper and engaged.

A couple dragging two thirteen-week-old Labrador puppies on leads stop to buy three rosemary plants and a white daisy. The dogs are soft and cuddly, their coats hanging loose on their bodies, just waiting to be grown into, and it reminds me that before Fat-Boy became an advanced eating machine he cost us hundreds of pounds in ruined shoes, chewed table legs and all the knobs on the lower drawers of a small chest of drawers which we keep cutlery in. The puppies, collapsed on the cobbles and panting from the heat, look incapable of any crime.

Dennis and I make £136.50 in four hours, far less than Sue Warrington with her jams and tarts and cakes and far less than Sue Tutton and her Gloucester Old Spot sausages and burgers. But, on our modest financial scale, it isn't a bad result. Back at home, the village fête is, if not exactly in full swing, at least jostling along merrily. I am pleased to see that my old black coat with the mink collar has been sold for a tenner. The coat was left behind in the vast cold store beneath Harrods where customers used to pay to store their furs through the summer months to stop the fur from moulting. The fur fridge was in operation for over a hundred years, until one day seven years ago Mohammed Al Fayed decided to stop selling fur in the store and to close down the store room beneath. Coat owners were contacted to come and retrieve their wares but, several months later, Al Fayed was left with about thirty furs in various stages of decrepitude and he handed them out to anyone who came by to visit. I went for lunch with him and he thrust three coats into my arms as I was leaving. They were strangely cut and looked awful. Two were long gone, consigned to the charity store in Westbourne Grove, but the third, which I had worn occasionally, hung on in my wardrobe for years, gathering dust and gradually moulting. I didn't see who had bought it but I wonder if I'll see it around town in the coming winter.

Charlie is doing a brisk trade in raffle tickets and Sophie is serving cream teas with scones and strawberry jam. The bric-a-brac stall, manned by Barbara and Steve and our friend Gillie, is overloaded with the unwanted contents of drawers and cupboards and shelves. There are a pair of green chintz curtains patterned with pink roses, three rolls of white em-bossed wallpaper, a pair of brass oak-leaf candle-holders, a cream and white wedding hat, a set of Henna Body Art, a thousand-piece jigsaw of the Houses of Parliament still in its plastic wrapper, a watercolour of St Margaret's Bay, Kent, painted by Linnie Watt in 1879, a wine rack, a relaxation bath pillow, a pair of bedside lamps with white shades covered in yellow roses, and two electric hand-mixers with a pictures of Antony Worrall Thompson on the side. The contents of the tables have the same unexpected intimacy that comes from seeing the faded wallpaper of a stranger's bedroom suddenly exposed after a building has been ripped apart by bomb blast.

Daisy has arrived from London while I've been at Montacute and she and her friend Rowland have organised a game of cricket with Miranda's two children, Fen and Jessie (Daisy's niece and nephew), and some other children whose parents have dragged them along to the fête. David has corralled two pigs, a young saddleback and an older Gloucester, behind a wooden gate in our garage and Joss is busy selling tickets to the 'guess the weight of the pig' competition.

I'd wanted to bring the Empress over to the garage so, like her namesake, she could star in a fat pigs event, but she is now *too* fat to be moved in the small trailer, so smaller pigs were called up for duty. Four people ask Sophie if we're not leaving it a bit late in the day to kill the Gloucester ready for the evening's hog roast, which, as she says, just goes to show that even in the heart of the country, people know astonishingly little about how food gets to their plates.

It isn't the hottest day of June, but out in the full glare of the sun the temperature is in the mid-eighties and our wood garden becomes a welcome retreat from the glare. In the three years since we first hacked out the brambles, cut down the trees that were crowding too close and built the paths and the pond, nature has reasserted herself and the dense greenness of it all is like a plunge into cool water, the foliage muffling and muting any noise. The willow house looks slightly crazy, with the springy leaves clustering towards the light on the top of the house, leaving bare branches down below, but the plants round the pond, the gunneras, the twisted willow, the marsh marigolds, the wild irises, with their soft blue petals marbled with delicate black veins, and the smaller marsh primulas all look like they have been growing there for years. There are ferns, which unfold their curled-up tips every spring, there is an Indian bean tree whose autumn flowers smell like lily-of-the-valley, there are some spiky dark-green hollies, red-stalked brambles, day lilies in huge clumps and hostas in their myriad shades of green. The sunlight filters through the trees, casting shadows and reflecting off the pond. It is amazing how the plants are growing to fill the spaces between the trees, forming their own complicated patchwork on the ground. In a few years, the shrubs and small trees will reach upward to fill in the air beneath the overhead canopy. Here there are no straight lines: the paths bend and weave, the outline of the pond is the sort of wobbly circle a child might draw and the great big chairs made out of tree trunks are rough and misshapen. But it is lovely and it's our creation, something we've watched grow and change, seeing how the light plays along the edges of the trees, never the same at any hour of the day. Standing in the wood, looking out at the park, where some twenty people are eating cream teas sitting at trestle tables, it feels like being underwater, the bright intense light mercifully out of reach.

By 7.30 p.m., Sophie and I have set up the pig roast on the grass outside the village hall. We've heated up three of the huge joints, weighing about twenty pounds apiece, in our oven at home. I didn't realise that the small kitchen in the hall

doesn't have an oven and I've had to beg oven space off Margaret Morgan, whose house adjoins the gravelled car park. By eight o'clock there's a hungry line of people scooping up chunks of pork, placing them on fresh white baps, then smothering the meat with apple sauce and stuffing, coleslaw and lettuce, which we picked from the garden moments before leaving. Sophie carves the pork and I sit behind the bowl of stuffing, ladling out portions as I am worried that it will run out if left to a free-for-all. For fifty quid, I've hired the services of Ron, a musician from Beaminster who plays a medley of tunes on his accordion. 'My Old Man Said Follow the Van' flows into 'Galway Bay', then 'Roger de Coverley'. Inside the marquee David has laid out straw bales for seats, and by nine o'clock there must be over one hundred grown-ups and children, eating and laughing, and jigging around the tent to the strains of Ron's increasingly Scottish airs.

Inside the village hall there's a small, cosy bar, home of the Whitelackington Social Club. Behind the bar, there's a row of upended bottles along the wall: Glenlivet, Famous Grouse, Bell's, Smirnoff, Martini. On the wall beside the bottles there's an old black and white picture of one of the village houses on fire. Underneath it says 'Fire at Bill Spinks' Forge, 1935.' Another depicts the fallen Monmouth Tree, site of a legendary meal eaten by the Duke of Monmouth when he stayed at Whitelackington Manor in 1680. Legend has it that a great lunch took place under the spreading shade of a chestnut tree, thought to have been planted in the Norman Conquest. It grew to over fifty feet with a girth of twenty-five feet. Monmouth drew a crowd of two thousand who pushed over a hundred yards of wooden palings in their eagerness to hear him speak. The tree survived another two hundred years and was then destroyed in a hurricane on Ash Wednesday 1897. There are two well-loved pictures in the hall, one showing all the villagers outside the hall celebrating the Queen's Jubilee in 1977 and another showing the village again, twenty-three years later at the millennium. But tonight they're nowhere in sight, safely tidied away to make space on the walls for the paintings and photographs on display for the art show. I find a small watercolour of our house, painted the previous summer by Penny Hawkins, and I buy it for Charlie for our seventh wedding anniversary the following weekend.

I like being in the village, but I'm pretty sure that I wouldn't have liked the village at all when I was twenty-one. I like the feeling of safety it gives me, of being part of a continuous line of people who've lived, worked, partied, married and died within the confines of this single street with its single row of small houses. It's a feudal place where Ewen, our landlord, still owns many of the houses, as his mother and grandfather did before him, but it's all well looked after, with pretty gardens and neat front gates and a sense of knowing who everyone is and where they fit in. Its cosiness could alternately succour or swamp you, and I find myself thinking of the quote from Rebecca West's *Black Lamb and Grey Falcon* that hangs on the wall of my study to the left of the window which looks out over our London garden:

> Only part of us is sane; only part of us loves pleasure and the longer day of happiness, wants to live to our nineties and die in peace, in a house that we built, that shall shelter those who come after us. The other half is nearly mad. It prefers the disagreeable to the agreeable, loves pain and its darker night despair, and wants to die in a catastrophe that will set back life to its beginnings and leave nothing of our house save its blackened foundations.

If Professor Lovelock is right, then the human race is hell-bent on choosing the latter option, and I know that in my life I have veered between the two, frequently pulling the plug on safety and contentment for the seductive dangers of unknown shores. The older I get, the more I realise that planning the future is a largely useless exercise, as full of the possibility of disappointment as of fulfilment. The Buddha knew that all we can really count on is today and, just for today, I am happy and I am where I want to be and that, for now, is enough.

12

The Return of the Large Blue

Charlie and I spend the evening of our seventh wedding anniversary, 1 July 2006, crouched together on a tartan rug, waiting and watching out for badgers. We are with my old friend Mike McCarthy, who was the news editor at the *Independent on Sunday* when I first became editor and is now the environment editor of the daily paper. Mike and his two children, Flora and Sebastian, are sitting on an adjacent rug, under an overhanging tree beside a stretch of open water in nearby woods. David has assured us that it is a good place to see badgers.

There is a strong smell in the air, not the sharp, slightly acrid earthiness of foxes, but certainly of a wild animal. The day has been hot and the sky is quite clear of clouds. A fuzzy crescent moon is slowly shifting through the lower part of the sky, moving towards the west as the darkness falls. We sit quietly, listening to the furious chattering of the rooks, the crows and the ravens who are settling for the night in the trees above our heads. The darkness comes gradually, gently sucking the blue out of the sky and reducing the trees to outlines, just shapes, the curves broken by tendrils and branches. As the details fade, the English woodlands become as thick as any tropical jungle. A heron flies across the pond, its cry more like a dog's bark than a bird's call; settles heavily on to the branch of the fir tree that hangs over the water and perches there, poised against the darkening sky like a Japanese painting. Suddenly, the birds fall silent, as though they've all decided it is time to go to sleep, and in the sudden silence we hear rustling noises from the trees behind.

Charlie sees it first: a snout peeking out from the long grass and the brambles which edge the wood, barely discernible amid the dark shadows of the overhanging branches. But then it moves forward and is out on the path in front of us. It isn't a big badger; he was probably born earlier this year and he moves at a fast trot, low slung to the ground, his thick tail bumping along behind him. Flora and Sebastian gasp. He looks almost pure black but a badger's fur is actually white with black tips, and as he moves there is an occasional flash of lightness. He heads first towards the pond, but then he hears us or senses us nearby and breaks into a run, passing in front of us towards a dense thicket of brambles.

Round us, badgers are the most common road kill. Several times, driving home late at night down narrow Somerset lanes, we've come across one on the road, startled in the car's headlights. My friend John Mitchinson, who lives in my cousin's village of Great Tew, has eaten badger ham, which he said was delicious, and we once sat next to a woman at a Sunday lunch party who claimed to have made an edible stew from a dead badger she picked up off the road. We stay there in the darkness long after the badger has made his brief appearance. Flora and Sebastian fall asleep. I watch the moon move across the sky towards the west, sinking lower and lower till it disappears below the level of the trees and the blackness becomes complete.

The following day we meet Martin Warren, head of butterfly conservation in Britain, and Jeremy Thomas, author of
Butterflies of Britain and Ireland, to visit the sites where the
Large Blue, officially extinct in 1979, has been reintroduced
to the countryside. We meet in the car park behind the pub
in Compton Dundon, a small village just north of Somerton.
Our destination is a steep bank at the southern end of the
nearby Polden Hills. We climb up a hilly path, through
tangled trees and bristly shrubs where wild pale-blue irises
peek out of the boggy places under the heavy branches,
through a hunting gate and on to a dramatically sloping,
south-facing meadow above the railway line where the
London–Penzance train, the First Great Western, whistles
by every twenty minutes or so. The precipitous field is
carved into tiny terraces, created over the centuries by
snowfalls and etched further by the travels of sheep. At
first site it looks uninspiring, just an ordinary meadow, the
grass kept trimmed by grazing sheep, a scattering of trees
and brambles breaking up the turf. But in the hands of our
guides, it becomes anything but, and for a moment I'm
transported back to that day in Africa, looking down at the
insects with Daisy beside me, touching my elbow and saying,
'Mum, it's nature's SimCity.'

Beneath our feet the life going on is every bit as complex and
interdependent as on the African veldt. We're all just too
snooty to realise that our own backyards hold such riches. We
find flowers: the yellow bird's foot trefoil so beloved of
bumblebees, the purple sweet scabious which is also known
as the Mournful Widow, yellow rock roses, wild geraniums,
wild parsnips, clovers, thyme, the delicate mauve and white
flowers of eye bright, yellow spotted cat's ear, the pinky red
pyramidal orchid, yellow melilot, silver weed with its delicate
leaves beneath its strongly coloured yellow flowers, spiky
agrimony and salad burnet, which we grow in our herb garden
and sell on our herb stalls. There are chiffchaffs singing in the

branches of a field maple, swallows on the wing, a pair of magpies pecking the ground for grubs. We crouch to look into the tunnel of a funnel spider's web, its tightly woven cone-shaped web opening out to create a landing place for un-suspecting insects. Martin gently touches the outer edges with a piece of grass, sending vibrations back to the waiting spider. The small black insect quickly comes out, looking around for the prey which he believes has landed in his lair. There are Brown Argus butterflies feeding on the rock roses, a Six Spot Burnet Moth hovering near the brambles, an Emperor Dragonfly pulsing through the air. And then Jeremy points to a small blue butterfly, fluttering slowly across the hillside, maybe a foot above the ground. It keeps changing directions, hovering for a moment, then moving on, as though searching for something.

It is an astonishing colour. When at rest, with its wings folded up, it looks brown, with black spots and a blueish tinge near its abdomen. But in flight it is a beautiful blue, shimmering in the sunlight, changing colour as it dips and flutters through the sky. Jeremy follows the Large Blue as she drops down towards a low-growing bushy thyme plant and, closing her wings, lands on one of the deep purple flowers. 'She'll lay an egg,' Martin says as he crosses the hillside to another mound of thyme and points out a single tiny, white egg held between the rich purple flower heads. 'Look, here's one.'

The life cycle of the Large Blue is both bizarre and complex. Before laying her eggs, the female Large Blue will have mated. She will have found her mate earlier in the day and, following a brief aerial courtship, they will settle on the ground to pair for about an hour. When they part, she hides until her eggs are ripe. Then she sets off to look for a thyme plant on which to lay an egg. This is what we are seeing now: the delicate blue insect twitching and rotating on the flower. She curves her plump stomach almost double, pushing the tip into a young bud. This process ejects a single egg and she will lay, on average, sixty eggs in a day.

Jeremy takes up the story: 'The eggs will hatch after five or ten days and the tiny caterpillars will burrow into the flower to feed on the pollen and seed. Even though each egg is laid singly, many Large Blues may choose the same plant. It's not uncommon to find four or five eggs, and I once found a hundred!'

But, he explains, most will die as the caterpillars are cannibalistic in their first life stage, and only one will ever survive on each flower head. After two or three weeks, each surviving caterpillar will complete the skin changes and develop the organs needed for the next phase of its life. The most important of these is a tiny honey gland which secretes minute drops of sweetness to attract red ants.

Once its final skin moult is complete, and always in the evening, the caterpillar flicks itself off the thyme flower and drops to the ground, where it hides beneath a leaf or in a crevice. 'By doing this,' Jeremy says, 'it greatly improves its chances of being found by the red ants, who forage in the early evening.' When the ant does find the caterpillar, it taps its body, causing the honey gland to produce more secretions, which excite the ant. It recruits others and they crawl all over the caterpillar, milking the gland and licking up the juices. Eventually they wander off, leaving the original ant with its find. That ant is possessive, and Jeremy says he has seen fights to the death when ants from different colonies try to milk the caterpillar as well.

Eventually, the ant decides to adopt the caterpillar, tricked into believing that it is an ant grub by its touch, scent, hairiness and size. Seizing the caterpillar in its jaws, he takes it down into the nest with the ant brood. Once safely inside, the caterpillar quickly transforms into the parasitic monster he or she really is. Puncturing the skin of an ant grub, he starts feeding on the fluid tissues. Between feeds, like an Eastern potentate, he reclines on a pad of spun silk. Soon the cater-pillar has become a bloated white maggot that dwarfs both the ants and the grubs. In the winter he crawls deep into the nest to hibernate; in the spring he resumes feeding. By late May, when it is time to pupate, the Large Blue chrysalis is about one hundred times heavier than when he first conned the hapless ant. He will have eaten about twelve hundred ant grubs, a greed which kills off many who have landed in nests simply not big enough to support their appetite. In the last week of June or in early July, the adult Large Blue emerges between eight and nine-thirty in the morning, when the ants are sluggish, to begin his five-day life on earth. As the hatching adult struggles to split open its pupal case, it gives off rasping bursts of song, which whip up the ants into a frenzy of activity. Despite the Large Blue's murderous assault on their nest, they accompany the insect along the narrow passages towards the light, milling around excitedly while the butterfly makes its way up a shrub to inflate its wings. After a forty-five-minute rest, the wings have set hard and it is ready to fly.

While Martin and Jeremy alternately tell us the story of this strange, convoluted life-cycle, I watch the Large Blues fluttering above the thyme plants, occasionally dipping downwards, apparently checking whether this plant or that would make a good home for their eggs. After they were officially declared extinct in 1979, Jeremy led a team to Sweden in the early 1980s to regions where Large Blues were living in habitats almost identical to southern England. He brought back the grubs, placed them in the nests of the red ants on these banks and brought the Large Blue back to life in the British Isles.

The proceeds from the fête and the pig roast have meant a good month's cash flow. The plant stall at the Dairy House

took £195, Dennis and I made £125 at Montacute and the
honesty table earned £75. If it hadn't been for the problems
with the pig, the hog roast would have earned the nursery
about £150. In the event, on that bit of the proceedings we
have barely broken even.

By the beginning of July the garden is an anarchy of
rampant growth. The once neat rows of small seedlings have
grown into dense jungles of leaves, spilling over each other,
fighting for their share of light and soil. In the polytunnels
the fat ripe tomatoes hang like scarlet jewels from the vines.
The squashes, their leaves as big as pizzas, sprawl across
their beds, an exotic tangle worthy of a Rousseau painting.
The rows of pepper plants in the tunnels are heavy with huge
green, orange, red and purple fruit. On some plants there are
as many as ten large peppers, barely visible under the lush,
luxuriant foliage. The slugs are eating the lettuce leaves, but
the lettuce leaves are winning. Up on their straw bales, the
strawberries flourish. High on their trellis network, the
runner bean plants make shiny little red flowers and fat
juicy beans hang from the stalks in bundles of three or four.
The plants are going about their business, doing what they
know how to do and doing it well, reaching for the sun,
fighting for space in the soil, ripening their fruit so that the
seeds will guarantee them life in the future. The order of the
garden and the choice of what we grow may be David's
doing but at the same time it is not; another force has taken
over here, something that springs eternal, that carries on
through wind and rain, roots questing down into the earth to
find the right combination of nutrients to create the beans,
the carrots, the onions, the garlic – a lush, fecund world. We
might not think that plants move, but they do; they're as
alive as the pigs, just growing at a different pace.

Our potatoes, in rows along the west wall of the nursery,
bear their white, star-shaped flowers with the purple and
yellow flecks in the centre. When you reach down into the

earth and run your fingers round the cold moist spuds, or accidentally slice through one and let the smell of all that richness, that earthiness, float upwards, there is something primitive in the moment. We plant them, but they do the awesome business of growing; they're domesticated but they're wild as well. That's what the smell says.

Out in the fields around the nursery, it's a different story. Ewen Cameron grows industrial quantities of potatoes, and their process from seed potatoes to supermarket shelf is a tale of high-tech automation worthy of a factory manufacturing ball-bearings. I ask Chris Wilson who runs the farm to take me through the annual cycle. He gives me a print-out entitled 'Field Applications from 04/04/2006 to 14/09/2006' which sets out exactly what is applied to his crop of Main Field Estima potatoes throughout their growing season. Spraying begins before the potatoes are planted, on 4 April, with an overall dose of Nitram Fertiliser. Six days later, two more fertilisers – 2.8.28 + 30so3 and Amm N 34.5 – are sprayed on to the earth. On the day of planting, 18 April, the first fungicide of the season, Amistar, is deployed. Amistar protects against black dot, a disease that causes black splodges on the spud. Its damage is purely cosmetic. Amistar goes into the ground along with the seed, Estima Se2, and on top they spray Mocap, the only chemical Chris describes as nasty. It is an organophosphate and it kills the wire worms which might eat holes in the potatoes which supermarkets would immediately reject, again on cosmetic grounds.

Then there's a breathing space until 16 May, when the first of the weedkillers are applied after the potatoes have germinated but before their leaves have emerged above ground. Linuron inhibits germination of any invading plant life and Pdq, a contact killer, makes sure that anything that has germinated and started to grow is stopped in its tracks.

On 3 June, just before the rows close – when the leaves of one row of plants meet those of the next – Chris begins spraying for blight. Blight is the disease which wiped out the Irish potato crop, turning the plants and spuds into black sticky goo. It is a fungus and its spores travel so quickly that a ten-acre field can be completely destroyed inside of five days. Blight germinates only when the weather is sufficiently humid and warm, and on a small hill outside Chris's office there's a weather station which records temperature, humidity, wind speed and the dew point. The device is paid for by Branston, the UK's largest potato packer and one of Tesco's biggest suppliers. The information from the station is relayed to climatologists in Holland who in turn feed it back to Chris via a forecasting software system he subscribes to for £600 a year. He shows me how it works. On his computer screen a series of brightly coloured graphs with red jagged blocks indicate the potential for high humidity and a purple and yellow series of graphs monitor how much of the leaf area has been successfully sprayed with an anti-fungal agent and when it will need spraying again.

Thus, in the year 2006, anti-blight sprays were applied to the crops eight times between 3 June and 18 August. The fungicides used were Shirlan, Fubol Gold, Option, Rhapsody and Ranman Twinpack. Farmers without this sophisticated forecasting system tend to spray every week. With the monitoring device, Chris not only cuts down the number of times he has to spray; it also allows him to use the most appropriate spray for the current conditions. The crops get some more positive help too: on 9 June they apply a trace element called Maghos, which Chris describes as a tonic for the soil, and on 28 June and again on 7 July they apply a trace element called Root 66. Root 66 consists of magnesium, phosphorus and nitrogen, which the overworked soil runs out of – an appropriate name for the one relatively healthy part of the process.

On 8 July, a slug-killer called Omex Sluggo is applied to the crop. It is mixed with Adjuvant Oil, which makes the slug-killer easier to adminster. Then, when Chris judges that the potatoes are the right size, the crop is 'finished'. On 18 August a herbicide called Spotlight is sprayed over the plants. Finishing is farming speak for killing, stopping the natural growth of the potatoes when they are at the optimum size for sale to the supermarkets and thus to our plates. Neat, round, not too big, not too small, smooth, blemish-free, very much like the factory product they almost are. A mechanical strimmer takes off the leaves while Spotlight knocks off the stalks.

Two or three weeks later the skins on the dormant potatoes will have hardened to a point where they can be harvested by a huge machine which can collect up to twenty-five tonnes in an hour. Then they're transported on to a conveyor belt, which sorts out the sizes and shakes off the mud. The majority of the potatoes are then stored in one of three huge barns, lined with a dull yellow insulation material. Over roughly three weeks the temperature is reduced to less than $2\,^{\circ}\mathrm{C}$, the point at which the potatoes become virtually dormant. Left at room temperature, they would continue to grow, sprouting leaves and smaller tubers.

But those spuds destined to become crisps – which we prefer to be a cheery golden colour – cannot be allowed to chill. Chilling changes the chemical structure of the vegetable, and the resultant crisps would fry into a dull brown colour. So, to stop them sprouting, crisp potatoes are stored in an insulated barn and sprayed with CIPC, a sprout suppressant. CIPC mimics a hormone that makes the potatoes dormant. It's never used on potatoes destined for baby foods because it might have adverse side effects, but, as yet, no one really knows for sure just what its possible side effects might be.

All this doesn't come cheap. The chemicals cost £600 an acre, irrigation £100, planting £45 and harvesting £70. Add to that each acre's share of machinery which, bought new, comes to over £300,000. One-third of Chris's crop will be chucked away, deemed too bumpy, blotchy, small, big or generally misshapen to grace a Tesco shelf. Some of that will go to animal feed, but some of it will be literally left to rot. In Germany, he tells me, big potato growers now have plants on site which turn the rejected spuds into bio-fuel. Every acre yields about seventeen tonnes and for every tonne of potatoes they actually sell they receive £103. It sounds good; it's not. If a third of the spuds are rejects, that means each acre yields twelve tonnes. At £103 per tonne, each acre earns £1,236. Direct costs add up to £815 per acre, without factoring in the capital costs of the machinery, the storage sheds, fencing and so on. As ex-banker Andrew Moore, proprietor of the Somerset Wild Meat Company and purveyor of salt marsh lamb in country markets said, 'When your margins are low, you have to sell one hell of a lot of whatever it is to make any profit.' In 2006, Chris harvested 4,500 tonnes of potatoes, which made it a good year. Chris loves to farm because, like any good farmer, he wants to grow good food. Although the list of chemicals is long, it is less than many of his competitors, who add chemical fertilisers to the mix and spray for aphids every two weeks. Chris leaves nature to take its course with aphids, relying on natural predators to deal with the insects.

At the door to the barn there's a big box of spuds which are there for anyone who works on the farm to help themselves. Even though they all know that there is no difference, as far as taste is concerned, between smooth or lumpy potatoes, ones that are blemish free or ones that have black splodges on them, Chris says that the misshapen ones are always left behind.

Bramble's piglets have discovered that, after they've squeezed out of their pens through the squares in the pig wire, they can then squeeze themselves under the main wooden gate leading into the nursery. I find them there early one morning, their tails wagging with pleasure as they hoover their way along a line of green French beans, emitting little grunts of pure delight and pleasure. A game of chase ensues: through the celery, across the carrots, down to the bottom of the garden, round the raspberry cage, until finally they are cornered in between the polytunnels where the strawberries stand in boxes on top of bales of straw. They admit defeat without much of a fight, blinking in the morning sunshine, like a team of delinquent schoolboys who've been caught smoking behind the potting shed. They are in varying degrees of dishevelment: a muddy nose here, a bent ear there, an uneaten bean still protruding from the corner of one mouth. I walk towards them. They stand their ground for a moment, then turn and scamper off towards the gate and back to the safety of Bramble's accommodating and ample stomach.

The following day, Bramble is moved back into the girls' run. Her piglets are almost ten weeks old and it's time for her to have a break from motherhood before she goes back for another amorous encounter with Boris and his brothers. No one really knows how old pigs get to be, as even breeding sows are generally slaughtered once their fertility wanes. The exception was the pig of my friend Francis Wheen, the writer and broadcaster and one of the funniest men I know. In 1993, Francis and his wife Julia acquired a pig. They received a call from Julia's ex-husband, a farmer who lives a few miles away from their Essex home. He'd found a piglet running loose in the lane and no one knew anything about it. Would Francis and Julia like to give it a home?

She was the size of a puppy and, despite her squealing and wriggling, the family took the piglet to their hearts. They bought her a collar and lead and took her for walks down the lanes. But every few days, Francis recalls, he had to buy a new collar as Perdita, as they'd called her, from the Latin for 'Lost Girl', grew and grew until, within weeks, she was the size of a sofa. 'That's when we had to fence off much of the garden and designate it pig paradise. We built her a hut out of corrugated iron and concreted over a patio for her.'

For the next nine years she lived a pretty idyllic existence, befriending the dogs and ponies and chickens, and lying under the apple trees in the late summer waiting for windfalls to land in her mouth. She was fed a diet of pig nuts and boiled scraps: potatoes, carrots, cabbages. But her favourite meal was left-over pasta, particularly spaghetti. Francis and Julia had frequent discussions about whether they should look for a husband for Perdita, but they didn't know what they would do with the piglets. Their sow lived the life of a maiden, adored by the children and admired by their friends. Perdita's special friend was Julia. One freezing morning in the last winter of the sow's life, Francis woke up to find Julia gone. She'd got up early, found the pig shivering and snuggled up beside her on the straw to warm her up.

In her later years, Perdita became arthritic. The vet called regularly but could never answer any questions about her life expectancy because he, like other vets and pig-keepers, had never known a pig who had died of old age. Perdita died just before her tenth birthday. By then she found walking quite difficult, and she usually limped out of her house to eat her breakfast on her patio, where she'd sunbathe for the rest of the day. On this particular morning she wasn't there when Julia went out with her food. In the night she had somehow staggered about twenty yards to the far end of pig paradise and lain down under a tree. She refused all food, even bowls of milk and water and she turned her head resolutely outwards, away from the house and her home. In the evening, she was dead.

Not long before she died, a policewoman and an RSPCA inspector turned up saying that some passer-by had reported the Wheen household for neglecting their animals, specifically Perdita, aged nine, and Julia's old horse, Easter, who was then thirty-six. The policewoman said these animals clearly weren't in perfect condition and therefore should be put down. Francis retaliated by saying that they were just very old, like the Queen Mother. By the time she reached her hundredth birthday, would they like to see her put down too?

'We told the policewoman that if the animals became distressed, then obviously we would consider it, but that they were actually jolly happy and regularly visited by the vet.' As if on cue, Perdita started making her happy snuffling sounds and Easter whickered and nuzzled the WPC's ear. The following day, their vet rang up both the WPC and the man from the RSPCA to say that if they tried this again, he would sue them for slandering his professional integrity. Two years on, Francis and Julia still miss Perdita, with her expressive face and intelligent eyes which met you on the level, just as Winston Churchill said.

Three more pigs go off to Snells in early July. Charlie and I wait anxiously for the verdict from Rowley Leigh, who has received his pig via the fish lorry from Bristol. Three days later, he emails to say:

> Just cooked part of pig. Extremely good flavour, rich in taste and almost gamey. Skin and fat still a little thin for my taste. Any fat is too much for most butchers so never listen to Mr Bonner on this score.
>
> Beetroot and runners are excellent. Not mad about the courgettes. Turnips good and I haven't tasted the spuds yet, I'm afraid.
>
> What we want is fat – because it makes the meat so much tastier and lubricates it, you can cook it for four hours and it comes out like butter.

Mr Bonner describes it as a 'cracking pig' and, the day after the carcass is delivered, our name goes up on the noticeboard: 'Pork – Dillington Park Nurseries.'

We have four litters of piglets in less than two months from Bramble and Bluebell, and the two saddlebacks. Collette produces eight little piglets, all healthy and well, wonderfully attractive with their black and white markings. Her sister Cordelia, though, is a rotten mum. Late one Saturday afternoon Charlie comes running back from the farm to tell me that she's just given birth to nine piglets. It happened quickly, before there was a chance to move Cordelia out of the big wood, so she's given birth in the communal pig arc, surrounded by laurels and overhung by a big yew tree. I make my way across the rough ground towards the shelter. There is no sign of Cordelia: the nine babies are lying on top of each other in a pile, smooth black and white fur, eyes bright and open. I look around: the fat pig is on the far side of the wood, her head deep in a muddy hole, rootling for food. That night, the smallest piglet dies. The following day we move the newborns and their mum into the maternity shed, but Cordelia just isn't cut out for motherhood. She hardly ever stays in the shed, preferring to hang out near the drinking trough which she shares with the other female pigs, planting her two front legs in the water and making great efforts to heave her considerable bulk right into the stone trough, all the while keeping up a grunting conversation with her girlfriends in the next paddock.

The mewling piglets follow her outside into the baking sunlight. Two more die, of heatstroke we think. In the office there is a bottle of Nivea Factor 35 sunscreen which David rubs all over Josh, so we rub that on to the white parts of the little pigs. It does the trick and there are no more fatalities. As they grow bolder, the piglets discover that they can squeeze under the gate to visit their dad,

Robinson, who, unlike Cordelia, greets them civilly and doesn't object when they climb into his feeding trough, pushing his huge snout to one side to get at his rations. The Empress and Earl also give birth: a litter of nine, although one dies after two days. Unlike Cordelia, the Empress proves to be an exemplary mum, herding the piglets outside the hut for a feed if it is sunny, even washing them briskly with her tongue till they squeal for mercy.

At the beginning of August, David proudly hands us a sheet of paper on which he had itemised the cash flow for July:

Wages: Anne – £342
Dennis – £192
Adrian – £392
David – £1,000
Total: £1,926

Owing to David:
£416 – pipe work
£4.80 – stamps
£28.93 – mite spray
£66.56 – jam jars
£79.24 – wire posts for the turkeys we are planning to fatten for the Christmas market
£20 – diesel for Transit
£30 – diesel for red van
Total: £645.53

Money owed:
Dillington House: £1,350
Rowley: £1,207

Table: £110
Montacute market: £197
Total: £2,864

We had made a profit of £292.47. I look back at the
original monthly forecast, drafted in optimism when we
first had produce to sell in July 2005: £1,500 from Dillington House, £320 from eggs, pigs £600 from May 2006,
vegetable boxes £600, rare breeds £200. Clearly, we had
been over-optimistic. We sell less to Dillington House and,
to date, not a single vegetable box has left the nursery. The
rare breeds have also been a failure and we will have to sell
off all the birds except for the Orpingtons in the autumn
market sales. Our investment in fencing for small groups of
birds and the two incubators is, largely, a write-off. Our
pig-breeding has been successful but, in terms of having
pigs to sell regularly, we are five months behind our
original forecast. Boris, our chubby, spotted boar has
had so many courses of antibiotics in his short, unhealthy
life that he's probably infertile and will soon be turned into
sausages. One of his brothers has stepped into his place,
claiming his name in the process.

On the plus side, we didn't factor in selling vegetables to
Rowley, nor did we think that we would be able to
produce double the amount of eggs on a good day. Farmers' markets and the honesty table more than cover the
projected income from the boxes and, this autumn, we're
hoping to start taking orders for them as well. Our capital
costs have hugely exceeded our original plan, but our daily
running costs have been more or less consistent. Back in
the spring of 2005, we estimated that our plant stock
would build up to about £5,000 in 2006. We've exceeded
that and we've been selling plants steadily, if not in great
quantity, since April this year. It would be naïve to think
that Charlie and I might start getting a return on our

investment any time in the next few years, but I don't think we're going to go broke and that feels like a real achievement.

In the middle of August, while Charlie and I are away on holiday, a fox breaks into the chicken coop. The first time it happens, the electric fence is down because the pigs crashed through the wire and shorted the system. That night, the fox kills over fifty birds, biting the heads off four of them and killing the rest for the hell of it, chewing their necks or bodies. Some are still alive the following morning, weak with shock. David has to shoot them and burn the carcasses. Two nights later, the fox, no doubt egged on by his successful raid, digs a two-foot hole under the fence, approaching the chicken coop from the shelter of the wood. This time he destroys sixty birds, eating none of them and again leaving several half alive. In the nearby fields, the maize is shoulder height and the foxes are using the dense crop as cover. But David and Rodney, the estate gamekeeper, search through the maize and in the nearby woods and shoot twelve foxes over the following three days. The remaining chickens take almost three weeks to recover: they huddle in sad, frightened groups, staying near the chicken house and laying less than half their normal number of eggs. Our egg income, from a high of £160 a week, drops to less than £50. When Chris Wilson hears about the attack he says we are lucky to lose only chickens. His brother, who farms pigs in the south-east of England, has had newborn piglets stolen by foxes. Evidently they watch the mother giving birth and strike as the baby pig slithers bloodily to the ground.

One day in early September, Charlie and I are digging up weeds from a bed of leek seedlings. It is a warm day and in the polytunnel we're getting sweaty and hot. As we work we suddenly become aware of two black noses peering round the doorway. Two small saddleback piglets trot in and start munching on the lettuces. We shoo them out and they run off towards the feed shed. David shouts at them to get out. 'Those two,' he says, as he hustles them back into the yard, 'it's always those two. They're smart. They've decided to move in with the Empress and suckle from her along with her piglets.' Fat-Boy, who has been regarding the piglets with a bemused look on his face, joins in, helping to herd them along the path till they reach their own gateway. Later in the day, I spot the two of them hunkering down in the fresh soft straw that has been put out for the Empress and her babies, chewing contentedly on some beetroot leaves that were intended for the nursing sow. Later still, I see them lying on their sides, fast asleep and facing each other, their front hooves touching as though they are holding hands. One of the Empress's small black piglets has scrambled into the cosy space between their two stomachs and, lying flat on his belly, is sound asleep, too.

From trees lining the walls of the nursery we've picked peaches, apricots, nectarines and small plums. They've been juicy and delicious and as sweet as fruit grown in the Mediterranean sun. Next year there'll be enough to sell and, as the fruit is so good, this winter we're going to plant more trees. As the days draw in towards autumn and the hedgerows blossom with nature's own harvest of blackberries and sloes, and the squirrels give up their summertime thievery in favour of walnuts and beech nuts, we start making plans for next year.

Financially, we should be on a firmer footing: we'll have enough pigs to be able to sell at least one every week and we're talking to more pubs and hotels in the area about vegetable supplies. Once most of the rare-breed chickens have been sold, their runs can be turned over to more egg-laying birds. David wants to add beef cattle to our smallholding, rearing them in a two-acre field up by a tumbledown farm that we've got our eyes on. Bramble and Bluebell are pregnant again and we plan to buy one more breeding Berkshire, so Earl can look after a harem of two.

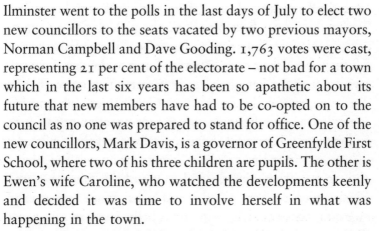

Ilminster went to the polls in the last days of July to elect two new councillors to the seats vacated by two previous mayors, Norman Campbell and Dave Gooding. 1,763 votes were cast, representing 21 per cent of the electorate – not bad for a town which in the last six years has been so apathetic about its future that new members have had to be co-opted on to the council as no one was prepared to stand for office. One of the new councillors, Mark Davis, is a governor of Greenfylde First School, where two of his three children are pupils. The other is Ewen's wife Caroline, who watched the developments keenly and decided it was time to involve herself in what was happening in the town.

In the first week of September, she takes her seat at the council table for a meeting to discuss plans for the road alterations. The meeting is being held in the hall at Swanmead Community School and I am surprised to see that well over a hundred people have turned up. We are all there to listen to Gerry Waller, managing director of the engineering firm that has been contracted by Tesco to build the store. Gerry is genial-looking, with a big smile on his flat face that reveals extensive, and expensive-looking, dental work. In order to change the slides on the carousel he has to keep walking in front of the white fold-down screen, and the coloured maps and diagrams make flickering patterns on his shiny blue suit.

'First we're going to build the new car park, then we're going to start work on the one-way system,' he begins with a brilliant smile. The audience starts to fidget. It soon becomes apparent that the agreement made between the council and the town at the Dillington House meeting no longer exists. The car park will be built by Christmas, but from January to Easter Ditton Street, the small street which connects the north and south of the town and currently a two-way thoroughfare, will be closed while Gerry's mob widen the pavements and change the traffic flow to one-way. The road will re-open at Easter, when work on the store itself will begin, but even though the store will not be open until the end of 2007, Ditton Street will be one-way from January onwards. There is a further act of treachery. While work is going on in Ditton Street, access from the new car park to the town is planned to run through Frog Lane, a small steep path that leads upwards to the east end of the town. Mr B's shop is the furthest away and this proposed 'access solution' is the worst possible result for him.

Gerry's bulky body keeps bobbing backwards and forwards in front of the screen. A woman in front of me mutters to her husband, 'Why doesn't he have anyone who can change the slides for him?' Gerry is at pains to say that anyone affected will be visited in due course by representatives from Tesco. He keeps on smiling.

At the end of his presentation, there are questions. Yes, Gerry says, he is happy to clarify that there *will* be access through Ditton Street while work is going on, but it won't be user-friendly, as the street will be full of bulldozers and machinery. When he has an answer, it tends towards imprecision. Often he doesn't have one at all. He can't answer questions about car park charges because he doesn't actually work for Tesco. He can't help Brian Drury, whose shop, B.D. Garden and Pet Supplier, is right in the middle of Ditton Street and who takes his deliveries of half-hundred-weight sacks of dog food and potatoes through the front door. In due course, Gerry says genially, Brian too will be 'getting a visit' from Tesco. He can't help at all when it is pointed out to him that, just two months ago, it was agreed that the traffic flow in

Ditton Street would remain two-way until Tesco actually opens, not altered irreversibly almost a year before.

There are currently 1,897 Tesco stores in Britain and in 2007 they plan to open another 153. Their expansion plans seem unstoppable, not just into the grocery business but into almost every area of life. Not content with 31 per cent of the entire grocery spend in this country, they also sell sofas, bikes, MP3 players, stuffed toys, arts and crafts, baby baths, pushchairs, nappies, tents, golf clubs, luggage, table-tennis tables, sports watches, power tools, pet food, car accessories, security alarms, high-pressure washers, shower units, shower curtains, towels, sheets and duvets, saucepans, mixers, cutlery, lighting, brooms, carpet sweepers, mats and runners, shelving and wine storage units, beds, dressers, cupboards, dining-room tables and chairs, pillows, cookers, ironing boards, sat-nav systems, broadband internet access, TVs, vacuum cleaners, car insurance, pet insurance, travel and life insurance, credit cards and loans, mobile phones with access to the Tesco network, gas and electricity supplies, holidays and flights, contact lenses, legal kits for making wills, conveying property, fighting small claims and getting divorced, flowers by post, low-calorie food, and they offer a diet club . . . and for every transaction you make, you earn points on your Tesco reward card which can go towards Tesco petrol, holidays, yoghurt, biscuits or home insurance, whatever you might want. Tesco, like it or not, are in our lives from cradle to grave.

I fear for Ilminster: 90 per cent of the money we spend in supermarkets leaves the local area. In 2000, the competition commission reported that if any one retailer accounted for more than 8 per cent of any one sector, then this was liable to lead to an abuse of power. Their recommendations were ignored.

When Tony Blair swept to power in 1997, the government went overboard to prove that New Labour would be a friend to business. But by allowing the supermarkets to grow so fast, New Labour has stifled the enterprise culture they claimed to support. They are a friend to big business, but not to business as a whole. In France, where supermarkets co-exist with thriving local economies, legislation limits growth. Even though the giant chain Carrefour fights for greater market share, the French government holds the line. No such measures currently exist in UK law and the presence of a massive supermarket in a small town not only jeopardises the businesses that exist but also stops other people from taking a chance. I know that John Rendell wants to sell his grocery shop, but I wonder who will be prepared to risk their capital on a vegetable shop knowing that Tesco is opening up five hundred yards away?

After the meeting ends, I walk up Ditton Street to the George in the Market Square with Henry Best, Clinton Bonner, Bryan Ferris and Aaron Driver from the wine shop. 'It's all done the Tesco way,' says Bryan, gloomily, as he and I negotiate the controversially small pavements. 'These aren't that small, are they?'

'The thing is,' Henry says, settling all six foot six of himself awkwardly on to a tiny chair by a small table in a corner of the public bar, 'if there were crested newts or dormice on the site we could hold it all up, possibly even stop it. Newts and dormice, they'll halt anything. Even the right kind of toad might do it.' He takes a long pull from his pint of Cottleigh, the local brew. Earlier that morning, in his endless quest for something to eat, Fat-Boy surprised a toad hiding behind the fifteen-kilo sack of dog food in the downstairs loo, but it wasn't the right kind. The right kind, from a conservation point of view, is the endangered natterjack, which has red spots on its back. Fat-Boy's small green discovery was just a common toad that probably started life in our garden pond. Still, it was exotic enough to give him a shock.

On the other side of the table, Aaron is trying his best to put a positive spin on the situation. 'We'll have to hold more festivals, organise shopping evenings. I could do wine tastings. How about barrel races? Pub Crawls? Cider and cheese? Raffles?'

I suggest buying brightly coloured plastic wheelbarrows, which could be left in the car park for anyone to use to cart their shopping from one end of town to the other. Aaron turns to Mr B, who's sitting at the end of the table. 'How about a raffle? I'll give a case of wine, you put up a whole turkey and if anyone can carry them all the way from our shops, up East Street, down Frog Lane and all the way to the car park without once putting them down, then they win!'

Mr B laughs, but despite Aaron's cheeriness we're a depressed group, sitting round the table while outside the window a full moon appears above the rooftops, bathing the Market Square in its silvery light. It feels hopeless. We are just a handful of local people, wanting concessions from a multinational, and we are losing every step of the way. Even the small but important agreement to keep the two-way system in place until Tesco opens its doors has now been ambushed by the engineers. On the way to the pub, Bryan has picked up that week's copy of the *Chard and Illy* from the garage. The same company which is developing the supermarket, Alborne Estates, has put in a planning application to construct 42 two-, three- and four-bedroom homes in the open area on the far side of the new car park. 'I wonder how long they've been cooking all this up,' he says gloomily, staring into his beer glass as though the rich amber liquid might reveal the answer.

'Isn't there an issue with the badgers?' asks Henry, reaching across the table to take the paper out of Bryan's hands. Holding the paper well out in front of him, he reads out the final paragraph of the article: ' "The planners say the northern part of the site will be kept free of development and will provide a foraging area for the badger community as well as a corridor linking the sett to the open countryside." Well, that's that, then, isn't it? Another bull's-eye for the planners.'

Henry gives me a lift back to the Dairy House. I stand by the gate, watching the tail lights of his car disappear through the park, the moonlight so bright I can make out the black and white markings on the young Friesians who are sleeping nearby under an oak tree. The evening has reminded me of an evening in late 2000, the day after it was announced that Richard Desmond had bought the *Daily Express*. With my friend and deputy editor, Chris Blackhurst, I had been in the Founders Arms, the pub across the road from the *Daily Express* building on Blackfriars Bridge. It was early evening, the busiest time in a newspaper's day as the office gears up for the eight o'clock deadline, but the two of us were shell-shocked by what had happened and this had been our first opportunity to get out of the office.

It had been an agonising autumn, knowing the newspaper was up for sale and living with rumours and uncertainty. Editing a paper means you are expected to know what's going on, often long before the rest of the world, and often you do. But in those autumn months, I was wholly in the dark about the future of the institution I worked for. Chris and I had been working together for almost six years by then; he'd come with me from the *Independent* to take on this seemingly impossible task. Now it was falling apart, our work and effort to transform the lumbering right-wing newspaper into a modern leftish publication that could challenge the supremacy of the *Daily Mail* just a distant dream. We felt both betrayed and powerless and, in my case, infinitely sad. In time, Chris returned to the *Independent* and is now the City Editor of the *Evening Standard*; he divorced and remarried and now has a new son called Archie. I often find myself missing his great humour, wit, intelligence and integrity. And as for me, unlikely as it might once have seemed, I now have a farm and own a part-share of sixty pigs.

I unlock the back door to let the dogs out into the garden and follow them along the grass path beside the long herbaceous border, and through the crooked metal gate into the wood. The moonlight is so bright that I can see the outline of the big oak tree in the flat reflective surface of the pond. The roots of an oak stretch for hundreds of yards and you are walking within the oak's domain long before you step under the first overhanging boughs. They branch frequently: the first roots are as thick as a man's waist, six feet from the trunk they're the diameter of a wrist, at thirty feet as thin as a pencil lead, at fifty feet as slender as grass and at one hundred feet thinner than a human hair. The smaller the roots, the less time they live: the thinnest are replaced several times a year but the hair roots, the almost microscopic ones that work in tandem with fungi to collect nutrients from the soil, survive for only a few hours. An average-sized oak has some five hundred million root tips which will graft themselves on to the root hairs of another tree of the same species. In time, an oak wood becomes a single living entity. If a tree is sick, or has been attacked, and can't feed itself through photosynthesis, the root system enables the other trees to keep it alive.

I lean against the gnarled trunk of the old oak. The night before the paper was sold I had invited Ewen and Caroline to dinner. It was the first time I had seen Caroline since the late 1970s. They came to our house in Notting Hill and the four of us walked round the corner to a now defunct restaurant in All Saints Road. I didn't often forget to take my mobile phone with me but I did that evening and when I returned, old friendships restored and promises to visit them in Somerset exchanged, I had twenty-three missed calls. On the front page of the following day's *Financial Times* was the story of the sale of the *Daily Express*.

What I didn't know then was that while those calls were going unanswered, I was rekindling a friendship which would, in due course, lead to this moment: leaning against a tree in a Somerset wood, watching the park glisten in the moonlight and listening to Fat-Boy rustling through the beech hedge in search of an old tennis ball, as he never considers it too late in the day for another game of catch.

FURTHER READING

Bakewell, Joan (ed.), *Belief*, Duckworth, 2005

Balfour, Lady Eve, *The Living Soil*, Soil Association, 2004

Baskin, Yvonne, *Underground: How Creatures of Mud and Dirt Shape Our World*, Shearwater Books, 2005

Bellamy, David, *Conflicts in the Countryside*, Shaw and Sons, 2005

Benson, Richard, *The Farm*, Penguin, 2005

Blythman, Joanna, *Bad Food Britain*, 4th Estate, 2006

Blythman, Joanna, *Shopped: The Shocking Power of British Supermarkets*, Harper Perennial, 2004

Carson, Rachel, *Silent Spring*, Penguin, 2000

Chatto, Beth, *Beth Chatto's Woodland Garden*, Octopus, 2002

Diamond, Jared, *Collapse*, Penguin, 2005

Don, Monty, *My Roots*, Hodder & Stoughton, 2005

Dunning, Robert, *A Somerset Miscellany*, Somerset Books, 2005

Flannery, Tim, *The Weather Makers: The History and Future Impact of Climate Change*, Penguin, 2006

Harvey, Graham, *We Want Real Food*, Constable, 2006

Hedgepeth, William, *The Hog Book*, Doubleday, 1978

Hillman, Mayer, *How We Can Save the Planet*, Penguin, 2004

Humphries, John, *The Great Food Gamble*, Coronet Books, 2002

Jenkins, Jennifer (ed.), *Remaking the Landscape: The Changing Face of Britain*, Profile Books, 2004

Kaminsky, Peter, *Pig Perfect*, Hyperion Books, 2005

Kohnke, Helmut, and D. P. Franzmeier, *Soil Science Simplified*, Waveland Press, 1994

Lawrence, Felicity, *Not on the Label: What Really Goes into the Food on Your Plate*, Penguin, 2004

Levitt, Steven D., and Stephen J. Dubner, *Freakonomics*, Allen Lane, 2005

Lien, Marianne Elizabeth, and Brigitte Nerlich (eds), *The Politics of Food*, Berg, 2004

Livio, Mario, *The Golden Ratio*, Headline, 2002

Logan, William Bryant, *Oak: The Frame of Civilisation*, W. W. Norton & Co., 2000

Lovelock, James, *The Revenge of Gaia*, Allen Lane, 2006

Mabey, Richard, *Nature Cure*, Pimlico, 2006

Maharaj, Niala, and Gaston Dorren, *The Game of the Rose: The Third World in the Global Flower Trade*, Institute for Development Research, 1995

Masson, Jeffrey, *The Pig Who Sang to the Moon*, Vintage, 2005

Maycock, S. A., *Livings from the Land*, C. Arthur Pearson, 1947

McIntosh, Christopher, *Gardens of the Gods*, I. B. Taurus & Co., 2004

Monbiot, George, *Heat*, Penguin, 2006

Pollan, Michael, *The Botany of Desire*, Bloomsbury, 2002

Porritt, Jonathon, *Capitalism: As If the World Matters*, Earthscan Publications Ltd, 2005

Prince, Rose, *The Savvy Shopper*, 4th Estate, 2005

Russell, Sir E. John, *The World of Soil*, Fontana, 1961

Schlosser, Eric, *Fast Food Nation*, Harper Perennial, 2002

Singer, Peter (ed.), *In Defense of Animals: The Second Wave*, Blackwell Publishing, 2005

Smith, Nancy, *The Story of Dillington*, Dillington House, 2000

Spencer, Colin, *British Food: An Extraordinary Thousand Years of History*, Grub Street, 2002

Stewart, Ian, *Nature's Numbers*, Phoenix, 1998

Taylor, Moss, *In the Countryside*, Wren Publishing, 2003

Thomas, Jeremy, John Heath and Ernest Pollard, *Atlas of Butterflies in Britain and Ireland*, Viking, 1984

Tudge, Colin, *So Shall We Reap: What's Gone Wrong with the World's Food and How to Fix It*, Penguin, 2004

Tudge, Colin, *The Secret Life of Trees*, Penguin, 2006

Watson, Lyall, *The Whole Hog: Exploring the Extraordinary Potential of Pigs*, Profile Books, 2004

Wiseman, Julian, *A Pig: A British History*, Duckworth, 2000

Young, Rosamund, *The Secret Life of Cows*, Farming Books and Videos Ltd, 2003

Young, William, *Sold Out: The True Cost of Supermarket Shopping*, Vision Paperbacks, 2004

Booklets and reports:

Conisbee, Molly, Petra Kjell, Juliam Oram, Jessica Bridges Palmer, Andrew Simms and John Taylor, 'The Loss of Local Identity of the Nation's High Streets', part of the *Clone Town Britain* report, New Economics Foundation, 2004

Gold, Mark, 'The Global Benefit of Eating Less Meat', Compassion in World Farming, 2004

Kingsnorth, Paul, 'Your Countryside, Your Choice', Campaign to Protect Rural England, 2005

Oram, Julian, Molly Conisbee and Andrew Simms, 'Ghost Town Britain II: Death on the High Street', New Economics Foundation, 2005

Picket, Heather, 'Supermarkets and Farm Animal Welfare: Raising the Standard', Compassion in World Farming, 2006

Pye-Smith, Charlie, 'Batteries Not Included: Organic Farming and Animal Welfare', Soil Association, 2003

Shah, Hetan and Nic Marks, 'A Well-being Manifesto for a Flourishing Society', New Economics Foundatin, 2004

Simms, Andrew, Julian Oram, Alex MacGillivray and Joe Drury, 'Ghost Town Britain: The Threat from Economic Globalisation to Livelihoods, Liberty and Local Economic Freedom', New Economics Foundation, 2005

Simms, Andrew, Petra Kjell and Ruth Potts 'The Survey Results of the Bland State of the Nation', part of the *Clone Town Britain* report, New Economics Foundation, 2004

Taylor, John, Matina Madrick and Sam Collin, 'Trading Places: The Local Economic Impact of Street Produce and Farmers' Markets', London Development Agency and New Economics Foundation, 2005

Tulip, Kathryn, and Lucy Michaels, 'A Rough Guide to the UK Farming Crisis', Corporate Watch, 2004

Woodward, David and Andrew Simms, 'Growth Isn't Working: The Uneven Distribution of Benefits and Costs from Economic Growth', New Economics Foundation, 2006

INDEX

Addis, Richard 126
African National Congress (ANC) 191
air travel 215–16
Alborne Estates 291
Alcoholics Anonymous 194
Al Fayed, Mohammed 262
Amazon rainforest 25, 106, 111
Anne, Princess 19
Armillaria root-rot fungus 107
Asda 218, 220
Ashdown, Paddy 164
Ashford Bowdler, Shropshire 7
Ashwell Farm, Dillington 243
Association of Convenience Stores 142
Atherston, Somerset 23
Attenborough, Sir David 120
Attlee, Joe 67–8
avian flu, see bird flu

badgers 268–9, 291–2
Bailey, David 233–4, 239, 244, 245
Bailey, Jennifer 233–4, 244
Bakewell, Cathy 245, 247
Balfour, Lady Eve 104, 105
  The Living Soil 105
Barker, Leslie 209
Barrington, Somerset 256
Battersea Dogs' Home 139
BBC 163, 175, 218
Beaconsfield Farm, Great Tew 80–87, 145, 154
Beaverbrook, Lord 132, 133
Beeching, Lord 227
Beedall, Thomas 207
beef 24, 25–6, 82–3, 86, 87
Bellew, Anne 12, 13, 93, 254, 255, 261
Bellew, David 152, 239–40, 249–50
  background 29, 65, 133

farm manager 6, 47, 93, 137, 155
  and farmers' markets 166–7, 229
  financial management 70, 94, 150, 251
  flying pigs notice 201, 249
  plans beef herd 286
  wages 13, 15, 93, 255
  work in nursery 9, 11, 32, 103, 257
  work with pigs 23, 50–51, 115, 134, 202–3, 226
  work with poultry 33, 60–62, 79, 97, 99, 103, 138, 249
Bellew, Dennis 23, 126–8, 134, 136, 154, 198
  background 132–3, 261
  and farmers' markets 252, 259, 261–2
  role at Dillington 12
  wages 13, 255
Bellew, Josh 9, 11, 67, 95, 151, 237
Bellew, Julian 33, 249, 250
Bellew, Mark 5, 6, 10–11
Bennett, Wayne 15, 35, 38, 140, 199, 218, 244
Best, Henry 197–8, 244, 245, 290–92
bio-fuel 278
bird flu 17–18, 23–4, 48, 97–8, 103, 115, 141, 173–5, 189
birds 119, 195
  eggs 100–101
  owls 258
  swallows 158, 252–3, 255–6
Blackhurst, Chris 185–6, 292–3
Blair, Tony 289
Blunkett, David 179
BNP 160–62
Bolehyde Manor 125
Bonner, Clinton (Mr B) 46, 63, 259

butcher's shop 24–5, 37, 143, 145, 175
and farm produce 65, 96, 117, 132, 149–50, 190, 282
and one-way system 178–9, 196, 213, 244, 246, 288, 290–91
Bonner Snr, Mr 149–50, 236
Borneo 120
Botswana 110
Boulder, Colorado 56
Boycott, Charlie (father) 80, 115, 135, 147, 192
Ludlow home 6, 7, 67–8, 100
old age 2–3, 4, 8, 145–6
Boycott, Collette (sister) 4, 74, 80, 146
Boycott, Mrs (mother) 68, 74–6, 81, 128
Boycott, Rosie
alcoholism 54–5, 57, 177, 230
car accident 52–7, 209, 230–31, 252
childhood 80–81, 85, 100, 115
depression 53–4
family background 81
financial insecurity 135
first marriage 133–4, 135–6
lack of interest in cooking 76
marriage to Charlie 2, 8
media career 3, 8, 17, 54, 76, 122, 133, 135, 175, 184, 227, 292, 294
religious views 56, 178, 191, 192–4
as single mother 36–7, 135–6
youth 7–8, 56, 203–5, 231
Bravais, Auguste and Louis 223
Brazil 25–6
Bristol University 122
British Meat Organisation 132
Bronx Zoo 23
Brown, Gordon 215
BSE 86, 174, 175
Buckmaster, Jonathan 126
Buddhism 56, 267
Bulgin, Mandi and Graham 196
butterflies 270, 271–3

Cameron, Alex 161
Cameron, Caroline 3, 287, 293

Cameron, Ewen 3–4, 10, 266, 275, 293
Campaign to Protect Rural England 45, 197, 245
Campbell, Norman 186, 233, 287
caravans 67–8
Cargen, Deirdre 196
Carman, George 2, 8
Carrefour 290
Carroll, Lewis: *Alice in Wonderland* 205–6, 207
Carson, Rachel: *Silent Spring* 86
cattle 133, 211, 286
Cellardyke, Scotland 173, 189
Chapman, Chris 179
Chapman, Lee 140
Chard, Somerset 29, 43, 46, 71–4, 159–64, 196–7, 235, 240–43
Chard and Ilminster Gazette 35, 142, 159, 160–61, 217, 291
Charlotte's Web 153–4
Charlton Mackrell, Somerset 3, 51, 227
Chedzoy, Somerset 169
Cheltenham Ladies' College 75
chemicals 219, 220, 275–8
Chester, John and Truda 133–4
Chicago Convention (1944) 215–16
chickens 11, 16, 17–18, 23–4, 30
bantams 62
battery hens 27, 71, 175
Brahmas 62
chicks 99, 115, 118
fox attacks 285
illness 97–8, 138–9
mating 141
rare breeds 11, 15, 62, 94, 99, 119, 137, 141, 151, 200, 201, 284, 286
rescue hens 138–9, 224
shed 103, 114
Sussexes 62
see also eggs
Christianity 190, 192, 194
Churchill, Winston 21, 281
cities 110–11, 239–40
climate change 119–20, 213, 215–17, 247, 248–9
Collier, Nan 44
Colombia 220
communities 234–5

Competition Commission 142,
    184, 289
Compton Dundon, Somerset
    270
Conegrey Wood, Oxfordshire
    81
Conservative Party 215
convenience foods 74, 77
Cooke, Alistair 84
Co-op, Ilminster 40, 43, 247
Cotehele Manor, Cornwall 139
Country Life 79
Countryside Agency 3
creationism 193
Cricket Malherbie, Somerset 132,
    142
Curzon, Lord 87, 167
Cyrus the Younger 208

Daily Express 3, 54, 123, 126,
    132, 133, 146, 174, 184–6,
    292, 294
Daily Mail 123, 124–5, 126, 179,
    184, 186
Daily Mirror 124
Daily Telegraph 110
Dairy House, Dillington 4–6, 16,
    253
    fête 252, 256–8, 262–4, 273
damsel flies 254, 255
Danish Crown 162
Davage, Angela 228, 232
Davies, Barbara 123, 124
Davis, Mark 287
DDT 89
debt 242
DEFRA 23, 97, 98, 115, 131–2
Denmark 74
Department of the Environment,
    Transport and the Regions
    (DETR) 41
depression 53–4, 112
Desmond, Richard 54, 292
Dickens, Charles 102
Diiulo, Arnaldo 124–5
Dillington Farms 93, 156
Dillington House 21, 218
    adult education college 4, 198,
        200, 244
    history 10, 207–8, 210, 246
    honesty table 198–200, 218,
        251, 255, 274, 284

produce supplied to 15–16, 32–
    3, 48, 69, 93, 96, 140, 156,
    251, 254–5, 284
public meetings 233, 234, 236,
    244–6, 288
Dillington Park Nurseries 6, 9–12,
    102–3, 206
    capital investment in 13–14, 70,
        93, 94, 113
    costs 13, 65, 69–70, 93–5, 140–
        41, 157, 255, 283
    employees 12, 49, 61, 70, 93,
        251–2
    expansion 69–70
    financial forecast 15
    income 16, 33, 63, 70, 93, 94,
        140, 150, 172, 200–201, 232,
        251, 254–5, 262, 273–4, 283–5
    potting shed 103–4
    problems 150, 154–5
    walled garden 9–11, 32, 94,
        207–9, 274
Dirt, Red 165
disability 230–31
disease 173–5
Dittisham Farm, Devon 135
Doble, Ellen 209–11, 212–13
Doble, Sandra 252
domestic cookery 75–8
Don, Monty 50–51, 52, 105
Dowling, Tony 72–4, 160, 162,
    163–4, 241
Drayton farmers' market 228
Driver, Aaron 37, 42, 143, 244,
    290–91
drugs 204
Drury, Brian 288
ducks 11, 30, 61, 151

Easter 190, 192
eggs 17, 78, 98, 103
    birds' eggs 100–101
    formation 99–100
    goose eggs 99, 190
    incubation 99, 115, 118, 141, 148
    production 33, 48, 61, 70, 95–
        6, 249
    sales 15–16, 23, 33, 96–7, 140,
        200, 254–5, 284, 285
    storage 103
    turkey eggs 148
Einstein, Albert 224

Elsworth, Callum 46
English Nature 39
Esquire 135
evolution 193
Excell, Margaret 187
Exeter 164
extremophiles 107

farm shops 169, 228
farmers' markets 87–92, 166–72,
    201, 227–32, 259–62, 284
Farmers' Weekly 212
farming 47, 82–7, 175
    agri-business 9, 44
Farrar, Andre 189
Feldman, Paul 198
feminism 76
Ferris, Bryan 46, 47
    head of Chamber of Commerce
        35, 186
    opposition to one-way system
        178–81, 187, 195–6, 213,
        238–9, 244–5
    opposition to supermarket 39,
        142–4, 290–91
    shop of 35, 42, 143, 181
Ferris, Elizabeth 35, 42, 144, 244
Fibonacci, Leonardo 222
Fibonnaci series 221–2, 223
Fielder, Sue 134–5, 136
Fisher, Stephen 179
fishing 67–8, 249–50
flowers 218–22, 270
food additives 71, 78
food miles 8, 15, 44, 71
foot and mouth 24, 26, 115, 212
Ford, Glyn 163
Fox, Richard 137
foxes 285
France 290
fruit trees 32, 94, 103, 286
Fry-Foley, Mike 142–3, 178–81,
    187, 196, 213, 246, 255
Fuller, Andrew 165–6
fungi 106, 107, 108

Gaia theory 248
Gallagher, Di 35
gardening 58–9, 208
geese 11, 30–31, 52, 65, 138, 153
    eggs 99, 118–19, 190
    killing 59–61, 62–3

Gellhorn, Martha 135
Genesis, Book of 193–4
Glastonbury Tor 91, 167, 191
globalisation 44, 235, 236
Glover, Charlie and Miranda 8,
    257
Glyn, Elinor 87
GM food 3
GMB 72, 160
Golden Number 223–4
Gooding, Dave 287
Gore, Al 247
Great Tew, Oxfordshire 28, 80–
    81, 85, 154, 269
Greaves, Gerard 123, 125–6
Green, Peter 42
Guardian 26, 77, 215
Guest, Henry and Rose 147
gypsies 51, 63–4

ham, processed 29, 165, 182–3
happiness 112, 236
Harpers Queen 135
Harris, Paul 125
Harrison, Sir Albert 104
Harrods 262
Hawkins, Penny 266
Hay-on-Wye festival 50, 247, 248
Heaven and Earth Show, The
    (BBC TV) 218
Hedgepeth, William: *The Hog
    Book* 102
Henley, Mike 187, 196, 197, 246–
    7
Henry VIII, King 234
herbs 91–2, 104, 150–51, 157–8,
    166–7, 170, 200
Hillman, Mayer 215, 216
Hollick, Clive 184
Homestead Act (USA) 188
honesty schemes 198–200
hornets 58
House of Commons 200
    Environment Committee 216
Howard, Charlie 20, 102, 170,
    257
    childhood 3, 5, 227
    children 7, 8
    cooking skills 78
    family background 147
    and farmers' markets 170, 228,
        229

financial management 70
as gardener 5–6, 8, 12, 55, 151
as lawyer 50, 56, 61, 175–6, 227
meets and marries Rosie 2, 8
personality 50, 56
teenage friendship with Rosie 2, 7–8
Hughes, Yseult 92, 171
Huish Episcopi, Somerset 228
Hunza Indians 104–5
Hygrade Meats, Chard 29–30, 71, 159–66, 169, 182–3, 235, 240–41

Ilizerof, Dr 53
Ilminster, Somerset 3, 24, 29, 34–9, 42–3, 46–7, 91
    arts centre 35
    Chamber of Commerce 35, 179, 186, 215, 233
    Christmas Shopping Evening 34–8, 42–3, 46–7, 235
    council 179–80, 186–7, 197, 214, 232–3, 234, 238, 287
    Ilminster in Bloom campaign 186
    local elections 287
    millennium celebrations 233–4
    minster 37, 234
    one-way system 35, 39–40, 142–3, 178–81, 186–7, 196–8, 213–14, 233–4, 238–9, 244–7, 287–9, 291
    Parish Hall 196, 234
    railway station 220–21
    supermarket development 35, 39–40, 42, 47, 141–4, 180, 197–8, 217, 234–6, 239, 246
Ilminster Democracy Action Group 233–4
Independent 292
Independent on Sunday 122, 268
India 203–4
insects 110–11, 270–71

Jacobs, Richard 187, 246
Jamie's School Dinners 27
Japan 135, 141, 249
Jersey 81, 121

Kaletsky, Anatole 184
Kathmandu, Nepal 203
Kelway, James 10

Kennedy, Adam 213–15, 233, 239
Kensington Place restaurant 16, 59, 63, 93, 97, 132, 150, 158
Kent University 8
Kenya 220
King, David 174
Kocyigit family 174
Kowalchuk, George 109

Ladak, India 35
lamb 88–9
Langport farmers' market 227–32
Langton, Peter 217–18
Large Blue butterflies 270, 271–3
Late Review (BBC TV) 175, 227
Lawrence, Felicity: Not on the Label 70–71
Laws, David 46, 142, 143, 164
Leahy, Terry 184–6, 238
Leigh, Rowley 59–60, 97, 150, 154, 158–9, 251, 255, 281, 284
Leitch, Daisy (daughter) 6, 8, 36–7, 68, 110, 111, 133, 135, 139, 146, 222, 257, 263
Leitch, David 133, 135, 257
    God Stand Up for Bastards 134
Levitt, Steven, and Dubner, Stephen: Freakonomics 198
local economy 43–5, 180
local produce 24, 45–6, 217–18
Lorch, Donatella 124, 126
Lovelock, James 248–9, 253, 266
Ludlow, Shropshire 2, 7, 67, 100

McCarthy, Mike 268
MacGregor, Ian 123
McLaurin, Lord 184–6
Malcolm, John 163
Malmesbury, Wiltshire 122, 124–6
Mandela, Nelson 191
Mansfield, Terry 135
Martin, Steve 159
Maycock, S. A.: Livings from the Land 96
Mayor, Steve 196
meat 24–8, 121–2, 169, 249
    processed 29–30, 169
Meat Hygiene Service 131
microbes, soil 106–10
migrant workers 71–3, 160–62, 242–3

Milk Marketing Board 83
Milton, Keith 160
Ministry of Agriculture 81, 82, 83,
    211
Mitchell, Steve 197
Mitchinson, John 28, 269
Monbiot, George 26
Monmouth, Duke of 265
Montacute House 87–8, 166–7
    farmers' market 87–92, 103,
        150–51, 157, 166–72, 200,
        252, 259–62, 274
Moody, Brian 80
Moore, Andrew 88, 260, 278
Morgan, Margaret 265
Morris, Steve 124–5
Morrison, Cathy 164, 165
Muchelny Abbey 233–4

Naivasha, Lake 220
National Farmers' Union 82
National Magazine Company 135
National Retail Planning Forum
    44
NatWest Bank 140
NBC 124 126
nematodes 107
Nepal 204–5
New Economics Foundation 41–2,
    180
New Labour 3, 289–90
New York 102
North, Lord 207, 246
numbers in nature 221–4

Office of Fair Trading 142, 184
Ogilvy, Mark 171
Okavanga Swamps, Botswana 110
Oliver, Jamie 26–7, 41
organic produce 65
organophosphates 86
Orwell, George: *Animal Farm* 22
Oscar Mayer Ltd 71–4, 75, 78,
    160–62, 164, 242

Parker, Ander (cousin) 80, 82, 83–
    7, 145, 146
Parker, Ben (uncle) 81–4, 154
Parker, Giogia (aunt) 80–85, 154
Parker, Mark 84
Parker, Richard (cousin) 80, 84,
    86–7

pesticides 220
pheasants 145, 195, 243
Phelips family 166–7
photosynthesis 106
pig clubs 211–12
pig rustlers 51–2, 63
pigs 18–23, 27–30, 49–52, 80,
    86–7, 101–2
    Berkshires 19, 127, 134–5, 136,
        287
    boars 18–19, 117, 148–9, 152
    breeding 33–4, 68–9, 101, 141,
        225, 237
    death 66
    factory farming 30
    flying pigs 205
    food 121, 122, 154, 212–13
    Gloucester Old Spots 1, 11, 18–
        19, 24, 170, 237
    health problems 101, 114–15
        118, 148, 225
    income from 15, 94, 136, 140,
        190, 284, 286
    intelligence 121, 122
    life expectancy 279–80
    new stock 134–7, 148, 200
    piglets 1, 18–19, 66, 155, 175,
        176, 187, 194–5, 202–3,
        226–7, 278–9, 282–3, 286
    pregnancy and birth 155, 175,
        176–8, 188, 224–5, 237, 287
    saddlebacks 80, 113–14, 134,
        137, 153, 212, 226, 282, 286
    sense of smell 67
    slaughter 117, 121, 126–32,
        281
    smallness 149–50, 152, 158–9
    Steinbeck and 205–6
    tagging 202–3
    Tamworths 51, 122–6, 127
    Truffle-hunting 64–5
    tusk removal 136–7
    in USA 102, 189
    in wartime 211–12
    Wilburys 154, 155
    see also pork
plants 15, 94, 200, 254–5, 284
    numerology 221–3
    photosynthesis 105–6
Polden Hills, Somerset 270
politicians 87, 200, 215, 216, 235,
    236

Popp Inn 16, 70, 93
population growth 146-7
pork 117, 149-50, 152, 154, 158-
      9, 170-71, 182, 281-2
Portuguese migrants 71-3, 160-
      62, 242-3
potatoes 275-8
Prince, Rose 88, 90
      The New English Kitchen 88
Prior-Sankey, Hazel 244-5, 247

rabbits 11, 210
racism 160-62, 242-3
Rayment, Sean 123, 125
ready meals 71, 72, 74, 75, 77-8
redundancy laws 240-42
religion 163, 178, 190-94
Rendell, John (greengrocer) 16,
      37, 38, 42, 98, 143, 177,
      218-21, 290
Rendell, Mary 38, 42, 219, 256
Riggs, Darren 127-8, 151-2
Rinpoche, Chogyam Trungpa 56
Rolfe, Colin 160, 162, 164, 169,
      181-3, 235, 240-43
Rolfe, Zoe 181, 183, 240, 242-3
Rowe, Marsha 76
RSPCA 27, 280-81

Safeway 91
Sai Baba 203-4
Sainsbury, Mr 150, 154
Sainsbury's 40, 41, 43, 71, 77,
      184-5
St Peter's Hospital, Chertsey 53
Salisbury Hospital 52
Sardis 208
Saxmundham, Suffolk 44-5
Selborne estate, Somerset 207
Shalom (rabbi) 231
sheep 22, 80, 81
      see also lamb
Shepton Mallet prison 61
shooting 145-6
SimCity 110, 111
Simonis, Bob 53, 56, 57
Small Pig Keepers' Council 211
smallholdings 96
Smith, Dick King: *Babe* 122
Snell, Charles 128
Snells abattoir 66, 117, 121, 127-
      32, 152, 154, 256, 281

Snuggle Pot and Cuddle Pie 36
soil 104-10
Soil Association 71, 104-5
Somerset County Council 4, 196,
      244
Somerset Levels 91, 132, 167-8,
      191, 227
South Petherton, Somerset 9, 200,
      255
South Somerset Climate Group
      213
South Somerset District Council
      39
Spare Rib 8, 76, 78
Spencer-White, Elaine 91, 260
spring 158, 202
Spry, Constance 75-6, 219, 220
Steinbeck Jnr, John 56, 203-5
Steinbeck Snr, John 205-6
Steinbeck, Thom 205
Steve (South African) 191-2
Stewart, Ian: *Nature's Numbers*
      222
Stinchcombe, Kevin and Debbie
      124
Storace, Francesco 98
street food 91
Stroud, Glos. 91
Sun 123
supermarkets 8, 24, 25, 40-46,
      70-71, 164, 170
   and climate change 217
   competition inquiry 142, 184
   convenience foods 71, 74, 77
   effect on independent retailers
      41-2, 44, 142, 180, 239,
      290
   environmental record 218
   flowers 218, 219
   government and 290
   Ilminster development 35, 39-
      40, 42, 47, 141-4, 180, 197-
      8
   impact on local economy 43-4,
      46, 180-81
   'just in time' 71
   out-sourcing 72
   prices 91, 92
   suppliers 48, 71-4, 86, 159,
      160, 275-8
Sweet, Ray 167-8
Symes, Trevor 128-32

tadpoles 202
Tamworth Two 122–6
Taunton, Somerset 151, 152, 164, 182, 233–4, 248
termites 110–11
Tesco 43, 72, 144, 170, 171, 183–6
  CEO 184–5, 238
  competition with Sainsbury's 184–5
  environmental record 217
  expansion plans 289
  Ilminster development 197, 213–14, 234–6, 239, 246, 287–8, 290
  international operations 185
  loyalty card 185, 289
  market share 41, 142, 180, 184, 289
  metro stores 71, 142
  prices 91, 92, 160
  producers 160, 235–6
  suppliers 30, 159, 162, 165, 182, 183, 276–8
  West Country stores 196–7, 239
Thomas, Jeremy 270, 271–3
Thomas, Tina and Paul 89
Thorpe, Laura 142
Times, The 118, 123, 184
Tiverton, Devon 144, 238
Tottenham Pudding 212
town planning 39–40, 178, 239, 291–2
trees 57–8, 60, 178, 293
Tricker, Marilyn 163
Trollope, Anthony: The Warden 228
truffles 64–5, 119
Tucker, Gordon 212
Tulip Corporation 159, 162–3, 183, 236, 240
turkeys 61, 65, 78–9, 119, 138, 148, 151
Turner, Kim 39
Tutton, Mark and Sue 170–71, 229, 262

unemployment 241
USA 7, 26, 84–5, 112, 188, 215

Vaser, Pieter 82
Vaughan Lee, Vaughan Hanning 10
vegetables 48, 250, 274–5
  eighteenth-century 207–8
  five-acre field for 65, 69, 103, 206–7
  organic 65
  planting schedule 155–7
  problems with 32, 102–3, 150, 195
  sales 15–16, 33, 94, 140, 200, 201, 254–5, 284, 286
vet 48, 97, 148, 225

Wadham, William 37
Wallace, Revd Alistair 46
walled gardens 207–9
Waller, Gerry 287–8
Warren, Martin 270, 271, 273
Warrington, Sue and Keith 168–9, 171, 260, 262
water 220
Weldon, Faye 244
Wells Cathedral 190–91, 192
Wessex Highlanders 228, 232
West, Rebecca: Black Lamb and Grey Falcon 266
Western Morning News 44
Westworth, Richard 238–9
Wheen, Francis and Julia 279–81
Whitelackington, Somerset 265
Wilson, Chris 5, 156, 178, 275–8, 285
Wilson, Edward O. 106–7
Wilson, Rosie 5
Windwhistle, Somerset 132
Winnie the Pooh 194–5
winter 115, 118, 139
Wodehouse, P. G. 20
Women's Institute 44
Woodstock Museum 82
Woolton, Lord 82, 211
World War II 81, 82, 120, 121, 192, 211–12, 216
Wright, Phil 5

Yeovil, Somerset 43, 46, 164
Young, Malcolm 213

A NOTE ON THE AUTHOR

Rosie Boycott was one of the founders of *Spare Rib* magazine and Virago Press. She was the editor of *Esquire* magazine, as well as of the *Independent on Sunday*, the *Independent* and the *Daily Express*. She is a frequent contributor to the *Late Review, Woman's Hour* and the *Politics Show*, and has presented her own show on BBC2, *Life Etc*. She is also the author of *A Nice Girl Like Me*, an autobiographical story of the '60s and '70s. Rosie is married to the barrister Charles Howard and they live in London and Somerset. She has one daughter, Daisy, four stepchildren, Miranda, Luke, Alex and Francesca, two dogs, Bingo and Dylan, and numerous pigs, chickens, geese and turkeys.

A NOTE ON THE TYPE

The text of this book is set in Linotype Sabon, named after the type founder, Jacques Sabon. It was designed by Jan Tschichold and jointly developed by Linotype, Monotype and Stempel, in response to a need for a typeface to be available in identical form for mechanical hot metal composition and hand composition using foundry type.

Tschichold based his design for Sabon roman on a font engraved by Garamond, and Sabon italic on a font by Granjon. It was first used in 1966 and has proved an enduring modern classic.